Our Wish for You and for Us

May the favor of the Lord rest upon us; establish the work of our hands for us; yes, establish the work of our hands.

They did what was right in the eyes of the Lord. They held fast to the Lord and did not cease to follow Him; they kept the "Successful Principles for a Healthy Life" the Lord had given, and the Lord was with them, and they were successful in whatever they undertook.

As I reflected upon the book's cover design, I asked myself, "What's the message you want to send to your readers?" It became clear it was to promote the mentoring concept. As I crafted the more than 200 blogs included in this book, I realized the phrases used to capture each idea and the related stories frequently came from one of my mentors. During my life, I've been blessed with many mentors — older individuals, peers, and people who are younger than me. For the book cover, I've selected six people I want to recognize and thank for their significant contribution to my life.

So here goes:

Al Doescher

Clearly, I won the lottery when it comes to fathers. My dad was the "real deal." After living an impactful 86 years, we said goodbye to him in 2013. His parents were first-generation German Americans. Grandpa was a career skilled tool and die worker who retired from Chrysler, and Grandma was in charge of the home front. My dad and his brother retired from the Mount Clemens (Michigan) Post Office. Although my dad's formal education ended at high school, his work at the post office and home kept him from reading much. Still, he was born with a lot of wisdom and an extra dose of common sense. He was a philosopher whose thoughts were rooted in the Bible. Much of that rubbed off onto me.

Uncle Pete

My Uncle Pete was a successful high school football coach. He had four daughters and then a son. I never asked him, but I think he unofficially adopted me, at some point before his son was born, thinking I may be the closest he would get to a son. He was a combination of a second father and a coach; growing up, I spent a fair amount of time with him. In high school, I became an honorary member of the Detroit Henry Ford High School football team. During the summers I would ride back and forth to Detroit with "Coach" five days a week and got to work out with his team. Uncle Pete modeled being a successful coach. He focused on the "whole person," a concept I learned about years later at Plante Moran. He was a student of his players, their strengths, and areas for improvement. He treated each player respectfully and uniquely.

Sage Business Advice from a Lucky Guy

Bob Maciejewski

Coach Bob came to L'Anse Creuse High School my senior year to become our wrestling coach. He was a big guy with an even bigger personality, and my classmates and I grew to love him. Coach Bob was really knowledgeable about wrestling, but probably even more so about coaching. He always knew what to do and when — like whether to kick you in the butt or give you a big bear hug. Coach Bob taught me a lifetime of lessons in only one short season. Here I am, honoring him more than 50 years later. He defines an impact player. The trait I would like to single out is goal-setting. He was a fanatic. For every match, each wrestler had a goal: pinning their opponent, winning by points, or not getting pinned. Probably one of my fondest memories relates to our match against Roseville. For reasons I never understood, from the beginning of the season, Coach Bob targeted the Roseville match, which was scheduled for about halfway through the season. He made it our Super Bowl. Finally, the week came and we were well-prepared. Unfortunately, Coach Bob was in a serious auto accident and was laid up in the hospital the day before the big match, so my co-captain, Steve, and I stepped in for Coach Bob and followed his plan — and we won! After the victory, the whole team raced over to the hospital to share the good news with Coach. Although he was hurting, I can still see that legendary smile on his face.

Frank Moran

I first met Frank as a Plante Moran intern in the summer of 1970. To say our chance meeting was life-changing would be a gross understatement. At that time, I knew almost nothing about business or the accounting profession, but I was drawn to Frank and his dream. I remember getting his Annual Firm Conference speech on a cassette tape and taking it home to have my parents listen to it. It wasn't until my dad died that I realized that although Frank's life was quite different than my dad's, they were both philosophers with similar beliefs. Plante Moran was small firm back then, so I had the privilege of working with Frank on client matters. He knew my family and I knew his. It was pretty special. Frank's dream of building a firm where professionals loved to serve matched my own goals. I was a team guy raised with Judeo-Christian beliefs, so Plante Moran became home for me; I feel so lucky to have spent four decades there. Because of Frank's deep life study of philosophy and psychology, and his ability to articulate and connect the concepts to the business world, I drank the Kool Aid. In my more than 200 blogs, Frank Moran is my most-quoted authority. I hope you enjoy my stories about him.

Ken Kunkel

At Plante Moran, each new staff member is assigned to a partner's team. Once again, I hit the lottery when I was assigned to Ken Kunkel's team. If you're a regular reader of my blogs, you know how important I believe it is to have good mentors. If there was a Nobel Prize for mentors, Ken would easily win. He, like me, bought into Frank's dream and made it a reality. For each "Frank Principle," I could offer numerous real-life examples of how Ken applied it in his daily life as a partner/mentor. You might say he put flesh on the bones. He also became another father to me. Like so many successful people, Ken's life had its share of hardships, including his mom's premature death and working at the post office to support his family and pay for his college tuition at the University of Michigan. Never once did he complain. Despite his commitment to family and his work, Ken received the Paton Award for achieving the highest score on the CPA examination. Probably the greatest compliment I could give Ken would be that he continues to mentor and share his wisdom with me after five decades.

Roger VanNoord

After having a Nicodemus experience in 1987, I met Roger VanNoord in a Bible discussion group that met in a Plante Moran conference room. Roger worked for the Navigators, an organization that provides Bible teaching with life applications. Although my dad had provided the basic foundation for my faith, Roger helped me study the Bible and apply its principles to my everyday life. As they say, Roger "walked his talk," modeled for me, and became my spiritual mentor. Although it's been 30 years since we spent significant time together, almost every week I think to myself, "What would Roger do?" In addition to his mentoring, he is on my short list of heroes who have stayed active. He's in his ninth life decade and still going strong as a spiritual mentor. He's setting the bar really high.

Hopefully, these brief bios will give you an idea of what a lucky guy I have been, and why I chose to honor these mentors.

Sage Business Advice from a Lucky Guy

Introduction

It's hard for me to believe my business life has already encompassed five decades. Ten years ago, when my wife, Barbara, and I launched Doescher Advisors, I sensed that a periodic blog to our network of former clients, referral sources, and friends would be a great way to stay in touch. During my first career at Plante Moran, I had the advantage of having many colleagues who were active in the business community, but now there are just two of us. On November 7, 2011, I posted my first blog, "Intimate Customer Service." It would be fair to say the blog started as a marketing tool, and I'll confess it was just another item on my growing to-do list. However, at some point, a few things happened. First, I actually began to enjoy crystalizing my thoughts. Second, I became more deliberate about the subjects. Third, as weird as it sounds, I started using previously posted blogs as a tool to address clients' business issues.

Many of my blog posts include key takeaways from business books I've read. Several of my readers have thanked me and said, "I love your book summaries. They're very useful and save me a lot of time." As the years have gone by, many readers have suggested I write a book. My standard response has been, "Thank you for the encouragement, but I read so many 'bad' books, I'm not going to write a book unless I have something special and unique to share."

Time has raced on, and I've now written over 200 blogs — and, as I've mentioned, I routinely share them with clients. Eventually, the idea of a book of blogs began to germinate in my mind. I concluded a "book of blog posts" would be a useful tool in advising clients.

When I step back and look through the posts, I realize I've succinctly summarized my views and convictions on many of the most common business issues faced by owners. While creating a blog, I'm visualizing a business owner/executive and their company. I identify a common business issue and offer solutions, often referencing a business book or periodical. My goal is for my readers to be able to read the entire blog on their smart phone while stopped at a red traffic signal. Sometimes I fail and it requires two stops.

The blogs cover four main categories: 1) Extraordinary customer/client service; 2) Ideas to help build a solid team; 3) Nuggets and encouragement regarding strategy and focus; and 4) Sharpening your personal leadership skills. I've organized this book into four sections dealing with those topics.

When a business owner is considering hiring Doescher Advisors, I first take some time to get to know them a bit. Then I'll send them several blog posts on subjects relevant to their business, and I'll suggest that they read the blogs. Finally, I say, "After reading these posts, I think you'll get to know me fairly well, and you should be able to decide whether I'm the right advisor for you."

Although this isn't intended to be an autobiography, I think you'll feel like you know me pretty well after reading it.

Finally, a comment on the book title, *Sage Business Advice from a Lucky Guy*. I'm not sure when it started, but at some point, I verbalized what I had felt my whole life: I *am* a lucky guy! I hope that, as you read through my blogs, you'll come to understand why.

Contents

1 EXTRAORDINARY CLIENT/CUSTOMER SERVICE

Introduction

After posting more than 200 blogs since 2011, I thought it might be helpful to my readers to have ready access to each blog by topic. The result is this book, or manual, that includes the posted blogs with some additional commentary.

The first category is Clients (Customers). For those of you who are familiar with me, you know I am obsessed with client service. I will start this category with new business development, or what I like to call "Hunting" — because, obviously, you do not have a business until you have landed your first client.

New Business Development Principles and Philosophies
October 20, 2015

TOM DOESCHER //

Are You Helping Your Clients/Customers, or Selling Them?

In preparation for an upcoming blog series, I am reading a book that was recommended to me by a client: *The Challenger Sale* (the authors are Matthew Dixson and Brent Adamson). According to the authors, it seems like most B2B businesses want to obtain new clients/customers, but few are able to execute their plan.
Here are just a few helpful tidbits I discovered in the book:

1. A business services sales director told the authors his company has 100 sales reps, but just two of those individuals are responsible for 80 percent of the company's revenues.
2. At the conclusion of the authors' study of more than 6,000 sales reps, they decided on a name for the most successful reps — "The Challenger" — and determined that all of these individuals possess three strong traits: teaching, tailoring, and taking control.
3. In a survey of more than 5,000 B2B customers, the answer 53 percent of the time, when asked "Why do you select a particular supplier?" was "The sales experience."

4. The second most common answer (19 percent of the time) was "The company and brand impact."
5. Customer loyalty is won out in the field.

Here is what the clients/customers say about the types of sales reps labeled "The Challenger":

1. They offer unique and valuable perspectives on our market.
2. They help navigate alternatives.
3. They provide ongoing advice or consultation.
4. They help me avoid potential land mines.
5. They educate me on new issues and outcomes.

Suffice it to say that at Doescher Advisors, we believe the most successful new business developers "help" their clients/customers; they do **not** "sell" them.

Are You Easily Accessible to Your Clients/Customers?

A survey cited in *The Challenger Sale,* by Matthew Dixson and Brent Adamson, reported that the second most important factor (95 percent) driving customer loyalty is accessibility. I believe too many businesses, both large and small, have substantially reduced their accessibility by hiding behind technology. (Think about this: What does it *really* cost to have someone answer the phone during normal business hours?)

Today, you can easily distinguish yourself from the competition by simply answering your phone or responding to an email in a prompt and timely fashion.

Have you performed an evaluation of your client/customer touchpoints? Have you talked with your key clients/customers about their experience with your company's accessibility? I changed doctors due to my physician's lack of accessibility. (I can feel some of you pushing back right now; I know you are busy, but what's more important than being responsive to your clients/customers?)

Do You Have the Courage to "No Quote"?

When I've reviewed client data regarding successful quotes on new business, I've generally found a very low hit rate. In reflecting on why this might be the case, it seems that often we (yes, I fall into this trap, too) like being busy, and preparing a proposal or bid makes us feel good because we believe we're accomplishing something -- when, in fact, it's probably a waste of time.

In *The Challenger Sale,* Matthew Dixson and Brent Adamson stated that the successful "Challenger" reps continually assess the likelihood of closing the sale. If they determine there is a low probability of closing, they are quick to cut the sales effort short and move on to the next opportunity. In my observations, many companies do not put a high value on time. I would suggest applying the old adage of "quality over quantity" when it comes to new business. What is your success rate on new business quotes? If you were to spend more time on new business opportunities, would you guess your success rate would be higher? Rather than wasting your efforts on creating quotes for low-probability business, would you be better off if you moved along to the next potential new business client?

Here is a Doescher Advisors Proverb: "It is better to be profitable than busy."

Words, Words, Words

I have written on the subject of "words" before, but I recently spent a little more time thinking about the topic while reading some very good business books. I believe the words you use influence — and have a definite impact on — how you think and behave. In the books I was reading, many of the authors refer to their clients/customers as "accounts." I assume they mean accounts receivable — or maybe accounts payable? (Just kidding.) Seriously, though, if you were the client/customer, would you like to be referred to as an "account"? I would highly recommend proudly referring to the companies you serve as your customers/clients. I bet you worked really hard to obtain their business, and you continue to work hard to provide them with great products and services.

Strategic Selling: Ideal Customers

Later this year, I plan to post a series of suggestions related to the best practices for obtaining new customers/clients. As part of the preparation for that series, I recently finished reading *The New Strategic Selling* by Robert B. Miller, Stephen E. Heiman, Tad Tuleja, and J.W. Marriott. If your job responsibilities include business development, I think reading this book would absolutely be worth your time. The authors touch on several of my favorite subjects, which I will comment on in the next several blogs.

First, though, what is an ideal customer/client? (Honestly, is that something you have ever thought about?)
The authors offer the following list of "best customer" characteristics:

1. They trust my company's performance.
2. They have innovative, progressive management.
3. They are loyal to the vendors I have selected.

3

4. They are committed to quality control.
5. They are willing to pay for "value-added" aspects of my product.
6. They demonstrate the highest business ethics and integrity.
7. They want a win-win relationship on every sale.

The authors follow that up with a list of "worst customer" characteristics:

1. They are inflexible on price.
2. They are slow in making buying decisions.
3. They have no loyalty to my company or to me.
4. They have an authoritarian management system.
5. They are secretive and unwilling to cooperate.
6. They want me to lose so they can win.

It might be a good idea to evaluate your customers/clients using the above criteria, plus anything else that is important to you. And then take action. With the generally strong economy, now is a great time to separate from your worst customer/client. It is scary, but you will be glad you did it — and so will your team!

Strategic Selling: Influencers

Probably some of the best material found in *The New Strategic Selling* by Miller, Heiman, Tuleja and Marriott comes in the form of the tips the authors offer their readers on understanding how companies buy products and services. The authors suggest there are four buying influences:

○ **Economic Buying Influence** — Who at the customer/client will give the final economic approval to buy? There have been plenty of situations over the years where people have missed this one. Is there money in the budget? Will the owner/CEO have to approve? Is someone else's approval required? Do you know that individual?

○ **User Buying Influences** — This one is kind of obvious, but here is a recent example. I have a client who has strong relationships with the owner/CEOs at many companies, but he does not know the users yet. He needs to identify the users who have buying influence and develop relationships with them, too.

○ **Technical Buying Influences** — These are the gatekeepers. They may not always have big titles, but they have veto rights.

○ **Coaches** — The role of the coach is to guide you in the sales process. I like to call them "insiders." I recommend that you establish an "insider" relationship with every major customer/client. This should be someone who, for whatever reason, likes you and your company, and wants you to be successful. I am **NOT** suggesting anything unethical. I will probably touch on this subject more in my upcoming series of best practices for obtaining new customers/clients.

The authors do a great job of explaining each role. In my experience, many sales have been lost because there were not relationships in place with all four types of influencers. Have you lost any sales due to this?

Strategic Selling: Competitors

I have commented on this subject before. In my May 13, 2013 blog post, I recommended not bad-mouthing your competitors.

Meanwhile, in my April 23, 2012 blog post, I recommended the book *Blue Ocean Strategy,* by W. Chan Kim and Renee Mauborgne, and talked about the concept of listening to your customers/clients and providing them with something new and different to meet their needs.

Here are two quotes from my newest favorite book, *The New Strategic Selling:*

1. "We have long held that one of the commandments for losing in business is to concentrate on the competitor rather than the customer."
2. "The alternative is to think far less about what the competition is doing, has done, or might do, and more about what selling is about in the first place — the providing of customized solutions to individuals' problems."

My question is simple: Where is your focus — the customer/client, or the competition? What would I hear if I listened in on your Leadership Team meetings?

Strategic Selling: Hucksters

As I continue my series, here's a quote from *The New Strategic Selling*, by Robert B. Miller, Stephen E. Heiman, Tad Tuleja and J.W. Marriott: "If you are to be successful in strategic selling, you'll have to leave the old-time huckster philosophy where it belongs — in the past — and learn how to dig for a real fit between what you have and what your customers need." The authors provide the following common-sense advice:

1. The only competitive strategy that can bring you success is a strategy in which you keep your eye on the customer.
2. A Hollywood agent's advice to his actor client was, "We're in Tinseltown. If you can fake sincerity, you've got it made." The authors' response is, "Maybe in Tinseltown, but not in the world of selling. Not if you want to build a reputation for credibility — which, as we have said, is the one thing you **cannot** do without."
3. By establishing low-pressure relationships with numerous buying influences, you will be positioning yourself to capitalize on them when they are ready to buy.

If you are responsible for business development, is this how you think and behave? If you are an owner/CEO or a sales manager, is this the advice you offer to your new-business developers?

Strategic Selling: The Big Surprise About Motivating Your Business Developers

I will definitely be providing some suggestions for motivating rather than demotivating your business developers in my blog series related to best practices for obtaining new customers/clients. For now, in my final post based on *The New Strategic Selling* by Miller, Heiman, Tuleja and Marriott, I will provide another direct quote from the authors. In listening to business owners/CEOs for years, I believe this quote will come as a big surprise: *"In every survey we have seen, the researchers reach the same 'surprising' conclusion that what really turns good salespeople on is not their six-figure commissions but job satisfaction, recognition and challenges. The popular belief that the top salespeople are in it just for the money always turns out to be a misconception."*

I would suggest this might even be a controversial conclusion.

Do You Want to Be More Successful Developing New Business?

August 12, 2019 // Tom Doescher //

TOM DOESCHER //

I just finished reading a fascinating book, *Win Bigly,* by Scott Adams. For those of you who read the daily comic strips, you will recognize Adams as the Dilbert cartoonist. If I have not lost you yet, guess who the book is about? President Trump. Adams, a self-proclaimed ultra-liberal, was in a very tiny group that predicted Donald Trump's victory in 2016. He says he took a lot of heat and abuse, especially from his liberal neighbors in California.

I would highly recommend the book, which was very entertaining, but not for that reason. Adams, who would say he is a persuader as much as a writer, refers to President Trump as the Master Persuader — and possibly one of the best in human history. Reading along as Adams makes his case, it dawned on me that he is describing the best marketing/new business/Hunters I've ever known.

As you read the book, assume you have two products to choose from: Hillary Clinton or Donald Trump. Which would you buy? The choice has almost nothing to do with their positions/platforms. Now, I am sure I've offended many of you, but I suggest that you read *Win Bigly* as a "How to win that next big customer" playbook.

Here are a few of Adams' observations:

1. Trump is the most persuasive human he has ever observed. (Editorial comment: Keep in mind that Adams vehemently disagrees with most, if not all, of President Trump's positions.)
2. By the time, they were done criticizing Trump for the "error" of saying he would build one big solid **"wall,"** the critics had convinced themselves that border security was a higher priority than they had thought coming into the conversation. The reason the wall imagery was a good persuasion is that it was both **simple** to understand and **memorable**.
3. A big opening demand in a negotiation will form a mental anchor that will bias negotiations toward that high offer.

7

4. Humans think they are rational, and they think they understand their reality. But they are wrong on both counts. The main theme of this book is that **humans are not rational**.
5. Humans literally make decisions first, and then create elaborate rationalizations for them after the fact.
6. Trump is so persuasive; policies do not matter. People voted for him even though his policies were murky and changing.
7. **Visual persuasion** is stronger than oral persuasion. Trump always paid attention to the **colors** and **symbols** associated with his brand — his shirt was always white, and his tie colors were always from the American flag.
8. What you might not realize is that each of us is "marketing" all the time. (Editorial comment: For those of you who know me well, you know I struggle with "business casual" dress. Show me a great new business developer and I bet they **look sharp**.)
9. If you want to make a good first impression, do not jokingly complain about the traffic on the way over. Try to work into the initial conversation some positive thoughts and images. (Editorial comment: People love to be around the "sharp" new business developer because they always share a positive, uplifting, inspiring story.)

My challenge to you is:

1. After reading the book, evaluate your sales process, including handouts and pitch.
2. Is it a bunch of facts and details?
3. Does it appeal to your customers' emotions? Is there a *WOW* factor?
4. Would you buy anything from you?
5. Do people like being around you or do they hide when they see you coming?

I would love for you to send me stories of instances where your company has applied the principles in *Win Bigly* and has won new business.

Just Ask for the Business, Please
March 25, 2019 // Tom Doescher //

 TOM DOESCHER //

In writing the simple fictional narrative entitled *The Asking Formula,* author John Baker hit a lot of nerves.

His book is all about the third phase of new business development, Closing, which follows Finding and Building a Relationship with a new prospective customer/client. *(See the next article, which explains all three phases.)* As a prospective customer, we have all had an experience where we think, *Just tell me how much it costs, and then I'll decide.* In this short (99 pages in large font) book, the main character shares his simple formula for Closing. To be honest, I would be embarrassed to relate the many actual stories of instances where my colleagues and I *should have* used his simple formula.

I will not ruin the book, but I'll share the first two steps:

Step One — Know what you want. (Editorial comment: The best new business development professionals I know always are specific about what they want to accomplish in every meeting with the prospective client — which might even be to have the next meeting with the decision-maker.)

Step Two — Ask for it. (Editorial comment: Do not laugh; it isn't as easy as it sounds. I was fortunate because my mentors were so good at teaching and demonstrating this simple action.)

Baker states that "Directness is a rare thing these days." I'll quote my dad, who always said, "Ask. What is the worst thing that can happen?" I also remember one of my successful new business development colleagues, who would say, "My goal in this meeting is to get to the 'No.' " Once again, Baker and other sales gurus would say that most people spend too much time with prospects who are never going to purchase anything from them.

I have a suggestion: Consider buying multiple copies of Baker's book and have your new business development team read it. Then, facilitate a discussion and maybe do some role-playing.

Let us Stop Arguing About What to Call It

March 6, 2017 // Tom Doescher //

TOM DOESCHER //

How about if we call "it" obtaining a new client (customer)? In this blog, I would like to focus on obtaining new clients for professional services. I believe most of the comments would apply to any service or product, but for purposes of clarity, let us focus on "professional services," which I will allow you to define.

If you Google sales, marketing, and/or business development, you will discover all kinds of definitions the authors of various articles and books are passionate about. The reason I am commenting is because of the ambiguity that exists in many companies. I would suggest there are three major functions necessary to secure a new client (customer):

1. **Finding** (This is not my own term; I got this word from a colleague in my networking group) — Finding is the process of identifying a prospective client. You might use an outside resource/service, have someone internally perform this function, your Hunter may be responsible, or possibly it is the result of a combination of tactics. Question: Is how you obtain qualified leads and who is responsible for finding leads clear to both you and your team? Do you have enough leads? If no, why not?

2. **Relationship** — Often, this is the hardest part, but the goal is to get a new client. This may take a period of a few weeks or a few years. I am aware of situations where this period lasted for more than 20 years (sorry, I have to tell the truth). Again, I think Uncle Dan gave us great advice and tips. This is where the great Hunters excel. They introduce the prospective client to their colleagues, especially those who can offer industry insights and what is called "thought leadership" (simply stated, they say, "If I owned this company, I would do this or that to profitably grow the business."). I strongly believe that personalized contacts are more important today than they have ever been. I am not talking about mass emails, webinars, podcasts, et cetera. I am talking about face-to-face, voice-to-voice, and handwritten notes.
Question: Do you have people who can truly develop new relationships and transform them into clients? (By the way, I have met people who know a lot of prominent executives but cannot convert them into clients. How many new clients do you have this year? Last year?)

3. **Closing** — This is getting the ball over the goal line or ringing the bell — whatever you want to call it. Again, Hunters are best in class at closing, and Uncle Dan provided some thoughts on this function, too. Question: What is your close rate? Could it be higher? How? Do you really have the right people involved in the close?

Talking Down About Competitors

May 13, 2013 // Tom Doescher //

We all can fall into this trap. One example of a potential talking-down situation is after someone leaves our company, goes to a competitor, and uses (steals) proprietary information/knowledge (I'm not going to deal with the legal aspects of this situation; rather, I'm considering how we should deal with customers or prospective customers). Here are a couple of other examples of times we may be caught speaking negatively about a competitor: 1) We know our competitor has offered a lowball price, which they won't be able to sustain; 2) We know our competitor's product/service is inferior to ours, but the prospective customer cannot discern the difference.

There may be a way to tastefully educate your prospect and open their eyes to any misinformation/misrepresentations, but my experience is that when you step into this dialogue, you are usually the one who comes out looking bad. My strong advice is to focus on your prospect and your product/service and helping them understand why you are the perfect solution. Provide examples and use customer references — especially people your customer may know in their industry. How do you feel when someone else speaks poorly of his or her competitors? Have you ever made a sale by bad-mouthing a competitor? I would love to hear about it.

My Son's Name Is Kaka
January 17, 2012 // Tom Doescher //

Here is a story from China. I was meeting with a Chinese business owner and we were getting to know one another. In an effort to build the relationship and develop a better understanding of each other, I asked him about his family. He started to tell me about the various family members, and when he came to his son, he told me that his son's name "is Kaka." He quickly followed it up with, "I think that means _hit in English." Although that remark might seem "politically incorrect" and/or inappropriate in a business conversation here in the U.S., we had a good laugh and it definitely helped break the ice in a new relationship.

This gentleman's knowledge of our culture enabled him to use humor to make a connection and build a bridge. It reminded me of how important humor can be (I do not mean sarcasm, obscenity, or biting comments, but down-to-earth and genuine humor). Does your company's culture make room for a healthy dose of humor when warranted?

11

Announcing "Sandbox 'Hunters' Game Plan" Blog Series
January 19, 2016

In my work with clients, especially industrial B2B clients, I often find that we wind up discussing one particular issue: the lack of business from "new" customers/clients. Several months ago, I began jotting down my thoughts and ideas on the subject. As I reflected on what I wanted to say and how I wanted to share my thoughts, a new idea surfaced — why don't I invite a guest blogger to assist me? For the next several weeks, you are in for a very special treat. Our guest blogger is someone I have known his entire life. I have observed him in many different situations and environments, and his relationship-building skills are extraordinary. In case you have not already guessed his identity from those clues, I'm referring to "Uncle" Dan. Many of you know him as Dan Doescher — who, after an exceptionally successful and rewarding career, left Plante Moran and launched Sandbox Partners International.

Sandbox is a firm that represents companies and gives them this promise: "Bringing partners the lifeblood of new business." While at Plante Moran, Dan was often pointed to as the poster child for a new business development/rainmaker partner. Among a vast variety of different industries, he was successful in attracting new clients representing government, manufacturing, distribution, automotive, and service businesses to Plante Moran.

In preparing for this "Hunter" series, I have read a number of great books and articles (including some recommended by several of my readers) describing the "best" salespeople.

Dan and I have our thoughts on this topic, and we like to say, "The most successful business developers are professionals who meet the needs of others first." As I have studied this subject, I've thought of a number of you whom I believe excel in this area. For that reason, it was hard to narrow the choice to Uncle Dan, but when I benchmark him against the criteria of the experts, he — like many of you — is a bull's eye. I hope you have as much fun reading the Hunter series as Dan and I have had writing it.

Enjoy!

STEP 1 — What Is a Hunter?

 DAN DOESCHER //

What is in a Word — or, Rather, What the Heck do I Call Myself?

"Salesman" remains an uncomfortable label. To me, that focus has a "self-interest-first" feel. Initially, "Hunter" did not feel quite right, either. I believe it, too, connotes high self-interest — which is generally a win/lose proposition. Merriam-Webster finally got my attention. It defines "Hunter" this way: "A person who searches for something." So, in this series, consider that a "Hunter" is someone focused on searching for unmet needs. The emphasis shifts from "making a sale" to finding the place I believe the most successful business developers spend their time: meeting the needs of others first.

Hunters can be both inside employees and outside independent contractors/representatives. Regardless, what do the best Hunters look like? Thoughts on this vary, but given the definition above, consider the following:

1. Hunters are effective at developing relationships with and helping people — they are able to gain trust.
2. Hunters are great communicators who place a strong emphasis on listening (do the math; we have two ears and one mouth).
3. Hunters are smart, with an ability to think strategically and out of the box.
4. Hunters are inquisitive when it comes to identifying unmet/unsatisfied needs — they are able to create "pull" scenarios to meet needs, versus "pushing"/selling.
5. Hunters are calculated risk-takers.
6. Hunters are disciplined, persistent, and competitive.
7. A Hunter believes in and is passionate about what they do.
8. A Hunter is able to balance the short- and long-term; they realize sometimes it is better to back off. Pushing may destroy an opportunity permanently.

Finding the right person is important. Equally important is how you treat them once they join your team. A few considerations:

1. Make sure you have a clear understanding of the Hunter's role in pricing. It helps avoid miscommunication, unmet expectations, and lost opportunities.
2. Do your homework when it comes to compensation. Treat these individuals commensurate with the value they bring. If you want better candidates, think upper quartile in the marketplace.
3. Beware of making the best Hunter the manager. The skills that are required for each role are very different, and not necessarily interchangeable.

13

STEP 2 — Let us Get Growing

Maintaining status quo as a sustainable option is a risky strategy. Compared to your competitors, you are either growing or you're declining. Knowing why you want to grow is a critical first step in developing your plan — just be aware that growth for growth's sake is not a recommended strategy. In this series, my focus will be limited to new customer/client attraction.

Thinking that growth automatically results in higher profitability is tempting, but it is not necessarily true (think GM). While increasing profits is a great reason — and often a driver — for growth, there are other reasons to consider growing.

Some of them might include:
1. Building a stronger base and critical market mass for entity continuation.
2. Increasing specialization to better meet customer/client needs.
3. Expanding product/service offerings to become a full-service solution.
4. Entering new geographic markets to build/expand competitive advantage.
5. Increasing your opportunity to acquire competitors or as an exit strategy.
6. Increasing opportunities for current and future staff.
7. Increasing pay to help attract the best talent.

As noted, increasing profits is a worthy pursuit. Even so, a balanced approach is advisable. Be mindful of Arthur Andersen's infamous demise, which was set up by the company's unreasonable focus on growth for the purpose of increasing profits. When properly approached, strategic planning will define the "why" you want to grow, provide alignment for how to allocate resources, and focus your team's efforts. However, this does not mean you're ready to engage in growth-oriented efforts. There are several fundamental questions you should consider before proceeding, such as:

1. Are you scoring better than average, or perhaps even in the upper quartile, with existing customer/client satisfaction and profitability? The worst thing you can do is put your current customer/client base at risk due to the potential distraction of chasing new business.
2. Who will lead the new business development? Are they truly empowered to make things happen, and do they have the time to devote to such an effort? This is not easy stuff to begin with, so not having the right team properly equipped is likely a doomed effort.

14

3. Are your systems (operations and administration) sufficient to respond to new business?
4. Are you prepared to invest the additional money needed to ensure the effort has a sustainable opportunity for success? On this point, budgets/plans are always recommended to help define success, to set expectations (both your own and those of others), to provide a compass showing your current position, and to give you the opportunity to change directions when needed — which is inevitable.

If your responses to these questions are not clearly affirmative, it's likely more work is needed in these areas, and proceeding without additional thought and planning could result in more harm than good.

STEP 3 — Who We Are and Why We're Here

Assuming growth is a priority and you understand why you want to grow, it is critical to ensure that your most important resource, your team, is on board with you. Inherent in "on board" is reaching a clear understanding and alignment of "why."

Call it whatever you like — mission, purpose, vision — but define it. If you already have a mission/purpose/vision, review it for reconfirmation and redouble your commitment. It should be very specific, brief — preferably a dozen words or less — and easy to remember. Ideally, its creation is a team effort that will result in shared alignment and passion. Ultimately, it drives a "way of life" in your business.

Be disciplined in this process. Some team members will have laser-like focus, while others can take you into the weeds. Consider capturing your core values first. Whether you have ever considered core values or not, you have them — you believe them, you operate by them — so simply reduce them to writing. Keep the list reasonably brief, three to six ideals, and make sure they are a reflection of what really matters to your organization — how you want potential customers/clients to see you. Why is the "why" so important? The alignment of your company's efforts begins with an alignment of thoughts. Developing tactical efforts requires making decisions about resource allocation, and a clearly defined consensus of thought becomes your compass for decision-making. This enables you to make the tough choices when developing your action plans. James Dibler, an owner, and CEO of BlueRock Technologies, has taken this effort to a whole new level. As team members join the firm, they are required to read Jim Collins' books *Great by Choice* and *Good to Great,* and Tony Hseih's book *Delivering Happiness.*

Then the new members are asked to summarize what stood out to them. James is trying to help reinforce his company's values and purpose, as well as benefit from any new ideas that reading the books may trigger.

Can you state your core mission, purpose, or vision? If not, it is likely your team can't, either. If you can clearly verbalize your mission, purpose, or vision, do you know if your top leaders can? Regardless, it may be time to step back and capture it in writing or reconfirm your collective commitment to it. With a clearly aligned view of where you and your team are headed, you will be ready to proceed to the next planning stage.

STEP 4 — What We Do and How We Do It

For years, my big brother Tom and I have been intrigued by businesses we have encountered whose leadership is convinced their company is unique in certain ways — and then, upon further research, we find the contrary to be true.

Successfully attracting new customers/clients requires a clear understanding of what you do and how you do it. That seems simple enough, right? But is your mission, your purpose, in writing? Does your team understand it enough to explain it? Even more importantly, do they embrace it?

Some call the process of aligning these aspects of your business strategic planning. Others consider it SWOT analysis documentation:

- **S**trengths: aspects of your business that provide advantage over others.
- **W**eaknesses: aspects of your business that put you at a disadvantage compared to others.
- **O**pportunities: aspects of your business that could be leveraged for further advantage.
- **T**hreats: aspects outside your business that could cause you difficulty.

Regardless of what it's called, it's a necessary process. Engage your team in such an effort. Be careful, however, because this is a process that can take on a not-so-helpful life of its own and backfire unless you have given it plenty of thought and preparation. Here are a few things worth considering:

1. Include the appropriate people — the approvers and/or those who will be responsible for implementing plans.
2. Do not include so many people that you stifle input and candor.
3. Plan the timing for the entire process, from beginning to end. Include lock-down dates and get a firm commitment from participants.

4. An offsite meeting location is advisable, to avoid daily distractions. Perhaps one of your company advisers can provide a conference room in their offices.
5. An outside facilitator can sometimes be useful.
6. Warn participants that "homework" before and/or between sessions may be necessary.
7. Commitment by all, backed up by accountability, is key to getting this task accomplished.

Ultimately, you are trying to come out of this process with action plans — to-do lists — that focus your team's efforts on bringing in more new customers/clients.

Some practical, useful outcomes might include:

1. Can your potential customers/clients clearly understand who you are and what you do?
2. How can features of what you do create benefits?
3. Remember that relatable success stories are powerful.
4. Describe how you serve customers/clients — including who, their roles, communication lines and where "the buck stops."
5. Demonstrate any synergies within your company that will benefit customers/clients.

Once you have engaged in this process, you will be:

1. Encouraged by an increased confidence and recommitment to leveraging your strengths to seize untapped opportunities.
2. Aware of areas to either shore up or avoid altogether.
3. More informed about your competition and the related implications (which we will talk about next time).

STEP 5 — But We're Different

Many years ago, I asked my wife, Jan, if she thought I was competitive. The look on her face said it all. I got it. I am as competitive as most. Admit it — you think your business is different from everyone else. That is great; it is an important mindset. Equally significant, however, is how you respond to competition. Miller and Heiman's book, *The New Strategic Selling*, acknowledges the need for being aware of the competition, but warns of the danger of sending an unintended "reactive/me-too" message to a potential new customer/client (we'll call them the "target"), rather than the preferred "better than" position. The authors note the potential negative repercussions of too much focus on competition:

1. It allows the competition to write the rules of the game.

2. It advertises your weaknesses, not your strengths.
3. It invites price-slashing.
4. It makes you look unimaginative or uncreative.
5. It deflects attention from the target's concerns.

I also like their definition of the "competition":

1. They buy from someone else.
2. They use internal resources.
3. They use their budget for something else.
4. They do nothing.

This provides a broader view of the potential barriers you may need to address. In sports, playing offense is essential to winning. Proactively focusing on leveraging your differences is critical. Ultimately, you want your target to see that you know what differentiates you from all other options. Focusing on your strengths is how you begin developing what really sets you apart from your competitors.

Begin by listing the features of what you do and how you do it that you think makes you stand out/differentiates you from all others. Then succinctly describe how your differences have created benefits to existing customers/clients. Documenting actual cases where customers/clients have benefited from these factors can be potentially powerful information that you will want to share with targets.

As always, it is beneficial to have your key team members involved in developing this type of information. More importantly, it is critical that your team is fully aware of these differences, embraces them, and easily communicates them to current customers/clients as well as targets.

Incidentally, if you do not think you're different, or you haven't given it much thought, it's time to consider the possibilities and related implications.

STEP 6 — Do You Know Your "10" When You See It?

OK, let us get to the point: They can't all be "10s." However, beware of chasing whatever comes along. Defining your perfect target isn't meant to restrict you; rather, it creates a guideline for determining where to proactively invest your time and resources for hunting, and it acts as a filter for deciding whether you should respond to opportunities that come to you.

Some of the target criteria you'll want to consider includes:

1. Determine the product or service providers you already have, or with whom you intend to develop a specialized capability in serving.
2. What is your potential new customer/client size?
   o Number of employees
   o Number of locations and where they are located
   o Revenue
3. Think about their culture — the way they do business.
4. Do you have recurring and/or single-project work?
5. What work may lead to other opportunities?
6. Remember that clients of your potential new customer/client may be new opportunities for you.

Part of defining your perfect target includes determining the least desirable target. Robert B. Miller and Stephen E. Heiman's book, *The New Strategic Selling,* suggests making a list of the following, in the order noted:

1. Current and past:
   o Best customers/clients
   o Worst customers/clients
2. Characteristics of the above clients:
   o Best characteristics
   o Worst characteristics
3. Now define your ideal customer/client from these four lists.

Before you pursue new clients, a next step — and one also recommended by Miller and Heiman — is to review your current customer/client list against your ideal profile. The purpose is to consider whether you should continue these existing relationships. This is a healthy process that you should go through periodically, perhaps every year or so. There may be some clients you should dismiss, and others that you will keep after making certain changes to the relationship. Regardless, it helps you focus your limited resources.

With your perfect target defined, a refreshed list of current customers/clients and renewed commitment to serving them, you are now well-positioned to begin effectively and efficiently hunting for new ones. Choose your analogy — shotgun or rifle, hurricane, or tornado — the more you narrow your definition, the more likely you'll find your "10."

STEP 7 — Goldilocks Was On to Something

You are confident you'll know your "10" — that perfect potential new customer/client — when you see it, because you've taken the time to define your target. The real test, however, is figuring out where you can find your 10 — or even the 7s, 8s or 9s. Given the many ways to hunt, consider experimenting until you determine the most effective and efficient approach for your business and your team. Brainstorming with team members who are in any way involved in the hunting process, including the inside administrative members, can be extremely useful.

With your ideal target profile in clear view, consider:

What companies, both generically and as far as specific names, best meet your criteria? Aspects to consider include:

1. Specific industries and/or professions — this may include those where you currently have or where you plan to have specialization.
2. Their location if you are trying to expand geographically.
3. Their size. While they cannot all be "10s," Goldilocks had the right idea: She tested the porridge, chairs, and beds until she found the one that was "just right."

Where do you find your target? This can be daunting, so break it down:

1. Generally, the narrower the field, the more difficult it is to connect. Experiment with a mix of both broad and narrow efforts.
2. Associations, community service organizations and clubs can provide networking opportunities.

Who are the likely influencers and/or decision-makers?

- Robert B. Miller and Stephen E. Heiman, in *The New Strategic Selling,* identify four potential influencers:
  1. Economic influencers — they have the final say.
  2. Users — they can kill a deal, but not close it.
  3. Technical influencers — they can keep a deal from getting to the Users, but they cannot close it.
  4. Coaches — they want you to close the deal, and they can provide some leverage.

- Current "loyal" customers/clients — with the emphasis on "loyal." These individuals are not likely to refer you if they are not completely delighted. Following up to ensure they are pleased is a great way to entrench your existing relationships.

- Referral sources — do not overlook some unsuspecting places! There is more there than you may think:
  1. All your staff
  2. Current suppliers and service providers
  3. Family and friends

If you want new customers/clients, the key is for people — all of the people you know, or at least most of the people you know — to understand you are "open for new business." Equally important is something my dad taught me. I heard it hundreds of times, and it's had a distinct and profound impact on my life: "Don't be afraid to ask. The worst they can say is no."

STEP 8 — "First I Look At The Purse" (Motown's The Contours)

A nickname I have earned from long, hard nights in places only the brave would dare to trod is Disco Danny. I admit it; I love all kinds of music, even disco. At the risk of even further dating — or, worse yet, downright outdating myself — I am reminded of a song by The Contours, of Motown Records: "First I Look At The Purse." We all know it; we have all done it. You get the proposal, and where is the first place you turn? To the page where you can check the price. Given its importance, the last subject of this blog series is pricing — an area where much thought is required. Some of the following guidelines just might be priceless.

Have you ever thought about why pricing is so important? Whether you are maximizing profits as a business, or services provided as a nonprofit, there are competing forces for the same dollar. Generally, that type of competition results in a win-lose situation. While that is not necessarily bad, focusing instead on win-win possibilities is a worthy endeavor. Consider what might happen:

1. New customers/clients, including owners and users, think their need is met — or, better yet, exceeded — for a fair price.
2. You build trust with new relationships; these new relationships may bring additional opportunities with them.
3. A win-win situation creates a potential booster — and perhaps referrals.
4. You — including owners and those involved in or impacted by the sale — think the price is fair.

The pitfalls of not having guidelines can cause irreparable harm, which often leads to lose-lose results. Try to avoid frustrating the following players:

1. Your "hunters," due to lack of clarity in the pricing process — including failing to specify their particular role, or lack thereof, as appropriate.
2. Those who have pricing responsibility, by interjecting 20-20 hindsight criticisms.
3. Yourself, by agreeing to take on work that has no profit — or, worse yet, work that has no marginal cash contribution.

21

Guidelines are like plans. They are essential and need to be viewed as subject to change if and when new information is compelling enough to warrant a change. Once you have your pricing guidelines, hold them with an open hand, rather than a clenched fist. Establish a process for pricing outside the boundaries — who has the authority, and under what circumstances? The reasons will vary, but may include:

1. Underpricing when trying to enter a new market.
2. Underpricing to fill capacity.
3. Underpricing to establish a new relationship.
4. Overpricing because you either think you must put in a proposal for other than profit motives, but you don't really want the work, or you're at capacity and would need outsourcing help if you were successful in obtaining the bid.

Whenever you are not successful, it is always helpful to try to understand why. Learning provides useful market data that may help you with future proposals.

Do you — and, equally important, your team — have guidelines for pricing your new business opportunities? Singing from the same song sheet may produce just the tune you want to hear.

By the way, just for the "record," the 1962 release of "First I Look At The Purse" came many years before my disco days of the '70s.
Thanks for following the series. It has been a privilege and a blast to do!

Tom's editorial comment:
If, while reading this series, you believe Dan could be helpful to your company, please contact him directly
at dan.doescher@sandboxpartnersint.com, or 248-701-8787.

The following are suggestions about how to best "Serve" your customers/clients.

Selling? Me?
June 23, 2014 // Tom Doescher //

I have always believed that every team member has a sales aspect to their job, be it internal or external. Unfortunately, when we say "sales," it often conjures up negative thoughts and feelings. In his latest book, *To Sell Is Human*, Daniel Pink (author of *Drive*) — once again citing some pretty compelling research — makes several surprising statements about those people who are most successful in sales.

The following are a few of his findings:

1. Thirty-five separate studies involving more than 3,800 salespeople found that the correlation between extroversion and sales was essentially nonexistent. In fact, the most successful salespeople are ambiverts — people who, on the extroversion/introversion scale, fall in the middle.
2. The most common thread in the people who are really good at selling is *humility*. Consider reading my March 29, 2012, Food for Thought article, which talks about the importance of humility for leaders and references a Patrick Lencioni article you may want to read.
3. Asking good questions and problem-*finding* are more important than problem-solving. Use the "Five Whys" — ask why five times, and you will be surprised what you will uncover. However, do not interrogate!
4. Listen, listen, listen. When others speak, we typically divide our attention between what they are saying now and what we are going to say next, and we end up doing a mediocre job of both listening and speaking.
5. Make it personal. In this high-tech, global economy, we often neglect the human element and adopt a stance that is abstract and distant. In the long run, relationships still matter.

Hopefully, you have picked up a tip or two and, at a minimum, you have a different attitude about selling. If you want more, I recommend reading Daniel Pink's book.

Editorial comment: In my experience, the associates in the best companies behave like owners.

Hire Owners
April 3, 2012 // Tom Doescher //

I hate to shop. In fact, I really hate to shop. But I needed to upgrade my wardrobe, so I ventured into Nordstrom's — and, to my surprise, I was delighted to meet Howard Klein. Klein probably deals with lots of guys like me, but he was amazing. He was direct, but not pushy. He offered a few choices, but not too many. He suggested items, but I did not feel like he was upselling me. He obviously really knew his business and was passionate about it.

Finally, I could not take it anymore, and I started interviewing him. I discovered that his grandfather had owned a men's clothing store, his father had owned a men's clothing store, and, for 25 years, he had owned a men's clothing store.

You would have thought he owned Nordstrom's, the way he behaved. So, should you try to hire "owners"? More on this subject next week.

Hire Owners, part 2
April 10, 2012 // Tom Doescher //

The crazy thing is that I actually looked forward to seeing Howard Klein at Nordstrom's again; meeting him made me want to return to the store, even though I hate to shop. The experience caused me to think about a possible strategy for hiring key associates. As I reflected on the subject, a manufacturing company with which I have worked came to mind. One day I met the sales manager, who used to own his own business. He was obviously excited about his new company and was glad to be there, and he told me, "I would do anything for Duane (the owner/CEO)." In a nutshell: If you want to have associates who really care about the business and act like owners, hire them. However, when you do that, you need to be sure to treat them like owners. Are you aware of a small competitor or a vendor whose owner would be a natural fit with your team? Think about it.

Another Owner Story
February 7, 2012 // Tom Doescher //

Last summer, my car windshield was the target of a stone that cracked the glass. The next morning, I went to the grocery store and, in the parking lot, I noticed a pickup truck with a sign advertising "glass replacement" on the side of it. The service this guy provided was world-class. He told me to go ahead and shop while he took care of the crack. When I returned, he called the insurance company on my behalf — and a few minutes later, I was on my way. (Well, not really. You know me; I had to find out more.) As it turns out, this is a franchise business and the man who fixed my windshield is the owner. As the owner, it's not surprising that he's willing to do whatever it takes to do the job well and make each and every customer happy. The question is, how do you get your associates to behave like you?

When Associates Behave Like Owners, Good Things Happen
January 24, 2012 // Tom Doescher //

A number of years ago I was on a plant tour, which I really love to do. When we arrived at a particular machining station, the owner asked the operator to explain what the machine was doing. The operator gave the most complete explanation I had ever heard, including the business case for purchasing this $250,000 machine. After she completed her explanation, I made the comment that she really knew a lot about this piece of equipment. Her response was that she had researched it and had recommended that the company purchase it.

Later on, as I was reflecting on our conversation, I thought of this rhetorical question: Do you think the operator was motivated to get that new equipment up and running smoothly, fast? How about you — do you create an environment where your associates behave as if they were the owners? Perhaps you should think about giving them the responsibility to act. If they feel empowered to act on behalf of the company, their sense of personal investment can move the entire organization further ahead, faster.

Service, Service, Service

May 7, 2012 // Tom Doescher //

I'm becoming obsessed with great service and am increasingly intolerant of **bad** service. I recently received great service in a completely unexpected place — the T.G.I. Friday's in the Atlanta Hartsfield-Jackson Airport. (You know what airports are like — crowds, lines, cranky people.) When I approached the hostess and gave her my name, I was told there would be a 10-minute wait. My wait, however, turned out to be less than 10 minutes. That was the first pleasant surprise. Then, when I was seated, the waitress politely asked for my order. My food arrived in less than 10 minutes and it was fresh, hot, and delicious. Surprised, I asked my waitress, Monique, "What's going on here?" She replied, "Our guests need to get in and out quickly, so we have to move fast to get them to their planes." (Monique also said she has worked at other restaurants, but this place has been, by far, the most financially rewarding.) My overall experience was refreshing, especially considering I had just left a pricey Florida resort where, poolside, I waited almost an hour for my food. I guess the resort staff wasn't overly concerned, maybe because no one needed to catch a plane. Do your customers/clients feel like I did at T.G.I. Friday's? Are your associates, like Monique, working hard because they are proud to be affiliated with your business?

They Make Me Feel Like I am the Only Member (Customer)

August 5, 2013 // Tom Doescher //

Last year, my partner and I joined the Detroit Athletic Club (DAC), which was established in 1887 and has occupied the same clubhouse since 1915. It's a great time to be at the DAC, with the rebirth that's taking place in the city of Detroit. When we joined the 3,800-plus-member DAC, we fully expected we would just be a "number." Wow were we surprised! Somehow, they (the doormen, the locker room attendants, the wait staff, and on and on) make us feel really welcome, as though we're the most important members.

Recently we had a chance to speak with the executive manager, and we took the opportunity to share our wonderful experience.

During our discussion, he told us that every team leader is challenged to help their team members get better, both personally and professionally, every year. What he described is the classic win/win situation: The member (customer) wins, and the team member wins.

Do your customers feel like we do about the DAC staff? Whether the answer is yes or no, we bet it has a lot to do with how your *associates* feel about their personal and professional development at your company.

That is Good Business. Or Is It?
November 25, 2013 // Tom Doescher //

My internet service is directly billed to my credit card, and I earn points that enable my wife and I to go skiing. A few months ago, the charge to the credit card unexpectedly increased 50 percent — so I contacted the service provider. After a lengthy, awkward conversation, the customer service rep actually reduced my monthly fee by 15 percent from what I had paid the prior year.

I was sharing this story with some business colleagues and told them that what really upset me was the fact that I knew many people who would just accept the charge, and not ask questions or jump through the required hoops to get it adjusted. At the end of the conversation, my colleagues stated that what my service provider had done was, in their estimation, "good business." Indeed, if maximizing profit in the short run is your business goal, then this sneaky tactic is a fantastic idea. But those of us who are in business for the long run believe it is a horrible practice.

I checked my service provider's website, and they clearly profess that their customers come first. Take a minute to consider this: Do your business practices *really* put the customer first? I have written about the idea of integrity. If that is not a trait, you're willing to vigorously pursue, please don't promise that the customer is No. 1, and then turn around and behave like my internet provider. In my opinion, it would be better to remain silent on the subject.

I am Sorry
November 11, 2013 // Tom Doescher //

Why are those words so hard to say? I am currently reading a great book, *Crucial Conversations: Tools for Talking When Stakes Are High*, by Kerry Patterson and several other authors.

It is a book I would recommend to almost anyone because it will help you in business, at home, or in any relationship.

I will probably comment on it more in another blog, but today I want to highlight one of the authors' recommendations. They suggest that when you realize you have made a mistake, it is important to start with an "**apology**," which they define as a statement that sincerely expresses your sorrow for your role in causing difficulty for others. Many of us have received what we called "qualified apologies," and maybe we've even delivered a few — something along the lines of, "I'm sorry you felt that way about me embarrassing you in front of your friends."

The other day I had an episode at my auto dealership. I have done business with them for a long time, and I've always received great service and had positive experiences. I was leasing a new vehicle, and I noticed a slight problem in the transaction. When I brought the problem to their attention, the finance manager took total responsibility and offered an unqualified apology for his oversight. He also solved the problem immediately. Do you and your team take total responsibility for customer/client problems, or do you place blame elsewhere?

In the story above, the dealership made a mistake — but the way they handled it has made me an even bigger fan of their establishment. We all make mistakes; it is how we handle them that separates the great from the average.

Can I *Please* Talk to Someone?
September 24, 2012 // Tom Doescher //

If you regularly read my blog and newsletter, you already know about my struggles with technology. Based on the feedback I receive, many of you can relate. Well, here is an issue I am still processing. I have an opinion about it, but I concede I may be wrong. I am not sure yet. Anyway, many of the online services which are free to subscribers fail to provide a phone number you can call if you have problems with any aspect of the service. You need to ask your questions via email, or by contacting an online help desk. Often, I do not know specifically what question to ask without being able to fully explain the circumstances, and I do not understand the written answers I receive. I just want to talk to someone!!!! I am sure Scott Klososky, a technology consultant who writes a very interesting newsletter for businesses trying to retool old dogs like me, would say, "Get over it." But I still wonder, is there a middle-ground solution for people like me, who sometimes struggle to stay on top of technological advances? Is it too much to ask for some degree of direct human contact?

How Accessible Are You?
August 19, 2013 // Tom Doescher //

In today's world, things move so fast that we believe it is very important to be (and to clearly appear to be) accessible to your customers/clients.

27

Despite all the new technologies, I continue to hear customers/clients complain that the people they do business with are hard to get ahold of. Sometimes that is true, but often it's merely perception. For example, do you frequently use email and cellphone greetings to let people know you are unavailable or on an extended absence? Why? Today, you can return emails and phone calls from anywhere in the world. Before we had cellphones, we put our home phone number on our business cards and told clients to use that number if they needed to get in touch with us. In more than 10 years, my partner and I only received one phone call at home — but our clients knew we were always available to them. Contrast that with our former doctor's office. It was impossible to get through to our doctor. So, even though we liked him, we left his 20-doctor medical practice. We now have a new doctor, and we have his cellphone number (we've never used it but knowing that we can if we ever need to is very comforting). What do your customers/clients say about the accessibility of their key contact at your company?

How Does Your Company Handle Customer/Client Complaints?
April 15, 2013 // Tom Doescher //

Last winter, my wife and I returned to our favorite place to ski in Colorado. In order to utilize our many frequent flyer miles, we had to take a flight that deposited us about three hours away from our destination. That meant we had to reserve a shuttle. Prior to our departure date we were contacted multiple times by the shuttle service, confirming our reservation — sometimes with the wrong date and/or time. Honestly, we thought we had a 50-50 chance of getting picked up. To our delight, the shuttle driver was waiting, with our name on a placard, upon our arrival. During our three-hour journey, we told the driver about our experience with his shuttle service. We related the story of the many phone calls we had received and told him how the calls and misinformation had created a great deal of anxiety. He gave us the name of the owner and said she would love to know about our experience.

On about the fourth day of our vacation, despite the fact that the sole purpose of the trip was relaxation, I decided to call the owner of the shuttle service. Due to our driver's strong encouragement, I thought it would be the right thing to do. And what was the owner's reaction? You guessed it. She was very defensive and cut me off several times. I finally terminated the call. When I got off the phone, I was angry, frustrated, and offended. After all, I was just trying to help a fellow businessperson.

How do you and your associates respond to legitimate service complaints? Are you willing to listen?

I believe world-class businesses convert these situations into opportunities to create loyal customers/clients.

Do You Really Believe What You Say?
December 17, 2012 // Tom Doescher //

I just read an article about Japan's Fukushima Daiichi nuclear power plant entitled "Japan Utility Says Nuclear Crisis Could Have Been Avoided." I then went to the Tokyo Electric Power Co.'s (TEPCO) website, and this is what it says: "TEPCO strongly wishes to be a nuclear power plant operator which has the world's highest level of safety awareness, engineering capabilities, and risk communication ability with society."

Before I make my point, I want to stress two things: First, I realize the company may have added this wording to their website in response to the accident that occurred in March of 2011; and second, my intention isn't to pick on TEPCO.

However, the wording on the company's website hit a nerve with me. As businesspeople, do we really believe what we say, or are we willing to stretch the truth strictly for the purpose of looking good? My experience tells me that you cannot answer this question with any certainty until you're really tested.

The other day I was talking with a business owner who told me he needed to remove one of his senior executives because of some unacceptable behavior that had violated the company's values. The owner told me that several years earlier, the expelled executive had been warned about his behavior. The owner went on to say, "I hated to let him go, since this executive ran a very profitable division and we really need him right now. But it was the right thing do."

This is where the rubber hits the road. Do you have a situation like TEPCO, where you know there are problems and you should act, but are not? Do you have a senior member of your team who violates your principles, but you look the other way because he makes your company a lot of money? Do you really believe what you say, and live by your principles and values?

Quicker Does Not Always Mean Better
November 19, 2012 // Tom Doescher //

This story will really date me, but please hang in there. I was at a reception one evening some years ago and was engaged in a fascinating conversation with a prominent corporate attorney. The fax machine was the latest technology at the time (no smart-alecky comments, please).

He was talking about how it was making an impact on his work life. He said, "Before the fax, my client would call me and explain his problem or issue. He would put the paperwork in the U.S. mail, and I would receive it a few days later. In the meantime, I had several days to think about my advice. The documents would arrive, and I would review them. I would then place a call and discuss his options.

Now, my client sends a fax and calls me immediately to ask my advice. I have no time to really think through the issues, or maybe seek advice from one of my partners. There's no way my advice is as good as it used to be." Imagine this story today, with smartphones! My caution to each of you is to have the courage to know when to slow the process down. Having the ability to push things through quickly does not necessarily translate into doing a better job. Think about this: Have you ever regretted sending an email or text?

What's More Important, Customer Service or Efficiency?
September 10, 2012 // Tom Doescher //

Believe me, I understand how efficiency and technology have substantially reduced business process costs. But give me a break! This past year, my heart medication pills were running low, so I logged onto the online pharmacy service I was using and reordered the medication. The service sent me a message saying that, by their calculation, it was too early to get a refill; they could not (and would not) process my order. I counted the pills, which come with 90 in a bottle, to see exactly how many were left. Because the online drug service refused to send me the pills, and in an effort to make the medication last until a refill would be allowed, I skipped taking a dose every third day.

Several months later, I became aware of a small pharmacy in my doctor's office building by the name of Oakland Pharmacy. What a breath of fresh air! Lynn, who usually takes care of me now, will call me when I need refills, and she arranges same-day delivery to my home. This ordeal made me wonder, where am I being efficient, but totally ignoring the impact it makes on my client?

What Was She Thinking?
August 27, 2012 // Tom Doescher //

Starting in 2003, I had the privilege of traveling regularly to China. Prior to this, I would have said I was tuned into customer/client service, and I would have considered myself relatively easy to please. My experience in China, though, opened my eyes to a new level of customer service. For example, many times I was the only foreigner on domestic flights in China. The attention and care paid to me was over the top.

This was the case even by non-English-speaking flight attendants. Although I may not have fully understood what was being said, I was always treated with respect and graciousness.

At the close of one trip, after receiving phenomenal treatment everywhere I went in China, I boarded my international flight to return home. I was sitting in an aisle seat across from the bulkhead, where families with children often sit because there is more room. There was an elderly Chinese gentleman in the bulkhead seat, and he was holding an infant. His bags were on the floor, not in the overhead compartment. (If you are a frequent flier, you know that bags, etc., must be stored in the overhead compartments during takeoff and landing.)

The flight attendant came by and, in a cranky voice, told the man to move his bags to the overhead compartment. She left, but he was preoccupied with the baby and did not move his bags. The flight attendant came back two more times and barked out her orders. Finally, she moved the bags herself. During the flight, as I reflected on the situation, I thought, "I bet he doesn't understand English; maybe this is his first airplane ride." I was embarrassed by the poor customer service he received, especially when I contrasted his experience with the thoughtful service I was given in China. It made me ask myself these questions: Do I ever speak a "language" my clients do not understand? Am I focused on my clients' comforts or making my job easier? How would I like to be treated if I were my client?

85 Years of Great Customer Service
August 13, 2012 // Tom Doescher //

A lot has been written with regard to customer service. In fact, I have written about it numerous times myself. The June 25, 2012 Automotive News video: Dealer Dick Mullen at 75: No games with customers is a refreshing locker-room talk from a very wise man — auto dealer Dick Mullen, of Mullen Motors in Southold, N.Y. Although it has been in business for 85 years, Mullen Motors would not quite make the "Built to Last" study conducted by Jim Collins; the study's subjects were required to have been in business for a minimum of 100 years. Even so, I think there is a lot we can learn from Mullen. I invite you to watch the video. I guarantee you will gain a wealth of valuable, common-sense advice on how to take care of customers/clients.

Intimate Customer Service
November 7, 2011 // Tom Doescher //

We've all experienced intimate customer service, like you expect to receive at the Ritz-Carlton. When business owners lose firsthand contact with their customers, the goal of providing intimate service often suffers.

A few years ago, my wife and I hired a well-known landscaping service. Despite their quality reputation, it seemed my wife soon had a part-time job communicating our desires to a rotating stream of workers. We finally switched to an owner-operated team — mom, dad, sister, and brother. If we have an important need or request, we can contact them via cellphone, and they respond promptly. Are you confident your associates take care of your customers' needs the same way you do, as the owner?

This Is "Really" Being Focused on the Customer

September 19, 2016 // Tom Doescher //

TOM DOESCHER //

My wife, Barbara, recently took her leased vehicle in for service. As the customer service rep was checking her in and reviewing the vehicle's history, he noted that she had previously been charged for maintenance that was included in the lease. Really? He then went on to tell her that he would process a check to refund her for the erroneous charge. Really? About a month later, the dealership check arrived in our mailbox. Really? As a regular reader of my posts, you know how hung up I am on customer service. This may be one of my best stories so far. You also know that I talk a lot about having your team members behave like owners. Think about it. No one would ever have known the difference — not us (the customer) or the boss (dealer/owner).

Wow, Glad They Had an Insider!

November 28, 2016 // Tom Doescher //

TOM DOESCHER //

In Uncle Dan's Hunter series, he talked about the importance of having an "insider" among your clients/customers. One of our clients recently experienced a nightmare, but fortunately they had a couple of great "insiders." The client has served an automotive OEM for many years and has enjoyed a true partner-type relationship. This past year, team members in our client's internal quality control system made a discovery.

32

A major assumption in their work was wrong, and it had resulted in some incorrect conclusions/data being provided to the OEM. Once they were certain of the facts, they immediately informed the OEM and began to redo their work at no cost to the client.

If that was not bad enough, a few weeks later the ultimate catastrophe struck. Unbeknownst to our client and their immediate client contact, the OEM's CEO was using the incorrect conclusion from their work as the basis for a presentation he was scheduled to make on the world stage of the New York International Auto Show. The good news is that the erroneous conclusion was discovered before the inaccurate facts were presented at the auto show. The bad news is that, at the last minute, the Hollywood-type presentation, with all its glitz and glamour, had to be significantly modified.

No, I am not kidding. You are probably ahead of me at this point, and you're correct: The CEO wasn't at all happy about the situation. (Actually, I would love to know what he said.) After a very tense week filled with awkward conversations, the storm blew over. Based on what I know, our client's insiders are the main reason they survived. Whew! So, I ask again: Do you have an insider among each one of your major clients/customers? We never know when a storm will strike.

p.s. This story has some other teaching points, such as confirming the value of providing **outstanding service** to a client over an extended period of time and informing clients **immediately** when a potentially disastrous situation is discovered.

Would You Recommend It to Your Mom?

February 20, 2017 // Tom Doescher //

TOM DOESCHER //

In my September 19, 2016, blog post, I told a story about an auto dealership's customer service representative who behaved more like an owner. Well, now I have another story about that service representative, Chad. Barbara and I took our vehicle in because of some issues we were concerned about. During our time with Chad, he said, "I always try to treat the vehicle owner like my mother. In other words, what would I do if it were my mother?" His comments triggered a fond memory for me. My dad spent his career as a mail carrier. With a little encouragement and mentoring, who knows what he could have done?

But he was proud of his accomplishments, and he was a wise man with an extra dose of common sense. Anyway, when Chad made his comment, it reminded me of the lens I have always used with my clients. If they (the client) were my dad, would I make this or that recommendation? It has been like a speed controller on a school bus, and it has helped me "do the right thing." Chad, thanks for the reminder and for being a wonderful example of excellent client focus.

Setting the Table

January 21, 2019 // Tom Doescher //

 TOM DOESCHER //

If any family members or good friends were to come to me and say they want to open a restaurant, I would beg them to pick another business. But Danny Meyer, owner of the Union Square Cafe in Manhattan and author of *Setting the Table: The Transforming Power of Hospitality in Business*, has somehow survived — and even thrived — in one of the most competitive markets in the world.

Recently I had the pleasure of hearing him speak, which provided some insight into his success. I believe many of his philosophies, some of which are listed below, apply to all of us in business. As always, I will offer some editorial comments:

1. Business, like life, is all about how you make people feel. It is that simple and it is that hard.
2. Hospitality is the foundation of Meyer's business philosophy. Virtually nothing else is as important as how one is made to feel in any business transaction.
3. Understanding the distinction between service and hospitality has been at the foundation of Meyer's success. Service is the technical delivery of a product. Hospitality is how the delivery of that product makes the recipient feel. (Editorial comment: In the past, I have shared David Maister's famous concept of the difference between quality service and quality work.)
4. Meyer credits several mentors for his success. (Editorial comment: Who are your mentors? The older I get, the more I am reminded of the impact made by those who mentored me, including my dad. I find myself quoting my dad, a career postal worker, more than ever.)

5. Invest in your community. A business that understands how powerful it is to create wealth for the community stands a much higher chance of creating wealth for its own investors. (Editorial comment: As I have learned, investment in the community is also very important to your team members, especially those under 30.)
6. Meyer has a list of traits he looks for in his managers, and it includes an infectious attitude, self-awareness, patience, and tough love, and not feeling threatened by others.
7. Meyer provides a great list of trust versus fear, including empowering v. ruling, giving v. selfishness, listening v. telling, and hopeful v. cynical.

When I heard Meyer speak, the comment that impacted me the most was related to his 5-step plan for addressing mistakes with a customer: Awareness, Acknowledgement, Apology, Action, and Additional Generosity. It was this last step that really resonated with me. Meyer instructs his team to do something special for a guest whose experience has been less than stellar, such as offering them an extra dessert or even a complimentary meal, depending on how bad the mistake was. In my experience, this is where many of us fall short. We may already have lost money on the transaction, so giving more away is not natural — but I think Meyer is on to something.

Especially in today's tech-dominated world, I strongly believe businesses that are able to provide a personal touch have a major competitive advantage. As an example, I have a client who recently purchased a pontoon boat, and he received a phone call from the owner of the boat manufacturer. How do you think he felt? How many other potential boat-buyers has he told — and will he tell — about his experience? Better yet, this client started calling his own customers, which has led to great success.

Are Your Clients/Customers Raving Fans?

April 9, 2018 // Tom Doescher //

TOM DOESCHER //

I am a fanatic about client/customer service, and I have written on the subject many times. Ken Blanchard and Sheldon Bowles, in their book *Raving Fans! A Revolutionary Approach to Customer Service*, have provided a new label that I love: **RAVING FANS**.

Like a few other business authors, they have styled the book as a novel, in order to make their point. Blanchard — well-known for his book, *The One Minute Manager* — and his co-author suggest defining what Raving Fans means to your business by determining your response to two statements. These declarations are simple but profound.

Declaration #1: Decide What You Want
This may sound trite, but business owners often struggle in trying to describe what they want in a few simple words. The authors provide some practical stories that will help you craft your company's declaration. (Note: This is the do-not-say-you-can-do-everything-for-everyone concept.)

Declaration #2: Discover What the Client/Customer Wants
Again, the authors offer some excellent examples to help you complete your declaration. As I was reading *Raving Fans*, I thought of a famous 1993 article written by Harvard professor David Maister: *Quality Work Does Not Mean Quality Service*. In my experience, this is a very common problem. I would summarize it by saying, "Don't assume you know what your client/customer wants."

Here is a great story to make the point: One of my clients went on a sales call with a new business development associate. They met with the business owner, who described what he was looking for and provided his budget. The associate developed a solution for the client that was within the budget he had been provided. When the associate met with his boss (my client) to share his proposal, the boss said, "That's not what the client wants," and he proceeded to describe what he believed the client *really* wanted. The associate replied, "That's double the budget!" My client suggested to the associate that he present both solutions to the prospective client — and, you guessed it, the business owner selected the higher-priced solution. My client, who has been in business for more than 30 years, really listens to his clients. Do you know what you want and what your client/customer wants?

Still Relevant After All These Years

December 8, 2014 // Tom Doescher //

TOM DOESCHER //

As many of you know, I am an avid reader of business books. After hearing about Dale Carnegie's famous book, *How To Win Friends & Influence People*, for the 50th time, I decided I had to get my own copy of the book. It was actually first published in 1936. Wow! Add me to the Carnegie Fan Club! How can a business book that's more than 75 years old still be relevant? Well, it is! It also nicely complements *To Sell Is Human,* by Daniel Pink. As you know, I am almost obsessed with getting leaders to provide actionable developmental feedback. Hopefully, I have encouraged you to be prepared, thoughtful, and careful with your word selection in your conversations and communications. Along those lines, here are his **WARNINGS**:

1. Criticism is futile because it puts a person on the defensive and usually makes him strive to justify himself.
2. B.F. Skinner, the world-famous psychologist, proved through his experiments that an animal rewarded for good behavior will learn much more rapidly and retain what it learns far more effectively than an animal punished for bad behavior.
3. Hans Selye, another great psychologist, said, "As much as we thirst for approval, we dread condemnation."

37

How to Win Friends & Influence People By Dale Carnegie

Fundamental Techniques in Handling People	Six Ways to Make People Like You
1. Don't criticize, condemn or complain. 2. Give honest and sincere appreciation. 3. Arouse in the other person an eager want.	1. Become genuinely interested in other people. 2. Smile. 3. Remember that a person's name is to that person the sweetest and most important sound in any language. 4. Be a good listener. Encourage others to talk about themselves. 5. Talk in terms of the other person's interest. 6. Make the other person feel important — and do it sincerely.
Win People to Your Way of Thinking	**BE A LEADER**
1. The only way to get the best of an argument is to avoid it. 2. Show respect for the other person's opinions. Never say, "You're wrong." 3. If you are wrong, admit it quickly and emphatically. 4. Begin in a friendly way. 5. Get the other person saying, "Yes, yes" immediately. 6. Let the other person do a great deal of the talking. 7. Let the other person feel that the idea is his or hers. 8. Try honestly to see things from the other person's point of view. 9. Be sympathetic with the other person's ideas and desires. 10. Appeal to the nobler motives. 11. Dramatize your ideas. 12. Throw down a challenge.	A leader's job often includes changing your people's attitudes and behavior. Some suggestions to accomplish this: 1. Begin with praise and honest appreciation. 2. Call attention to people's mistakes indirectly. 3. Talk about your own mistakes before criticizing the other person. 4. Ask questions instead of giving direct orders. 5. Let the other person save face. 6. Praise the slightest improvement and praise every improvement. Be "hearty in your approbation and lavish in your praise." 7. Give the other person a fine reputation to live up to. 8. Use encouragement. Make the fault seem easy to correct. 9. Make the other person happy about doing the thing you suggest.

Client (Customer) Service Review Meetings

January 25, 2016 // Tom Doescher //

TOM DOESCHER //

I was recently reminded of the importance of this practice when a client reported they had just lost five large customers. After a series of questions, I told the client, "I'm not overly troubled by the loss of the customers, based on the facts (i.e., these events often seem to occur in waves); however, I'm very concerned that your company was caught by surprise. That really bothers me."

A best practice we frequently recommend to our clients is to conduct Client (Customer) Service Review (CSR) meetings for their clients/customers — and that is what we suggested to this executive. On our website, go to the Resource section and scroll down to Other Essays & Articles. There, you will find what I call a CSR Checklist. The checklist provides an exhaustive list of best practices.

One of the most significant conversations you can have during the CSR involves discovering the identities of your "insiders." In my October 5, 2015, blog post, I discussed what the book *The New Strategic Selling* calls "coaches." I like to call them "insiders." Consider the individuals at your major clients/customers. Who will tip you off and let you know that you are in trouble? Maybe you offended someone inadvertently, or maybe a competitor has made some inroads. Who will tell you?

Did You Have a Paper Route?

August 7, 2017 // Tom Doescher //

TOM DOESCHER //

Today, most newspapers — for the few still reading them — are delivered by adults. That, in some ways, is sad to me. I had a *Detroit News* paper route that was passed on to my brother, "Uncle Dan," and then to my two sisters. As a paper boy, I was running a small business. I had to order the correct number of newspapers, deliver them on time, and collect the subscription fees from my customers. The first two activities were relatively easy but collecting the money could be challenging. Fortunately, I had my dad as a mentor/advisor.

To this day, I think my paper route and certain customers sharpened my collection skills, and it became personal. During all my years at Plante Moran, collecting fees was a serious business. I took failure to collect personally — and, as a result, my outstanding receivables were generally quite low.

My advice to you is that if you have team members who are responsible for collecting receivables, make sure they have the right attitude. They can't all have had a paper route but teach them to act as if it's their own money they're collecting — otherwise, they're just going through the motions. Good collection people can really benefit a company and reduce your borrowing costs.

2 BUILD YOUR OWN DREAM TEAM

My second category is Team.

Customers vs. Associates

March 13, 2012 // Tom Doescher //

TOM DOESCHER //

Successful owners/executives realize they need to spend an equal amount of time developing their associates and winning and retaining customers. While it is a fact that without customers you have no business, it's also true that without knowledgeable, well-trained, and motivated associates you cannot keep good customers. I have observed that some executives focus solely on customers — and have noted that their businesses suffer in the long run. Are you appropriately focused on recruiting, training, and retaining your associates?

Editorial Comment:

Some argue that the Team is more important than the Customer/Client. Either way, in my experience and observation of hundreds of companies, the best team almost always wins.

I will start off with the Dream Team series.

Build Your Own Dream Team
June 16, 2015

Most businesses are currently experiencing strong demand for their products or services. Very predictably, many say they are short of people at all levels, and some have even found themselves in a bidding war to hire top-quality team members. I often hear owners say, "Our people are our most important asset."

For that reason, it seems fitting to spend some time discussing people. I believe the best companies take into consideration the following elements when putting their team together:

1. **THE PERFECT CANDIDATE** — Clearly define the perfect candidate (skills, background, experience, etc.) and determine the best place to find them (a particular university, community college, high school, etc.).
2. **A GOOD FIT** — Establish a rigorous process to ensure the candidates you select are a good fit with your company and the position, and vice versa.
3. **CO-OP** — Offer internships, co-ops, and apprenticeships to attract great talent to your company.
4. **MENTOR** — Make buddy/mentoring programs available to your team members.
5. **FEEDBACK** — Offer clear, actionable developmental feedback to all team members.
6. **ADVANCEMENT** — Provide opportunities for advancement.
7. **RE-RECRUITING** — Develop and monitor your re-recruiting process.
8. **A SPECIAL PLACE** — Create a special place that people are proud of, and where they want to work.

THE PERFECT CANDIDATE

You may think it's obvious but take a minute to ponder exactly who you're looking for at all levels of your company. What background, skills, education, and experience do you desire in new hires? You already have team members, and that is good — but think about finding and developing a long-term dream team. Over the years, I have observed that most successful and profitable companies develop their own players.

As an example, you may be looking for high school students who have shown an interest in making things — and maybe have participated in school-to-work or co-op programs — for your shop floor team. If that is the case, have you developed relationships with your local high schools? Several years ago, I heard the owner of a very successful auto supplier give a presentation on this subject. I will never forget when he said, "If we can convince a high school student to join our company instead of going directly to college, we have a chance of developing a great team member. As they progress at the company and show promise, we send them to college. However, if they go directly to college, we don't even get a shot at them — or they with us." He went on to add, "As they continue to take on more responsibilities and grow, they make pretty good money, too."

I have a technology client who has had some nice success recruiting at Kettering University (formerly known as GMI). The client is looking for smart, hard-working software developers, and has found that Kettering attracts those types of students. Are you thinking about developing your own future team members? Do you know what you are looking for? Do you know where to find them?

FINDING A GOOD FIT

Years ago, I received some sage advice from a guy who hired a lot of great people. One day he said to me, "If someone is smart enough, they can probably perform well in most jobs. The trick is to find the perfect fit for the company and for the candidate." The following are some suggested methods for you to use when you want to increase the likelihood that your candidates are, indeed, great fits for your company.

1. Be able to clearly articulate the vision/mission/dream of the company. For example, I joined a small, local firm because I did not want to travel excessively. If the vision of the company had been to serve clients throughout the world, I would not have been a good fit.
2. Make sure you have a good job description.
3. Engage a company executive who can help you determine what you are really looking for.
4. Define what success will look like as concretely and clearly as you can and share these ideas with the candidates.
5. As you interview candidates, be open-minded and reflective. Maybe you will find an outstanding person you can use somewhere else, if not in the job you're looking to fill at the moment. This happened to me once, and I almost missed it. We hired a great person to solve another problem we had, rather than what I went into the interview looking for. Remember: The team with the best players usually wins.
6. Consider using personnel assessments.
7. Think about enlisting retained search consultants when you want to fill senior executive positions.
8. They are usually able to find talent that you cannot. Plus, they are very objective and focused on achieving a good fit for the company *and* the candidate.

If you do it right, the process is a lot of work. But on the other hand, what are the costs of bad hiring decisions and their impact on your customers/clients and your team?

As the old television commercial said, "You can pay me now, or pay me later."

CO-OP

To be successful building your own dream team, I believe a best practice includes offering internships, co-ops, apprenticeships, or similar experiences. This provides you and the prospective team member with a chance to kick the tires. According to a survey conducted by the National Association of Colleges and Employers, 40 percent of respondents' new hires came from internships or co-op programs.

I would encourage you to follow a structured approach; students today have lots of options, and you want to ensure that their time with you is a quality experience. Often, they can become your best recruiters when they return to the classroom.

Sometimes companies complain that they invest a lot of time and money training someone who then ends up going to work for a competitor. I have a colorful answer to this concern, but my polite answer is: "They're yours to lose. If you take care of them and give them a good experience, they won't leave." In my mentoring discussion below, I will recommend a system that will almost guarantee the students you want to work for you will stay.

I'm aware of a $400 million professional service firm that had two managing partners who began working at the firm as summer interns, where they were proofreaders. Fortunately, their supervisor was wise enough to observe their potential and he made a special point of introducing them to the right partners. As they say, the rest is history.

As many of you know, apprenticeships for shop floor team members, which were very common years ago, are rare — so you can really distinguish your company from your competitors in this way and attract the best students.

Do you have a pipeline for new hires such as internships, co-ops, or apprenticeships?

I believe there is no downside to this best practice!
MENTOR

Over the years, I have observed that team members do better if they have a "sponsor." By that, I mean someone senior to the team member who takes a special interest in the younger (or newer) person and their career.

Why not adopt that as a standard practice? Assign someone senior to each new person, to mentor and look out for them. A buddy or mentor is someone safe; it's someone a new hire can go to and comfortably ask sensitive or even embarrassing questions. Senior team members can give their mentees tips and talk about their own career. Our experience is that most buddies/mentors like the role.

If you decide to start a mentoring program, make sure you provide training to the mentors. Some people are naturals, but do not assume everyone will know what to do.

p.s. My longtime mentor, Ken Kunkel, is still advising me.

FEEDBACK

The best companies are exceptional at giving team members regular, clear, actionable, and developmental feedback. Ideally, the suggestions are offered as close to the time the observation is made as possible. I have noticed that many of the feedback forms companies use are potentially quite negative. Many people say their annual review is a negative experience, and I believe part of the reason is because of the forms.

I like to refer to a review as an "annual career development and planning session" (CDPS). Here is a list of tips supervisors might want to keep in mind:

1. Prepare, prepare, prepare.
2. Make sure you spend the appropriate amount of time on the team members' strengths and unique contributions. Write them down. The written word is powerful!
3. Most CDPS meetings are with team members who are doing great, so please be positive and upbeat.
4. The CDPS is a great time to re-recruit the team member. (More on this idea later.)
5. Be very clear with any feedback and offer concrete, actionable developmental suggestions.
6. Ask the team member for feedback. What are they observing and thinking?
7. Thank the team members for their contributions to the company in the past year(s).
8. In a few situations, there will be a need to deliver a strong performance message (i.e., I am concerned that you haven't made

progress in XXXX). These sessions require special care and preparation. I recommend that, after your discussion, you ask the team member to prepare a summary of the needed performance change(s), including listing specific dates for meeting their goals. How do your team members feel about these annual sessions? Consider asking them.

ADVANCEMENT

If you want to build a lasting organization, provide advancement opportunities for your team members. This is a huge differentiator in motivating and retaining good people. Just to be clear, I am not talking about promoting unqualified individuals. I could tell you countless stories about people who started in one position or department and progressed to another. Often, it is the supervisor or mentor who suggests the change, based on knowing the person's strengths. Here are just a few examples of how people advanced in their careers:

1. A woman who started with an automotive OEM as an administrative assistant and eventually became an executive was recruited away to serve as CEO/president of a number of companies.
2. An office helper became a key member of the marketing team as a result of his technology and social media hobbies.
3. A machine operator became director of quality at a middle-market automotive supplier.
4. An executive assistant became president of Southwest Airlines.
5. A professional service firm wanted to start a new service and offered the opportunity to a young professional who started a department that has grown to include more than 100 people.
6. A CPA became a marketing professional.

The point is that it's important to give your team members hope for their future with the company. Sometimes you may see traits in a person and challenge them to transfer to a new area where you think they could excel, thereby giving them a chance for advancement. If you have someone who you think is a really great worker and a good fit with your company, and you do not want to lose them, take the time to figure out where they would fit best. In all the cases mentioned above, many more team members were motivated and encouraged to stay with their current company just by seeing that there were new opportunities for them.

Do you have a process to identify key team members? Do you have a system to smoothly transfer team members from one department to another?

Do you ask your team members, in their career development and planning sessions, if there is somewhere else in the company they would like to work?

RE-RECRUITING

So, what is re-recruiting? It is a deliberate effort to retain your team members. It may be a negative motivator, but I always assume two things: (1) I need the team members more than they need me; (2) They have lots of other options to choose from.

Often, I have experienced and observed that the most important team members are taken for granted. More often than not, leaders spend time with the people who have issues, not their stars. I recommend taking a continuous, thoughtful approach that might include the following:

1. Have dinner with the team member and, if appropriate, include their spouse.
2. Send hand-written notes to the team member's spouse about a job well done or after a long, difficult assignment.
3. Send hand-written notes of praise or encouragement to the team member.
4. Single out the team member in front of others and mention a special job that was done well.
5. Ask if you can relieve some of their workload.
6. Visit their personal office.
7. Visit them on a job site.
8. Use travel time with them to praise them for a recent job well done.
9. Share positive feedback from a customer/client or from another senior executive.

If you notice, nothing on this list costs much money — the only thing these suggestions require is a little time. Are you regularly re-recruiting your team members, especially your stars? What would they say?

A SPECIAL PLACE

It may seem obvious, but to build a great team you must create a special place to work. Much has been written on this subject; one of my favorites is *Drive: The Surprising Truth About What Motivates Us*, written by Daniel Pink. I have written about his work several times and would highly recommend reading his book. In addition, Marcus Buckingham, in *First, Break All The Rules*, provides a very practical list.

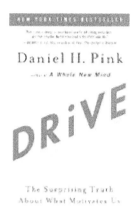
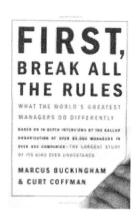

In summary, I highly recommend that you build your own "Dream Team" and, when you do, have a plan that includes the following: Know the team members you want, and where you can find them; utilize a rigorous interviewing process; offer internships and apprenticeships; formalize mentors; provide clear, actionable feedback and advancement opportunities; constantly re-recruit your team; and create a special place where people love to work.

p.s. I believe "celebrating successes" and healthy humor are important, too, and I may discuss those subjects in the future.

Great People/Companies Deserve Great People

July 25, 2016 // Tom Doescher //

TOM DOESCHER //

Over the years, I have spent time observing top-notch companies such as Southwest Airlines, The Ritz Carleton, and Plante Moran, among others. One thing I have noticed is that these companies tend to hire outstanding people. Too often, I come across great people who are working for less-than-great companies, and vice versa. With my clients, I encourage them not to settle for less than the best.

I have committed myself to connecting great people with great companies.

While I hate to use clichés, it is a fact that when great people combine their collective experiences and skills, one plus one equals three.

48

If you own or are leading a company, would you say that your team members are "great"? If you are a team member, would you say that you are with a great company?

It is All About "Attitude"

March 7, 2016 // Tom Doescher //

TOM DOESCHER //

Over the past year, Barbara and I have had a chance to experience/observe a landscaping company that provided world-class service to us on three different projects. We were so impressed, we asked to meet with the owner/founder of the company. We told the owner how amazed we were by his employees' professionalism, knowledge, and personal attention to our projects. Our question for him was, "Why?"

To our surprise, he quoted the famous Notre Dame football coach, Lou Holtz, who said, "Your talent determines what you can do. Your motivation determines how much you are willing to do.

Your **attitude** determines how well you do it." Those of you who know me will understand that I have used a lot of adjectives related to team members, but I probably have never used the word "attitude."
As I reflected on the role of attitude, I thought, "He's on to something." Although he gave several reasons for and examples of why his team performs the way they do, I left the meeting thinking, "This guy has summarized a lot in one word: attitude." Are you tolerating team members with "negative 'tudes"? If your answer is "yes," this is my advice: **DON'T!**

We Need More Joes Today

July 30, 2012 // Tom Doescher //

Joe, born in 1948, has operated the shoeshine stand at Flint Bishop Airport since 1980. What a breath of fresh air he is! He provides an outstanding shoeshine — one of the best I have ever had. He wears a collared shirt and a tie, is very polite, smiles a lot, and works hard. Joe, originally a migrant worker from Texas, has only a third-grade education, but you would never guess that. Rather than dwelling on the burdens he has carried, in what certainly can't have been an easy life, he beams with pride when he shares stories about his six children, 13 grandchildren, and three great-grandchildren. All six children are college-educated and have good jobs.

One is a college professor, two are architects, two are self-employed in business, and one is a nurse. As I was leaving his stand recently, I asked him how much longer he was planning to work. He said, "As long as I can!" How refreshing it is to meet someone who is so enthusiastic, positive, and happy to be working. I hope his story is as encouraging and uplifting to you as it is to me.

p.s. I gave him a very large tip, and I'm sure I'm not the only one to do so. This is yet another example of how giving your clients great service pays off.

Are You Holding Your Team Accountable?
December 3, 2012 // Tom Doescher //

One of my favorite books is *Who Says Elephants Can't Dance?* by Louis V. Gerstner Jr. In his closing comments, he says, "People do what you inspect, not what you expect." I was reminded of this thought-provoking advice when I read "What Happened to Accountability" by Tom Ricks in the October 2012 issue of the *Harvard Business Review*. Instead of me attempting to summarize a great article please go to a 13-minute podcast interview of Ricks entitled "How a Culture of Accountability Can Deteriorate" on the HBR website. As a leader/business owner, would you say you're more like General Marshall or General Taylor?

There Are Leaders All Over the Plant
October 8, 2012 // Tom Doescher //

A number of years ago I was in a meeting with a high-profile Tier 1 automotive CEO. The subject was leadership on the plant floor. His premise was that there are leaders throughout our companies, but we — the chairmen, managers, and supervisors — do not see them. To make his point, he told those of us in attendance, "The other day I walked around one of our plants and randomly interviewed machine operators. I asked them about their activities outside of work.

To my amazement, most of the associates with whom I spoke had 'leadership roles' in their communities — they were Little League coaches, subdivision presidents, PTA presidents, deacons at their church, or owned small businesses." He went on to say, "We have untapped talent already on our team, and we need to get better at engaging them."

You may want to re-read my June 12, 2012, Food for Thought entitled "Levels of Leaders," and then ask yourself this question: Do I have a way to determine if my associates are working at their highest level? Do I have a future plant supervisor or even a plant manager already on the team?

What can you do to discover the potential leaders in your business?

I Did Not Think Linda Could Do It, But She Fooled Me

November 27, 2017 // Tom Doescher //

TOM DOESCHER //

Years ago, I was meeting with a longtime client who was also a business owner. He informed me that one of his key executives was planning to leave and asked if I thought her assistant, Linda, could handle the job. Without thinking much about it, I said, "I don't think so," to which he said, "I agree." Some time went by and, based on a number of factors, he decided to give Linda a chance.

Now, let me tell you a little bit about the executive who was leaving. I believe most people would have given her relatively high marks because her department functioned well. She had a very strong personality, and, in retrospect, she probably was overly controlling without causing any obvious issues.

You are probably ahead of me at this point. It turned out Linda was very successful, and I believe my client and I both would agree she outperformed her predecessor.

So, what is the point? After that experience, whenever a similar situation arose, I would attempt to determine whether the No. 2 individual was being held back and hiding their real skills and talents, just to get along with their boss. How many Lindas get passed by? Do you have any Lindas in your organization that you may be overlooking or underutilizing? As you know, leaders are hard to come by. Do you have a true leader who is hidden in your midst?

Do You Want to Turn Followers into Leaders?

March 5, 2018 // Tom Doescher //

TOM DOESCHER //

In *Turn the Ship Around!* L. David Marquet, a retired Navy nuclear submarine captain, proposes using a leader-leader model rather than a leader-follower model in the workplace. If you know anything about the military, the power of his contrarian point of view is revolutionary.

Based on firsthand experience, having survived U.S. Army basic training at Fort Ord a few decades ago, it seemed to me that the Army's goal was to get us to do whatever they told us to do, no matter how stupid or unreasonable it may have been. Some of the absurd things drill instructors said to us were laughable — although, for self-preservation, no one would dare laugh out loud. I recall coming home on leave for the first time and Barbara asking me, What is the matter? The opinionated fellow she had married suddenly was not able to make any decisions for himself. That is when I realized that, in order to survive, I had put myself in a mental state where I just did whatever my superiors told me to do, no matter what I personally thought. As a result, I had become — and remained throughout my military career — a really GOOD follower.

In his book, this former captain is proposing something very foreign to the military. Marquet says leadership in the armed forces has historically been all about controlling people, but he goes on to admit that there is a vast untapped human potential being lost under the leader-follower model. I know you are trying to figure out the business application. Well, if you're a regular reader, you know I've commented many times on the importance of listening to your team members.

Even when you don't like their input. Finally creating an atmosphere where team members at all levels are encouraged to share their ideas. Marquet offers an interesting point of view that I believe applies to businesses as well as the military.

In addition to the above, Marquet provides some insight into the how the leader-follower model is only effective in the short run. He gives examples of submarines with effective leader-follower captains who failed under a new captain. In the past, I have addressed the importance of business succession; Marquet believes the leader-leader model is best for succession. If you are like many of us who prefer to control, I would suggest reading *Turn the Ship Around!* I am certain you'll be encouraged by Captain Marquet's revolutionary ideas.

I believe the absolute best way to develop leaders and build a team is to create, both formally and informally, a mentoring culture.

What Does Mentoring Look Like?

June 18, 2012 // Tom Doescher //

There is no secret formula for mentoring someone, but one thing is certain: It requires spending a lot of time together. One of my favorite mentoring stories involves an owner-operated manufacturing business where the founder — an Ivy-League-schooled, impressive, enlightened individual — was preparing his son to run the business. One of the many examples of this owner's insight was the fact that he had an open-office landscape for his team, himself included. Because of this setup, I often had the privilege of observing the father/founder meeting with his son — and I admit I would try to eavesdrop on their conversations.

What I observed was the father asking a lot of questions, and then patiently listening to his son's answers. I also saw mutual respect, and never detected any form of lecturing.

I watched the interactions between a son who really wanted to learn, and a father who wanted his son to be successful. It was truly a wonderful picture, and a perfect example of good mentoring.

p.s. The father has since passed away, and the son is at least as impressive as his father. As a result, the company continues to prosper.

What Is a Mentor?

October 13, 2014 // Tom Doescher //

The term "mentor" has become popular in recent years, although it has been a concept forever. There are countless examples of business, political, religious, and sports leaders who credit their success to their "mentor" — or, like I like to say, their "coach."

As I have reflected on my own life, I have realized that I've been blessed with more than my share of coaches.

What are the benefits of a mentor? To me, a mentor is a role model who is someone further along in life than you. The mentor may provide values, skills, techniques, and possibly a network.

Most of all, a great mentor tells you things you may not want to hear.

Early in my career, one of my mentors suggested I improve my grammar. Instead of using the phrase "constructive criticism," or "weaknesses," another mentor emphasized personal and/or professional development.

Maybe a rhetorical question you could ask yourself is: Am I a better person because of a mentor?

I've been fortunate to have many great mentors over the years, including my dad, my Uncle Pete (Wesley C. Carlos, a successful high school football coach), Coach Bob (my high school wrestling coach), Frank Moran (founder and managing partner of Plante Moran), and Ken Kunkel (my Plante Moran team partner who is still mentoring me today). In addition, I have identified close to 20 others who I would say have had a meaningful impact on my life.

As I meet with executives, I am shocked by how many would say they've never had a mentor. This got me thinking and asking myself, Why do I have so many and others have none? Is it a matter of pure luck?

Is it possible there are potential mentors all around us, and maybe we are the ones who need to take the first step?

As I reflected more, I thought about the great advice I have received from so many "peers" — even those who are "junior" to me.

So maybe the real question is: Are you an island? Are you the Marlboro man? (For my younger readers, the Marlboro man was the image of a self-sufficient man who could do it himself; a true loner.)

Is There a Reason You May Not Have Any Mentors?
June 5, 2017 // Tom Doescher //

 TOM DOESCHER //

For decades, I have been fortunate to have so many mentors who have poured into my life, and I have written about it more than once. I have also observed that many executives I meet have very few, if any, mentors. So, me being me, I concluded once again that I am a "lucky guy."

The other day, I was expressing to a group of executives how fortunate I am and how sad I feel for those individuals without mentors, who go it alone.

One of the executives, a longtime friend and colleague who happens to be a clinical psychologist, said, "Did you ever consider that possibly you have so many mentors because you're open to and solicit input from others?"

Believe or not, I had never had that thought. So, I ask you: Do you have mentors? If your answer is no, then why not?

Fascinating Mentoring by a Dad

May 2, 2016 // Tom Doescher //

TOM DOESCHER //

Somehow, I missed Steve Wozniak's book *iWoz* when it was published in 2006, five years before Walter Isaacson's now-famous book, *Steve Jobs*. My regular readers know I have written several times about Steve Jobs, but I knew very little about his Apple co-founder, Wozniak. At the end of the book, Wozniak states that he wrote the book for two reasons. The first was to set the record straight. The second — and I quote — was "To give advice to kids who are like I was. ... Kids who feel they're outside the norm ... who feel it in themselves to design things, invent things, engineer things."

My biggest takeaway from *iWoz* was Wozniak's description of how his dad mentored/fathered him. His father, a Lockheed engineer, was the perfect person for this young, gifted inventor. In his own words, "My dad guided me, but I did the work. And my dad, to his credit, never tried to teach me formulas about gravitational power and electric power between protons, or stuff like what the force is between protons and electrons. That would have been way beyond what I could understand at that point. He never tried to force me to try and jump ahead because I wouldn't have learned it."

Wow. I am sure you can imagine how easy it would have been for his dad to push him, like some other famous fathers. Mr. Wozniak's perfect mentoring contributed to one of the greatest technological discoveries of all time.

Question: Would your team say this about you?

p.s. When Steve Wozniak was a child, he says his goal was to build something that would end up allowing him to do something really good for people. I would suggest he accomplished his goal and then some.

A Tribute to My Father and Mentor

March 31, 2014 // Tom Doescher //

On December 7, 2013, Al Doescher, a common man with a lot of wisdom, passed after enjoying a very fruitful life. In reflecting upon his life, I connected some dots I had never thought of before. The following is partially therapy, but hopefully some advice that will enhance your life and business. Enjoy.

As many of you know, Frank Moran, founding partner of Plante Moran, had an enormous impact on my life and my family; as a result, he has been mentioned or quoted many times in previous blogs or in the Food for Thought articles. The first time I heard Frank speak, it was special. His philosophies connected to something deep inside of me.

From that first moment, I said, "I'm all in" — and I never looked back for 40 years. Those of you who have been receiving my blogs know I identified four traits observed in the greatest leaders and labeled them the "Big 4." The first trait is a high degree of self-knowledge or, as Socrates would say, "Know thyself." A new insight for me has been the realization that my dad and Frank Moran were philosophically similar.

Now I know why I was so at home at Plante Moran!

Anyway, here are 10 Al Doescher proverbs:

1. Every day is a bonus.
2. Life is a bowl of cherries. Watch out for the pits.
3. One day at a time.
4. It is what it is.
5. What you gonna do?
6. You can't spend whatcha ain't got.
7. Save your nickels and dimes.
8. He puts his pants on one leg at a time, just like everybody else.
9. The Golden Years ain't so golden.
10. He's dumb like a fox.

Hopefully, there are one or two that will be helpful to you in your life or business. In recent years I have come to realize that, most days, I draw upon the mentoring I received as a child. So now you know more about me, too.

Buckingham's 8 Questions

December 11, 2017 // Tom Doescher //

TOM DOESCHER //

Those of you who personally know me or have been reading my blogs are aware that I have highly recommended using the **12 questions** found in the book *First, Break All the Rules,* by Marcus Buckingham.

This summer, I heard Buckingham speak, and discovered he has pared his 12 questions down to eight (fewer is always better). During his presentation, he explained that some of the original 12 questions were focused on the company, while others pertained to the team member.

He went on to say that the best employers encourage their team leaders to really understand their team members' point of view. In reviewing and reorganizing his original 12 questions, Buckingham classified half of the questions (four) as company-focused; the other half address the individual team member. Then, he paired up the questions and categorized them: Purpose, Excellence, Support, and Future.

	"WE"	"ME"
PURPOSE	I AM REALLY ENTHUSIATIC ABOUT THE MISSION OF MY COMPANY.	AT WORK, I CLEARLY UNDERSTAND WHAT IS EXPECTED OF ME.
EXCELLENCE	IN MY TEAM, I AM SURROUNDED BY PEOPLE WHO SHARE MY VALUES.	I HAVE A CHANCE TO USE MY STRENGTHS EVERYDAY AT WORK.
SUPPORT	MY TEAMMATES HAVE MY BACK.	I KNOW I WILL BE RECOGNIZED FOR EXCELLENT WORK.
FUTURE	I HAVE GREAT CONFIDENCE IN MY COMPANY'S FUTURE.	IN MY WORK, I AM ALWAYS CHALLENGED TO GROW.

As with the 12 questions, I would highly encourage leaders/supervisors to use the **Buckingham 8 Questions** as a tool for career planning sessions (annual reviews) and/or as a gut check to make sure you're thinking about questions from your team members' point of view.

One of the most important characteristics of a great mentoring relationship is a solid oral and written feedback culture.

I Want to Get Better!
June 9, 2014 // Tom Doescher //

After working with a number of clients, it has become clear to my partner and I that we are incredibly fortunate to have received more developmental feedback than most of our peers. That being said, we were also fortunate to have been the recipients of a *lot* of mentoring, which we admit we may have taken for granted. I benefited from the Plante Moran environment, which provided regular improvement suggestions and gave very specific feedback every six months. It was not a program; it was a way of life. I believe in outside training programs like Harvard and the Center for Creative Leadership, but the best way to improve your team and company results is to provide continuous developmental feedback. Why? Because it is very specific to each individual team member and your business. The question is, do your team members get regular, actionable feedback to help them be better? (And I am not talking about a program or forms.)

Get started this way. Twice a year, meet with your key team members and tell them two things they are really good at. Then, give them two suggestions for how they can become even better. People are dying for candid, truthful feedback. They want to do better, and they need your help.

World-Class Feedback
June 3, 2019 // Tom Doescher //

TOM DOESCHER //

is what Kim Scott, author of *Radical Candor*, is referring to when she describes how you can "Be a Kick-A__ Boss Without Losing Your Humanity." If you have been a reader for a while, you know that, on more than one occasion, I have encouraged team leaders to provide their associates with quality feedback. At Plante Moran, where I received great feedback from many different partners and associates (I did not say I always liked it), we referred to it as "Candor is Kindness."

Scott had the privilege of working for Apple and Google during their formative years and, per her book, both companies, although they used different styles, were havens for constructive feedback.

Here are two specific examples of quality, actionable feedback that I received. Early in my career, Plante Moran's founding partner, Frank Moran, encouraged me to work on my grammar. I was a young hotshot, a recent college graduate with a high-grade point average, and Frank's comments could have offended me. But he handled the situation in the most delicate way, and I am forever grateful for his feedback. Another time, my team supervisor and mentor, Ken Kunkel — who provided hundreds of great suggestions — gently told me that I had "coffee breath". I give these as simple but very personal examples. When I read Scott's book, I was reminded of both Frank and Ken.

Based on my observations and experiences with privately owned businesses, I have found that many bosses aren't providing good, actionable feedback to their team members. If you own a business or are responsible for leading a team of people, I highly recommend you read *Radical Candor*. Scott, whose mentor was/is Sheryl Sandberg, COO of Facebook, offers some great, practical examples and advice regarding feedback and career planning.

I am going to leave it there and encourage you, after reading the book, to take the risk of giving your team members developmental feedback (stuff you've talked to your colleagues about but have never shared with the specific person). If it would help, I would be happy to role-play a situation with you.

Do You Have a System to Get Input from Younger Associates?
March 4, 2013 // Tom Doescher //

Recently I had the privilege of hearing Angela Ahrendts speak about the transformation of the 150-year-old British icon Burberry. According to Ahrendts, Burberry's CEO, an important contributor to the company's success was the off-site meetings she conducted with the youngest and brightest Burberry associates. As I listened, I was reminded of Apple's "Top 100" retreats, conducted by Steve Jobs, and the "ranks off" meetings suggested by technology consultant Scott Klososky.

If you have a way of getting uncensored feedback from your younger team members, I would love to hear about it. If not, I would highly encourage following the lead of Ahrendts, Jobs, and Klososky in developing a similar process that will fit in with the character and culture of your company.

59

Are You Good at Giving AND Receiving Great Developmental Feedback?

May 12, 2014 // Tom Doescher //

I have read many books and articles about "giving" feedback. I have written about "giving" feedback. At the Center for Creative Leadership, my partner and I were trained on how to "give" feedback. But we have *never* read or heard any advice about "receiving" feedback. Once again, the *Harvard Business Review* January 2014 article "Finding the Coaching in Criticism" offers some very practical suggestions for Type A personalities like us. This is a must-read, even if you have to pay for it. (Just for the record, we do not get any kickbacks from *HBR*.)

I will begin with an observation, and then tell a story (you know I love to tell stories). One of many contributions Bill Hermann, managing partner of Plante Moran from 2001-2009, made was to change the company's internal language from having a focus on making constructive criticism to emphasizing developmental feedback.

In my 38th annual performance review (just two years before my retirement), Bill asked, with a smile on his face, "Tom, what are you going to do different this year to improve your performance?" How do you think I felt? It may surprise you, but I can honestly say it made me feel energized and enthusiastic! Setting goals for yourself is motivating; if there was nothing to improve upon, what value is there in working hard?

Now the story. Months before my retirement, I was involved in a number of the partners' annual performance reviews. As I was preparing for one of these sessions, another partner said, "We need to be careful in this annual review with Charlie so that we (the three of us) do not talk too much and Charlie has time to express himself."

This being my last performance review with Charlie, of whom I was very fond, I could not hold back — and I talked too much. I am certain those of you who know me aren't at all surprised.

About an hour later, one of the partners in attendance stopped by my office. He said, "You talked too much! Because you will be involved in several more partner performance reviews, you need to chill." I reacted in a way that was open to receiving the feedback, and rather than being defensive about the criticism, I modified my behavior. Eureka!!!

Please read the article and change the way you react to feedback. You will be better off — and so will those people with whom you interact.

The Re-Recruiting Gold Medal Award-Winner

February 6, 2017 // Tom Doescher //

TOM DOESCHER //

In my *Build Your Own Dream Team* Food for Thought, I encouraged company owners and senior executives to have deliberate re-recruiting activities. I suggested sending handwritten notes to team members, recognizing a job well done, and possibly sending notes to the individual's spouse or parents, as well. I emphasized that most of these acknowledgements don't need to cost any money; the gesture is simple but powerful, and the only thing it requires is a little time.

I recently became aware of a situation that is worthy of the Re-recruiting Gold Medal. A company with a very nice, spacious showroom offered one of its young team members the use of the facility for his wedding reception. Wow!!! These guys just set the bar pretty high.

Stephen Covey used the metaphor of making deposits in someone's Emotional Bank Account. The company owners mentioned above made a huge deposit to the Emotional Bank Accounts of this team member, his family, and even their other team members.

And what was the cost? Nothing! I would love to hear about other creative re-recruiting stories that I can share with my readers.

We Are More the Same than Different

December 20, 2011 // Tom Doescher //

I have had the privilege of interacting with people of almost every color, language, culture, and social status on six continents. My personal conclusion is that the people of the world are more alike than different. For example, children are important to parents from all walks of life and in every culture. I believe that, too often, we let form over substance — not to mention busyness — get in the way of developing relationships with co-workers. Most companies today have some type of global activity.

Do your associates respect each other's differences and embrace them? What programs do you have in place that assist in building a greater understanding of diversity of all types? I believe this leads to improvements in your company's bottom line and associates who are more satisfied with their work environment.

Would You Like to Be Referred to as Human Capital, or an Asset?

March 6, 2012 // Tom Doescher //

Words are important. Today, everything seems to have a fancy label — which was probably created by some well-intended consultant and then used, overused, and abused by everyone. But think about it: Would you like to be referred to as an asset, human capital, or "my guy"? Or would you prefer to be thought of as a really important team member, an invaluable player, or a key associate? How do you refer to your associates?

Do Your Associates Ever Voice Disagreement with You?

January 3, 2012 // Tom Doescher //

I read a fascinating article in the *Harvard Business Review* entitled, "What to Ask the Person in the Mirror: Critical Questions for Becoming a More Effective Leader and Reaching Your Potential," written by Robert Kaplan. The question I found most powerful was this: How often do your subordinates challenge or disagree with you? In my experience, the most effective leaders have at least a few associates who are willing to share contrarian points of view. When associates are willing to speak up and voice their concerns, it can lead to a process of working together to refine and perfect the end goal. It also says a lot about the leader if he or she can trust their team and truly listen, not be threatened, and consider the ideas suggested by other team members. How often does someone on your team challenge your views? What does this say about how you lead? What does this mean about the relationship and the trust you and your associates share? If you do not have anyone who truly challenges you in a healthy way, why do you think no one is willing to speak up? What would the outcome be if you truly welcomed others' observations and heard what your associates had to say?

Do Your Associates Feel You Have Their Back?

July 2, 2012 // Tom Doescher //

I believe great leaders help their key associates stretch and achieve their highest potential by "covering their backs." In other words, they are willing to say: No matter what happens, do your best and I will not second-guess you. A vivid example of this occurred when I was given an assignment, I did not feel qualified to perform, but my leader said he believed I was the best person to try to achieve this business goal. Another colleague and I developed a plan, sought the appropriate wise counsel, and prepared to dive into the assignment. I was scared to death. The next day, my leader showed up in my doorway. After exchanging pleasantries, he said, "I know you're launching that new initiative next week. You have a history of success over the years, and that is why I selected you.

By the way, if this project is not successful, it will not tarnish your record. I've got your back." I cannot tell you how grateful and confident his words made me feel. Do your key associates feel that way about you? Are they secure enough that they are willing to take appropriate risks?

Please, Let us Focus on People's Strengths

November 24, 2014 // Barbara Doescher //

BARBARA DOESCHER //

For years I have struggled with the incessant focus so many of us seem to have on people's weaknesses. The tendency has stretched from the working world to the classroom; I saw this firsthand when my son, a card-carrying introvert (just like me), was told by his teachers that there was a problem — and the problem was that he needed to talk more. My outlook on this issue completely changed when I heard the co-author of *Now, Discover Your Strengths,* Marcus Buckingham, speak at a conference. He, along with others, began a movement to train leaders to focus on building their team members' strengths rather than searching for ways they could overcome their weaknesses. In 2008, I discovered Leading from Your Strengths, an assessment tool within the strengths movement. After a little investigation, I decided to become a certified facilitator. Since then, I have had the joy of helping individuals all around the world. You may ask, How is this program different from other assessment tools?

First of all, it focuses on a person's strengths. It is not a personality test that labels you or tells you what you already know about yourself; instead, it predicts how you will behave when approaching problems, new information, change, and risk. While other assessments overlook the fact that some people are naturally optimistic while others are skeptical, the truth is that different people handle risk in different ways, and some team members move faster while others are more thoughtful. Leading from Your Strengths considers all these possibilities.

From what I have seen, the real power of the tool is most evident when working with teams, because it helps individuals better appreciate their differences when making decisions and/or dealing with conflict. I believe the best companies value all points of view.

Do you fall into the same trap as our son's teachers, who did not appreciate what was good about him.

63

They only commented on what they perceived as his negative trait? Do you ever find your team in conflict resulting from their different personalities and abilities? What are you doing about it?

Surveys Help Teams Improve Performance

August 21, 2017 // Barbara Doescher //

BARBARA DOESCHER //

In the March-April 2017 *Harvard Business Review*, there is an article entitled "Pioneers, Drivers, Integrators, and Guardians," which describes the tool Deloitte designed to improve team performance. Because of my client-focused advising, where I frequently use the Leading from Your Strengths tool, I was especially interested in their research, findings, and approach. Deloitte's clients told them they were not getting the performance they needed from their teams. Their conclusion (and mine) was that too many leaders fail to effectively tap the diverse work styles and perspectives of their team members, and do not recognize there truly are profound differences between how people work. Deloitte's tool, like Leading from Your Strengths, provides examples of behavioral styles:

- **Pioneers** seek possibilities, and they spark energy and imagination.
- **Drivers** seek challenge, and they generate momentum.
- **Guardians** value stability, and they bring order and rigor.
- **Integrators** value connection and draw teams together.

These four styles give teams a common language for understanding how people work. When I use the Leading from Your Strengths method with my clients, it, too, provides a common language for their teams.

My goal, like Deloitte's, is to help business executives realize that different styles can contribute to the success of a business.

Generally, you need to have representatives from each category.
If you want your team to work better together, consider getting help from Deloitte, Doescher Advisors, or another firm that provides this type of assistance.

I guarantee it will improve your profitability, and your workplace will become an environment where team members thrive because they are given the chance to achieve their fullest potential.

Perspective Helps
December 13, 2011 // Tom Doescher //

I was in a meeting one day, listening to all the problems resulting from the sudden growth of a business. As the conversation continued, many of the comments and observations became quite negative. You would have thought the company was having a bad year. During a pause in the discussion, I mentioned that in my experience, whether you are doing really well or performing poorly, there are always problems. I shared that I have decided it is a lot better to deal with problems during the good times. This seemed to change the mood of the team for the better. *Do you keep a pulse on the perspectives of your team?*

You Can't Put a Square Peg in a Round Hole. It is All About "Fit."
July 24, 2017 // Tom Doescher //

TOM DOESCHER //

Years ago, my wife, Barbara, and I were leading a mission trip to Ecuador. One of our 20 team members, "Charlie," was quite challenging to our leadership team. He often showed up late and missed several required preparation meetings, he struggled to get paperwork completed on time, he talked too much at our tightly scheduled meetings, he frequently offered unasked-for comments suggesting we do this or that differently, and the list went on. I think you get the picture.

The general policy with mission teams was that the leaders had the right to excuse someone from the trip if they believed that individual would be a detriment to the team. In the case of the Ecuador trip, we would be traveling through a number of airports to a developing country where the government was unstable. We needed team members who responded to us. A week before our departure, the leadership team expressed their concerns and said they thought it would be best to leave Charlie in Detroit. For reasons I cannot even explain today, I disagreed and assured the team that I could manage him, and the situation fell into my lap. (Let me tell you, working with Charlie really honed my leadership skills.)

During our trip planning and preparation process, Barbara had offered to administer the Learning from Your Strengths assessment to any team members who wished to complete it.

Charlie volunteered to participate in the assessment. One evening in Ecuador, Charlie came to me with his LFYS profile and asked if we could talk. Several hours later, after he had shared his life story, including telling me that he had worked at many different financial services firms, I said to him, "I am at least an average leader, and you're unable to follow me. After hearing your story, getting to know you over the past six months, and looking at your assessment, it is evident that you need to be in charge. I strongly recommend you start your own financial services firm."

When we returned home, he did just that — and over the next several years, I heard from multiple sources that his firm had become very successful. Why am I telling you this story? If you are a business owner or CEO, it is part of your job to make sure people "fit." In the past, I have spoken about the importance of "attitude"; now I'm adding "fit." Charlie was obviously talented, but all his life he had been a square peg in a round hole. Do you have any square pegs in your company?

p.s. Charlie was a very well-meaning and talented guy. He painted a beautiful mural on the back wall of the Ecuadorian church we were constructing and, privately, he gave a generous gift to the church.

Apprenticeships Work!!!

August 22, 2016 // Tom Doescher //

TOM DOESCHER //

Recently, I had the privilege of meeting and speaking with Brad Nycek at Clips & Clamps in Plymouth, Mich. General Manager Jeff Aznavorian provided a wonderful tour for a group of us, and when we arrived in the dimly lit Design Department, we were introduced to Nycek. He showed us, on his 3-D screen, a problem he was solving with a clip. I was amazed as he explained the situation in a way that even I could understand. I will not attempt to explain the fix to you but suffice it to say it was brilliant.

I could not resist interviewing Nycek, a 2007 high school graduate, to find out his story — and I am glad I did. While he was in high school, he said everyone encouraged him to go to college, but it just did not feel right. (By the way, no one suggested that he might want to consider going into the "trades.")

He did take some classes, including general studies, business, and auto body at two community colleges, but his "Big Break" came through family friends — the Aznavorian family.

One day, Jeff Aznavorian called and told Nycek his business was booming, and he wondered if Nycek would be interested in coming to work at Clips & Clamps. Nycek started out in assembly and, after less than six months, Aznavorian offered the Clips & Clamps three-year apprenticeship program to Nycek, who quickly accepted. Today, while still working at Clips & Clamps, Nycek has entered the University of Michigan's mechanical engineering program — sponsored by, you guessed it, Clips & Clamps. Nycek told me, "The real-world experience is making school easier, and more enjoyable."

This is one of the best examples I have seen of "Building Your Own Dream Team." Congratulations to the Aznavorian family and Brad Nycek!

Do Not Settle for Less than the Best

March 20, 2012 // Tom Doescher //

The most successful companies focus on developing the best team members possible. It is an ongoing process and includes both continually raising the bar on existing team members, and occasionally adding and grooming new team members. Businesses that become complacent and satisfied with their performance eventually lose to more innovative, aggressive competitors.

Do you have key positions in your company that you know should be filled by more capable players? As the leader, this is one of your most important — and probably most difficult — responsibilities.

That Guy

March 27, 2012 // Tom Doescher //

I recently heard Henry Cloud speak from his very powerful book, *Necessary Endings*. Cloud used the phrase "That Guy" to label the team member in every company who is holding the rest of the team back from greatness. Cloud's talk led me to reflect back on so many organizations where I have met "That Guy." The person is usually someone who has been with the business for a long time, maybe from the beginning, and has made invaluable contributions. The problem is that, as the company has grown and changed over the years, they have not.

Do you have someone like that in your company? (By the way, my favorite stories are those where the owner/executive has addressed the situation and successfully moved "That Guy" to a position where they can continue to put their talents to the best use.)

Leader vs. Manager
April 30, 2012 // Tom Doescher //

I may lose some readers over this one, but here goes anyway. Many leaders — including Frank Moran, former managing partner of Plante & Moran — have said you *manage tasks*, but you *lead people*. I believe this is especially true today because there are very few purely manual jobs. I have spent the past 20 years in manufacturing, and I love to go on plant tours. Do you realize everything machine operators have to know to perform their jobs today? Running a machine can be very complex work; some of the work cells I have seen remind me of Houston's Mission Control Center. So, what is my point? There probably are times when an activity is purely a task, and your role may be that of a manager — but I would suggest that, in most environments I have observed, what most associates need is leadership. A leader provides a clear plan/goal, offers relevant training, gives developmental feedback when something does not go right (I didn't say screaming!), is accessible to answer questions, and remembers to say "thank you" for a job well done. If you have subordinates, I challenge you to think of yourself as a leader, rather than a manager or a boss.

The Unmanageable Star Performer
July 22, 2013 // Tom Doescher //

One of the most universal concerns in many companies, especially in service-related businesses, is how to deal with the superstar team member who has an unhealthy ego. The May 2013 issue of the *Harvard Business Review* includes a great case study that addresses that all-too-common dilemma. If you have someone on your team like this, we would encourage you to deal with it now! You may even want to seek outside help. For those of you who have participated on any sports teams, you know that sometimes the team plays better without the big-ego superstar. I would love to hear your thoughts on this.

Is Your Employee Turnover Too High?
August 26, 2019 // Tom Doescher //

 TOM DOESCHER //

In this historically low unemployment environment, many business owners are struggling to keep their people. According to the leadership coaching team Bliss & Associates, the cost of employee turnover averages 150 percent of the employee's annual compensation. Wow!

In his book *The Dream Manager*, Matthew Kelly offers some very practical advice. The book is a fictional story/fable, similar to Patrick Lencioni books, and it's a powerful, quick, easy read. Kelly opens the book by quoting Thoreau: "Go confidently in the direction of your dreams. Live the life you have imagined!" He goes on to quote statistics on the high level of disengagement by employees in the workplace today.

Kelly states that people generally don't leave because of money. Remember Marcus Buckingham's Gallup results and his 12 Questions, now reduced to 8? (You can get a PDF copy of both the 12 and 8 Questions in the Resource section of my website.) Most of the book is about "dreams," but the fictional company owner reluctantly agrees to a one-question employee survey, recommended by his COO. Here is the question: Why do you think so many people come and go from our company? It is a very simple, but powerful, question, and although the results are shocking, they are relatively easily dealt with. However, as my mentor, Ken Kunkel, used to warn me, "Be careful what you ask for." By that, he meant that if you ask, you need to be prepared to do something, and not just "receive and file" the advice. You will probably be surprised, and it may cost some money, but do the math. How many people left your company last year? What was their average compensation? Multiply that result times 150 percent, and that is what it is costing now, if you do nothing.

Most of the book involves a revolutionary idea that may be more than you are willing to take on at this time. I would still encourage you to read it; it may stimulate an idea or two that you can implement. If you are concerned about your high turnover rate, I would highly recommend you and your leadership team read *The Dream Manager*. If you are a financial/wealth management advisor and you're looking for ways to use your skills and give back to your community, I would also recommend you read this book.

Field House Janitor Gets National Championship Ring

March 18, 2013 // Tom Doescher //

In a previous blog post, I promised to tell another Coach Tom Izzo story. As promised, here it is. There was a janitor who allowed the MSU basketball players to shoot hoops in the field house after the normal hours of operation, as a favor for the coach. Turns out the janitor would also let the coach know which players were actually investing their personal time this way. When the Spartans won the National Championship, Coach Izzo, with a huge smile, said he gave the first championship ring to this janitor. Now, just think about the positive consequences of this classy move by the coach. We probably all have janitors (or seemingly less-important team members) in our companies. Do we take the time to appropriately recognize them?

Creating the Best Workplace on Earth

July 8, 2013 // Tom Doescher //

You all know I am really into building great companies where people love to work. In the past, I have recommended the book *Drive*, by Daniel Pink, which focuses on how organizations can effectively — and successfully — motivate their teams. I discovered an outstanding article in the May 2013 *Harvard Business Review* that delves into the same issue. The article, titled "Creating the Best Workplace on Earth," was written by Rob Goffee and Gareth Jones, and its precepts are based on a three-year study. As a result of the study, Goffee and Jones have identified six common imperatives of great places to work. Here is their list:

- Let me be myself (i.e., I want to be the same person at work as I am at home).
- Tell me what is really going on (i.e., tell us all the whole story; do not spin information).
- Discover and magnify my strengths (i.e., give every team member a chance to develop).
- Make me proud I work for your company (i.e., I want to value what we stand for).
- Make my work meaningful (i.e., at work, it gives us purpose when we share a common cause).
- Do not hinder me with stupid rules.

Consider using this as a self-assessment tool for your company. Although these ideas may seem easy and rather obvious, very few companies manage to accomplish all six.

Shocking Information About Millennials

March 20, 2017 // Tom Doescher //

TOM DOESCHER //

By the year 2020, millennials will represent 50 percent of the workforce. Millennials are probably one of the hottest subjects talked about by business owners and executives today. I found a 15-minute Simon Sinek December 27, 2016 YouTube video entitled "The Millennial Question - Millennials in the Workplace" to be incredibly insightful (he's the author of *Start with Why*). As a result of watching the video, I have a completely new attitude.

70

If you do not have 15 minutes to watch the video, here are Simon's four main points:

1. **Parenting:** In Simon's words, there have been too many "failed parenting strategies." Since they were children, millennials have been told they are special and can have anything they want (i.e., everyone gets a trophy or medal just for participating). The actual effect of these types of strategies? Low self-esteem, a shattered self-image, and depression.

2. **Technology:** Interacting with Facebook, Twitter, texts, etc. releases a chemical called dopamine, which makes us feel good — similar to the feeling we experience when we drink alcohol.

3. **Impatience:** Millennials grew up getting everything they wanted instantly (Amazon, Netflix, etc.), so they have no patience or appreciation for delayed gratification. The result has been an increase in suicide rates among young people. They do not know how to deal with disappointment.

4. **Environment:** Unfortunately, many workplaces are more focused on the financial results than the people.

Simon says, "It sucks to be you, but leaders have to pick up the slack and build millennials' confidence." Hopefully, this shocking list will cause you to listen and give you pause before jumping to conclusions about the younger generation.

Editorial comment: I find this to be an exciting opportunity for enlightened business owners. If you and your leaders engage millennials using Simon's advice, your company will soar past your competitors.

Happy Associates Equal Delighted Customers/Clients
September 30, 2013 // Tom Doescher //

I was going to write a blog that would connect the dots between happy, motivated associates who love their jobs and delighted customers/clients, and then I read the Patrick Lencioni book, *The Three Signs of a Miserable Job* (it's an easy read, and I would recommend it to anyone leading a team). In his inimitable way, Lencioni makes a significant point by telling a fable.

He identifies three factors that create job misery: anonymity, irrelevance, and immeasurement. To combat the first of these, anonymity, great leaders need to show a genuine interest in their team members by asking themselves: What is on my team member's mind? How can I contribute to them becoming a better person?

71

When I read the comments made by Lencioni, it reminded me of the 12 questions/discoveries highlighted in Marcus Buckingham's book, *First, Break All the Rules*, which I have recommended reading in previous blogs. In Buckingham's book, Question No. 5 asks: Does my supervisor or someone at work seem to care about me as a person? I have been on plant tours with owners who ask very specific questions of machine operators about their spouse or their children by name, and I've noticed that these places always seem to be some of the most profitable businesses.

On a similar note, Hank Paulson, the former CEO of Goldman Sachs and former U.S. Treasury secretary, tells a story in his book, *On the Brink: Inside the Race to Stop the Collapse of the Global Financial System*, about how a senior partner paid special attention to him early in in his career; it's something Paulson credits for the fact that he spent his entire career at Goldman. What do you know about your immediate team members? What are their special interests? What are their special needs? When is the last time you offered a tip to help make them a more effective and successful associate?

Happy Associates Equal Delighted Customers/Clients, part 2
October 14, 2013 // Tom Doescher //

The second job misery indicator, according to Patrick Lencioni, is irrelevance. Lencioni would say that human beings need to be needed, and they need to be reminded of this pretty much every day. Remember the story about the janitor at Michigan State? Did Tom Izzo find a way to help make the janitor's job more relevant?

As human beings, we see similarities between relevance and purpose — which is one of three traits that motivates us, according to Daniel Pink in his book, *Drive: The Surprising Truth About What Motivates Us*. Pink defines purpose as a desire to be involved in a cause larger than oneself. I know a lot of you are probably saying, "Yeah, right." It may be easy to motivate the team if you are sending a man to the moon, but what most of us do on a day-to-day basis is pretty plain vanilla. Still, Frank Moran, founder of Plante Moran, was able to create just that — the feeling of being involved in a larger cause — at an accounting firm, of all places. He would say, "Plante Moran is the Mayo Clinic for businesses. At one end of the building is a long line of successful business owners looking for help with their businesses, and at the other end of the building is a long line of well-educated, talented, resourceful professionals desiring to help businesses achieve their goals."

How do your associates feel about the relevance of their job? When they refer to the company, do they say "we" or "they"?

If you have a profitable business, you are very relevant to your customers/clients. As the leader, do you connect the dots for your team?

Happy Associates Equal Delighted Customers/Clients, part 3
October 28, 2013 // Tom Doescher //

The final job misery factor, according to Patrick Lencioni, is immeasurement. Team members need to gauge their progress and level of contribution for themselves. Question/discovery No. 1 in the book *First, Break All the Rules*, by Marcus Buckingham, is: Do I know what is expected of me at work? This one is somewhat counterintuitive. It seems like accountability has become a bad/evil word. But the truth is, people want to be held accountable.

Another one of my all-time favorite books is *Who Says Elephants Can't Dance?* written by Louis Gerstner. It is the story of how the author and his team saved IBM in the early 1990s.

In his concluding comments, Gerstner speaks about measurement. He says, "People do what you inspect, not what you expect."

Do you measure what is important to your business success? Do all of your team members have clear goals? I cannot tell you how many times I have heard stories about team members who were demotivated because they did not receive any specific — or even any fuzzy — goals. They did their best, only to be criticized by their supervisor, who would say, "That's not what I want or what we need."

The cool thing about attacking these three traits — anonymity, irrelevance, and immeasurement — is that they are not rocket science or proprietary, and they do not cost any extra money. As a well-known advertisement proclaims, "Just Do It!"

Three Life Lessons Learned from Team Sports
March 17, 2014 // Tom Doescher //

Recently I was asked by a former Plante Moran colleague, Brian Kirby, to give a locker-room pep talk to the Sacred Heart School's eighth-grade boys basketball team. After thinking about it for a while, I realized that almost every week I find myself in a situation where I draw upon my team sports experience from decades ago.

When it came time to meet with them, I told the student athletes that although their focus today is appropriately on basketball, the lessons they are learning will make them successful in life.

The following are the three lessons I selected to highlight:

1. **Set goals and prepare.** Those of you who regularly read my blogs know I'm obsessed with being focused. I asked the student athletes if they were familiar with the famous line from Alice in Wonderland, "If you don't know where you are going, any road will get you there." We also discussed the concept of "deliberate practice" from Geoff Colvin's book, *Talent is Overrated*, and the importance of practicing.

2. **Put the team's interests first (as the cliché goes, there is no "I" in team).** I told the young men that in so many companies today — like Google, Apple, etc. — associates frequently work on global project teams with co-workers who speak different languages and come from different cultures. The lessons they are learning from Coach Kirby at Sacred Heart are preparing them to be successful in today's collaborative world.

3. **Win and lose gracefully (i.e., learn to overcome adversity).** We discussed celebrating their victories appropriately and learning from their defeats, but never giving up.

Fortunately for me, this was a very mature group of 13-year-old young men. I could tell that thanks to the tutelage of Coach Kirby, their parents, and their school, these guys get it already!

I left really encouraged about the future generation and, as often happens, I may have learned more from them than they did from me. Have you learned these three life lessons? Are you applying them in your company?

Stars and Rotten Apples

October 17, 2016 // Tom Doescher //

TOM DOESCHER //

"Stars and Rotten Apples" is the title of Chapter 4 in *Good Boss, Bad Boss* by Robert Sutton. Sutton also wrote *The No A _ _ hole Rule*, which I would not recommend. His language is a little rough and harsh (not my style), and a conundrum to me — kind of surprising, since he is a professor of engineering and business at Stanford.

All that being said, *Good Boss, Bad Boss* may make my Top Book Picks list. I have written a lot about having the "right" team, which is code language for hiring the best talent you can and stepping up to people who are not performing. If you can get past the rough language, Sutton makes some great suggestions. I will attempt to summarize them for you:

1. **Bring the energizers.** Interactions with some people can leave you feeling drained, while others can leave you feeling enthused about the possibilities.
2. **Rotten Apples: Bad is Stronger than Good.** The best bosses eliminate the negative, because even a few bad apples and destructive acts can undermine many good people.
3. **Show Them the Love.** When people talk about leaving a company, they often are not feeling sufficiently appreciated.
4. **Assume the Best.** The power of believing that good things will happen to your team and communicating that to them — the self-fulfilling prophecy— is supported by much research.
5. **Cut Loose the Real Losers (ouch!).** Bosses sometimes make excessively glowing judgments about people they have invested a lot of time and money in, or who they simply find to be likable and admirable. (Editorial comment: I have observed this a lot!)
6. **Keep Teams Together.** Sutton used the first U.S. women's national soccer team, which won numerous championships, as an example. Per Sutton, the key to their amazing success was the fact that they were a tight-knit and stable group of players who had played together for a dozen years or so.
7. **Take a Look in the Mirror.** On page 124, Sutton provides a 20-question "EGOS Survey" (Evaluation Gauge for Obnoxious Superstars). (Editorial comment: I haven't gathered up the courage to take the assessment yet, but I'll bet it's revealing.)

My question is this: If I were to confidentially interview your key team members, would they all give me the same name of someone who should leave? And, just as important, would they all agree on someone (generically) who should be added to the team? You already know the answers, so save your money and just do it!

Work Rules from *Fortune's* Best Company to Work For

January 8, 2018 // Tom Doescher //

TOM DOESCHER //

I have to admit I reluctantly read *Work Rules! Insights from Inside Google,* by Laszlo Bock. Once again, I was confronted with my deep biases, this time related to certain tech companies. To my surprise, the 19-year-old company described in the book was more similar than dissimilar to my 40-year experience at Plante Moran (the Firm).

Bock organized the book in such a way that it's easy to reference back to certain subjects, and he provides a great summary at the end of each chapter.

In this blog, I will highlight a few of Bock's major points and share my personal experiences related to them. In 2015, I posted the "Build Your Own Dream Team" Food for Thought. The ideas presented here could be considered a supplement to those thoughts.

1. **CHOOSE TO THINK OF YOURSELF AS A FOUNDER — AND ACT LIKE ONE:** Frank Moran, founder of Plante Moran, wanted everyone to feel like a partner in the Firm and, from the time I started as an intern, I felt that way for the majority of every day. Instead of me embellishing this subject, I thought the 2014 blog posted by Gordon Krater, Plante Moran Managing Partner succinctly captured Frank's ownership concept.

2. **THINK OF YOUR WORK AS A CALLING:** I have written often about purpose/mission, or whatever you want to call it. I most recently addressed this topic in my "Man's Search for Meaning" post, where I mention Plante Moran as the Mayo Clinic for businesses.

3. **GIVE PEOPLE SLIGHTLY MORE TRUST, FREEDOM, AND AUTHORITY THAN YOU'RE COMFORTABLE GIVING THEM. IF YOU'RE NOT NERVOUS, YOU HAVEN'T GIVEN THEM ENOUGH:** I do not think it's written in the handbook, but I always believed the Firm "gave me enough rope to hang myself," allowing me to decide when to ask for help. Said another way, I had a ton of freedom to choose — but I always had a safety net. I strongly believe this accelerated my personal and professional development. Hopefully, I treated those juniors to me the same way.

4. **HIRE ONLY THE BEST BY <u>TAKING YOUR TIME</u>, HIRING ONLY PEOPLE WHO ARE BETTER THAN YOU IN SOME MEANINGFUL WAY, AND NOT LETTING MANAGERS MAKE HIRING DECISIONS FOR THEIR OWN TEAM:** The Firm was committed to hiring the smartest and most talented candidates. Actually, near the end of my career I used to say, "I probably wouldn't get hired today, since the standards have been

raised so high."

Our process was very rigorous, involved multiple interviews and, depending on the position, several partners participated in the final decision. We know we lost good candidates due to the process, but our retention rate was one of the highest in the profession, which benefited our clients.

5. **USE A CALIBRATION PROCESS TO FINALIZE PERFORMANCE ASSESSMENTS/RATINGS:** Like Google, the Firm utilized a calibration process. This added a step, but it was critical to ensure fairness. As a supervisor, you did not always get your way, but the decisions were better.

Although a 19-year-old company would not normally make a Jim Collins or Daniel Pink list, I think Bock offers some interesting and practical advice to those of us leading businesses in the 21st century.

Man's Search for Meaning

October 16, 2017 // Tom Doescher //

TOM DOESCHER //

No, *Man's Search for Meaning* is not the title of a current *New York Times* bestseller; it is something that was originally published in 1946 in German. I am guessing some of you have read it, maybe for a college psych class.

I finally read the timeless book, which was written by Viktor Frankl, and I admit it was a hard read — but it was well worth the time and effort, for many reasons. Frankl, an Austrian neurologist, and psychiatrist born in 1905, was an Auschwitz concentration camp survivor.

In the beginning of the book, Frankl states that he did not intend for this to be another history book about the concentration camps, although he does provide some chilling personal stories. Instead, he wanted to share his professional conclusion that man's primary motivation in life is to find "meaning." He quotes Friedrich Nietzsche, a German philosopher, as concluding "He who has a *why* to live for can bear almost any *how*." He also quotes a Johns Hopkins University survey, where students were asked what they considered "very important" to them. Seventy-eight percent responded, "Finding a purpose and meaning to life." (Although it may

sound like I am quoting Daniel Pink, Marcus Buckingham, Jim Collins, or Patrick Lencioni, I really am talking about a holocaust survivor.)
Owners and senior executives, I'm asking you to think about what Frankl is saying. Then, realize he had no idea that, more than 50 years later, millennials would come along. I have commented on the topics of purpose, your why, and your mission several times. You probably started your business with a passion for something. What is it? Do your team members know, and are they as excited as you? You may say what you do is pretty plain vanilla, but I do not accept that.

In the past, I commented on how Frank Moran created an accounting firm using the metaphor of the Mayo Clinic for businesses — and, to this day, it still inspires hundreds of professionals.

When I tour manufacturing facilities, I always ask a few operators where the part they are making goes. To my shock, most do not know. To them, it is just a metal or plastic fastener. Owners, please figure out a way to inspire your team members. They could easily work somewhere else and probably make similar money. You have an opportunity to appeal to their need for meaning in life. Do not miss it. It will not cost much, but it could make your company an even better place to work.

p.s. Actually, I will make you an offer. Contact me and, at no charge, I will help you communicate your "meaning" to your team.

Another Employee Retention Idea
November 4, 2019 // Tom Doescher //

 TOM DOESCHER //

In the August 27, 2019, issue of *Inc.* magazine, Bill Gates is quoted as saying the most important perk companies can give their employees is "flexible work arrangements" (FWA). The article goes on to report on a new Harvard Business School study that says companies that let their employees "work from anywhere" and work "whenever they want" wind up with employees who are more loyal, more productive, and cost less.

I can feel the cynical pushback from some of you but bear with me. The starting point for any policy would have to be to include guidelines for "who" and "when" employees would qualify for FWA. Examples of exclusions that I can think of would be office receptionists, those whose work is performed at the clients'/customers' place of business, and those who are on teams that continually collaborate, to name a few.

Probably one of the challenges of adopting an FWA would be allowing some employees to have this perk, while denying it to others. Obviously, whatever you do has to be a win-win. I know a young market research professional who started at her employer's Detroit headquarters, but after a year asked if she could work remotely from Colorado. Today, she works remotely from the East Coast.

At my former firm, Tailored Work Arrangements (TWA) have been ragingly successful for years — and the firm has been able to retain very talented professionals. My all-time favorite TWA is an amazing story. A young tax partner and her husband had adopted an infant daughter and, as time went by, she asked if she could reduce her work hours to spend more time with her daughter. The firm gladly agreed. Then she asked if she could work part-time, and the firm gladly agreed. She was a very valuable professional in a highly specialized area of tax. Sadly, for us, she eventually decided to resign from the partnership and stay home full-time. A couple of firm partners continued to stay in touch with her, and even had her perform some contract work in her unique specialty area. As her daughter grew up and went to college, she was excited to rejoin the firm as a non-partner. After several years, she was asked if she would like to become a partner again, and she said yes. She went through the partner selection process, and once again was offered a partnership. As a matter of fact, she is the only person, in the 90-year history of the firm, to have been promoted to partner twice.

In this competitive world, I happen to agree with Bill Gates; I believe companies that figure out ways to accommodate employees' special needs will be the winners in the long run.

3 NUGGETS & ENCOURAGEMENT REGARDING STRATEGY & FOCUS

At Doescher Advisors, in general, we don't develop strategic plans. We have found that our clients know what they need to do to become more successful. In our initial meetings, we find out what those items are, and then we help them execute. With that being said, the following are blogs related to Strategy and Focus.

It Is All About Execution

November 5, 2012 // Tom Doescher //

In his first year as managing partner of Plante Moran, Bill Hermann visited many of the major accounting firms in the country. One day, after he had visited with most of the firms, he and I were talking. He said something like, "You know, Tom, the strategies and tactics of the other firms look very similar to ours. It's all about execution." I believe he was right. Most of the companies I have worked with have pretty good strategies and reasonable tactics. What distinguishes the best performers from the average performers is execution, or the way they go about achieving their objectives. Do you have clearly defined goals? More importantly, are you and your team achieving your company's goals? Although technology has enriched our lives and businesses, it has also created a lot of new distractions that easily divert our attention and interfere with our plan of action. We know what we should be doing, but are we actually following through?

EXECUTION, EXECUTION, EXECUTION
September 27, 2016

In the past three years, I've read more than 60 business books. Ten of those books were special (i.e., new concept, new point of view of an old concept, or what I like to call a "fresh" idea) and, of those, five were "high impact" – including *The 4 Disciplines of Execution* (4DX), which addresses an issue with which most businesses struggle.

In my **November 5, 2012, blog post, entitled "It's All About Execution,"** I discussed this problem – but now I can offer a solution. I have summarized the key points. Enjoy.

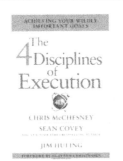

The 4 Disciplines of Execution: Achieving Your Wildly Important Goals

by **Chris McChesney**, **Sean Covey**, **Jim Huling**

Addresses an issue with which most businesses struggle.

Purchase book from Amazon.

What is more challenging for your company, strategy or execution? Most owners/senior executives say execution. In your formal education (business school, etc.), how many classes did you attend where you learned about execution? Probably none. In your postgraduate training and development programs, how much of the time was devoted to execution? Most likely, the answer is very little. According to the authors (Chris McChesney, Sean Covey, and Jim Huling), there are three primary reasons why businesses fail to execute: the lack of clarity of the objective, commitment, and accountability. 4DX defines a significant initiative/strategy/goal as a "Wildly Important Goal" (WIG). The authors suggest leaders make a major mindset change and think of the WIG as an activity that's above and beyond their day-to-day operations, or day job, which the authors have appropriately labeled a "Whirlwind." *(Editorial comment: I think the fact that many people fail to recognize their Whirlwind is one of the greatest contributors to WIG failures.)*

81

The authors propose spending 80 percent of your time on your Whirlwind and 20 percent on your WIG(s). (*Editorial comment: In my experience, 20 percent seems high for most owner-operated businesses, which are already pretty lean.*) Based on the results of surveying more than 300,000 leaders and team members, the authors have identified four disciplines that exist in organizations that consistently achieve their goals and strategies:

Discipline 1: **Focus** on the Wildly Important
Discipline 2: Act on the **Lead Measures**
Discipline 3: Keep a Compelling **Scoreboard**
Discipline 4: Create a Cadence of **Accountability**

Discipline 1: **Focus** on the Wildly Important

- Most organizations have too many goals and do not complete them:

Number of Goals	2 to 3	4 to 10	11 to 20
Goals Achieved with Excellence	2 to 3	1 to 2	**ZERO**

- Steve Jobs' focus at Apple was legendary.
- People who try to push too many goals at once usually wind up doing a mediocre job on all of them.
- In selecting your WIG, ask this question: If every other area of our operation remained at its current level of performance, what's the one area where change would have the greatest impact?
  -Something so badly broken that it must be fixed.
  -Leveraging a strength.
  -Launching a new product or service.
- The battle (WIG) you choose must win the war.
- All WIGs should include a specific finish line that must be reached within a certain time frame; in the early 1960s, for example, President Kennedy pronounced the intention to "Land a man on the moon and return him safely to the earth before this decade is out." (Paraphrased)

- (*Editorial comment: This is easier said than done, but it will increase your chances for success.*)
- As a result of Kennedy's clear proclamation, accountability in the space industry soared —and morale and engagement

went through the roof.

Discipline 2: Act on the **Lead Measures** (LM)

- Lag measures tell you if you have achieved the WIG, while an LM tells you if you're likely to achieve the goal.
- An LM is predictive (i.e., if you do this, then that will happen) and influenceable (i.e., you and/or the team have 80 percent control over the measure).
- Think about the story of Billy Beane, the Oakland Athletics manager, which was chronicled by author Michael Lewis as well as in the popular movie, "Moneyball."
- Does the LM start with a verb (i.e., make, raise, improve, increase, etc.)?
- Is it simple?
- Review your processes to identify LM candidates (i.e., bottlenecks).

Moneyball

by Michael Lewis

The story of Billy Beane, the Oakland Athletics manager.

Purchase book from Amazon.

Discipline 3: Keep a Compelling **Scorecard**

- People play differently when they're keeping score. Simply put, people tend to disengage when they do not know the score. (*Editorial comment: In* Who Says Elephants Can't Dance, *Louie Gerstner says, "People do what you **inspect**, not what you expect."*)
- To drive execution, a player's scoreboard needs a few simple graphs, indicating: We need to get from **here** to **there**.
- In five seconds or less, anyone should be able to determine whether the team is winning or losing.
  (*Editorial comment: I am a huge fan of Dr. Deming, the founder of the modern-day quality movement.*

Unfortunately, leaders did not hear his total message, so in the quest for total quality management, ISO, QS, and all these standards resulted in many companies creating way too many complicated charts. Keep it simple.)

- Think of a time when you were most excited and engaged in what you were doing. Now ask yourself this question: At that time, did I feel like I was winning?
- Editorial comment: The leader may have other scoreboards to assist them, but often so much information overwhelms the team. I once had a client indignantly say, "I can track whatever I want!" My response was, "Absolutely. Just don't confuse your team with it."

Who Says Elephants Can't Dance

by Louie Gerstner

People do what you inspect, not what you expect.

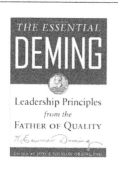

The Essential Deming: Leadership Principles from the Father of Quality

by W. Edwards Deming

Discipline 4: Create a Cadence of **Accountability**

- Great teams operate with a high level of accountability.
- The authors recommend meeting at least weekly but recommend that you have a set agenda and that the meeting lasts no more than 30 minutes. (*Editorial comment: Later in my business life, I had an epiphany: Why do we schedule all meetings for at least an hour? Instead, think of 15-minute, 30-minute, or 45-minute meetings when appropriate.*)
- Suggested weekly WIG meeting agenda:
  1. Account: Report on commitments.
  2. Review the Scoreboard: Learn from successes and failures.
  3. Plan: Clear the path and make new commitments (one or two actions per person that will positively impact the lead measures).

The first third of the book presents the 4DX concept, while the balance of the book shares lots of specific, real, common issues related to 4DX implementation, how-to's, and helpful checklists and forms.

Although I loved the book, it was written by consultants and is more like a textbook. Go ahead and read it if you want more details and examples. Whether you choose to read it or not, I would challenge you to select a WIG in the next month and give it a shot. Let me know what happens. Good luck!

Is the Problem Time Management or Sticking to Your Priorities?
October 22, 2013

I work with many busy executives who continuously have to decide where to spend their time. As I observe those who are the most successful, my conclusion is that they know what is vitally important and they have the discipline to stick to it. I have also realized that there's no magic time management system, no matter what the consultants promise. Successful executives all have different systems — some are sophisticated, others are quite simple.

My longtime mentor amazes me because he knows exactly where to spend his time. As I have studied him and others I respect, have read countless books on the subject, and have attended my share of presentations, I've developed the following opinions.

Why Is It So Hard?

First, it is important to understand what the problem is. It may not be obvious. I hate to use clichés, but in this case, it may be appropriate to quote Benjamin Franklin, who said: "If you want something done, ask a busy person." Presidents, CEOs, business owners, and other executives are busy people. They are like enormous magnets that attract big problems that need to be solved.

Second, it is important to understand a phenomenon called the "Tyranny of the Urgent," identified by noted author Charles Hummel. He challenges us to not allow *urgent* matters to drown out the *important* matters. I find that many people do not properly value their time — every minute of it. They come to me for help but then shoot down every suggestion we offer with the phrase, "Well, it only takes a few ..." Actually, some of the urgent items are activities the executive loves to do (I will talk about that subject another time).

Finally, it is hard to say "no," but it's a requirement for those who want to achieve their best. I love to hedge my bets.

So, What Should We Do?

1. **Know what an important priority for you is and write it down.** I have not met with one executive who has told me they don't know what to do. Usually, within 15 minutes they can clearly articulate what they should be focused on.

   Bill Hybels, the leader of a global nonprofit organization that's growing exponentially, writes down the six most important things he needs to focus on for the next six months on a 6x6 index card he always carries in his pocket. In Andy Stanley's book, *Next Generation*, he quotes Dr. Howard Hendricks — a notable professor, speaker, and author — who said, "There are many things I can do, but I have to narrow it down to the one thing I must do."

2. **Learn to say "NO."** When Steve Jobs returned to Apple, he cut the product line from 350 to 10. Based on market capitalization, Apple went on to become the most valuable company in the world.

3. **Have a trusted advisor(s) who speaks the truth.** This may seem like self-serving advice, but I have found, for a variety of reasons, that even a board of directors/advisors does not provide the tough, tailored messages that are necessary at times.

86

4. **Measure your progress.** In his book, *Who Says Elephants Can't Dance?* Louis Gerstner Jr. says: "People do what you inspect, not what you expect." That applies to us leaders, too. Review your 6x6 card (or whatever your system) regularly. Depending on your routine, consider doing this at the beginning or at the end of each week.

Business Lessons Learned from a Successful Coach
November 19, 2013

Many of you know I love to tell sports stories to make a business point. I found a fascinating story about a famous coach in, of all places, the *Harvard Business Review's* October 2013 issue. Harvard Business School professor Anita Elberse interviews Sir Alex Ferguson, who recently retired after serving for 26 years as the manager of the Manchester United football club.

You may not be familiar with his achievements, but he would be in the same category as Vince Lombardi, John Wooden, or Scotty Bowman — in fact, he is maybe even more accomplished. Professor Elberse summarizes Coach Ferguson's approach in eight leadership lessons. As I read his story, I thought of the obvious relevance to a business.

Below are Coach Ferguson's lessons, followed by my business application:

1. **Start with the Foundation** — The coach reports that the first thought of most newly appointed managers is to make sure they win; that ensures they will survive. To accomplish their goal, they bring in experienced players. That is simply because they're in a results-driven industry. (Editorial comment: Does that sound familiar?) Coach Ferguson's focus was on building a club, not just winning a game. He went on to say that his team's youth development efforts ended up leading to their many successes. **Application:** Most companies seem to need more supervisors, skilled associates, and even a few high-level executives. Often their only solution is to hire from the outside. The most successful companies, however, have a "youth development" program. They have a well-oiled developmental system at all levels, from operators to future C-level executives, including apprentice programs and internships. They are always looking for raw talent they can develop. They take risks. If they are successful, they know they will need lots of great people. They take it upon themselves to grow their own.
   Note: I often hear executives complaining that they invest all this money in developing their people and then those people leave for more money. According to 1 million people interviewed by Gallup, that is not true.

2. **Dare to Rebuild Your Team** — Coach Ferguson admitted that managing the talent-development process inevitably involved cutting players, including those he had a personal attachment to. **Application:** If you want to succeed in the long term, don't settle for less than the best.

3. **Set High Standards — and Hold Everyone to Them** — Coach Ferguson wanted to inspire his players to strive to do better and to never give up — in other words, he wanted to make them winners. **Application:** First of all, do you provide clear direction to your team? Once that has been done, do you hold them accountable?

4. **Never, Ever Cede Control** — An important part of maintaining high standards across the board was Ferguson's willingness to respond forcefully when players violated the team's

standards/values. In 2005, a longtime captain publicly criticized his teammates, and his contract was terminated. Ferguson recommends responding quickly, before situations get out of hand.
Application: Once again, the coach provides us with some sage advice. Often a team is better off without a big-ego superstar.

5. **Match the Message to the Moment** — Ferguson found it useful to remind players how far they had come. He would tell them that having a good work ethic is very important. He went on to say, "As a manager, you play different roles at different times. Sometimes you have to be a doctor, or a teacher, or a father."
    Application: Needless to say, everything Coach Ferguson said applies to business.

6. **Prepare to Win** — United practice sessions focused on repeating skills and tactics. Coaches and players looked at the training sessions as opportunities to learn and improve. With this type of mindset, there is also an underlying signal that you're never quite satisfied with where you are and are constantly looking for ways to improve.
    Application: Ferguson's advice reminded us of Geoff Colvin's book, *Talent Is Overrated*. Colvin coined the phrase "deliberate practice," which is where you really prepare and focus on what you are competing in. He used Tiger Woods as an example. We have all read stories of how Tiger began playing golf as a young boy and, even today, he spends a significant amount of time on the practice green. A business example comes from David Gergen's book, *Eyewitness To Power*, where he provided his views of the four U.S. presidents he served. He talked about the many hours President Reagan spent preparing to speak. In this example, you have a former movie star and a gifted communicator who was following Coach Ferguson.

7. **Rely on the Power of Observation** — Ferguson said, "I don't think many people fully understand the value of observing. I came to see observation as a critical part of my management skills. The ability to see things is key — or, more specifically, the ability to see things you don't expect to see."
    Application: When I read this lesson, I immediately thought of the 1982 Tom Peters and Robert Waterman book, *In Search of Excellence*. It was the first time I was exposed to the phrase "Management by wandering around," which was originally used at Hewlett-Packard. All great business owners/executives that I know find a way to get out of their office and into the plant, other offices, and other countries — and, yes, they visit customer, who love the attention.

I observe far too many executives who are managing from their office, even though their team and customers love to see them.

8. **Never Stop Adapting** — Finally, the coach would say, "One of the things I've done well over the years is manage change. I believe that you control change by accepting it. Most people with my kind of track record do not look to change. But I always felt I couldn't afford not to change."
   Application: One of the most refreshing and inspiring change stories is the transformation of Encyclopedia Britannica.

I hope you have picked up at least one idea to improve your business and increase profitability. As one of my colleagues used to say, it is all in the execution. Good luck — and just do it!

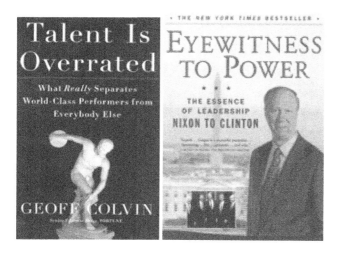

What You Can Learn from a Family Business
January 15, 2013

More than 20 years ago, I asked a highly respected CEO at a Tier 1 auto supplier this question: If I only read one magazine/periodical, what would you recommend? To my surprise, his answer was the _Harvard Business Review._

Since then, I've been a subscriber. I must say, however, that I have considered canceling my subscription more than once — especially when they went from six issues per year to 10. (Why would I consider canceling a magazine when I seemed to be getting more for my money? It is because there is so much information, I struggle to finish reading the entire magazine before the next issue arrives.) But then, just when my guilt is about to cause me to pull the trigger, an amazingly relevant, fresh article about a topic that is not covered anywhere else appears.

In fact, that happened as recently as this past November.

Three professionals from the Boston Consulting Group (BCG) reported their findings from studying 149 publicly traded, family-controlled businesses (as compared to similar companies that are not family-controlled) in an article entitled, "What You Can Learn from Family Business."

The *Harvard Business Review* has very strict rules prohibiting me from sending you the article, but most of you are involved in family-owned businesses, and I would highly recommend obtaining reprints.

Quoting from the article, "Our results show that during good economic times, family-run companies don't earn as much money as companies with a more dispersed ownership structure. But when the economy slumps, family firms far outshine their peers. And when we looked across business cycles from 1997 to 2009, we found that the average long-term financial performance was higher for family businesses than for nonfamily businesses in every country we examined. The simple conclusion we reached is that family businesses focus on resilience more than performance."

They identified the following seven differences that set family businesses apart:

1. They are frugal in good times and bad. (Editorial comment: It is their own money they are spending.)
2. They keep the bar high for capital expenditures. (Editorial comment: Did I mention it is their money?)
3. They carry little debt. (Editorial comment: Over the years, my experience has been that companies with less debt make some of their best investments during economic downturns, when their competitors cannot come up with the capital.)
4. They acquire fewer (and smaller) companies. (Editorial comment: I cannot prove it with data, but anecdotally, I have observed that most acquisitions fail. So, usually, bigger is not better.)
5. Many show a surprising level of diversification. (Editorial comment: As Mark Twain once said, "Don't put all your eggs in one basket.")
6. They are more international.

(Editorial comment: When your business goes cross-cultural, there is often a lot of mistrust. In my experience, family-owned businesses are better able to develop deep, healthy relationships with customers and associates in other countries.)

7. They retain talent better than their competitors do.
(Editorial comment: In my experience, in well-run family-owned businesses, the "family" goes well beyond "the family.")

For those of you who own and operate family businesses, I hope the BCG's findings are encouraging and will give you the courage to keep going.

Is It Better to Be Smart or to Be Lucky?
February 28, 2012 // Tom Doescher //

As many of you are aware, I am fond of asking this rhetorical question, and often I go on to say that I believe I'm a lucky guy. My partner, Barbara, likes to take issue with me, saying I am *blessed* rather than merely *lucky*. In 65 B.C., Seneca — a Roman dramatist, philosopher, and politician — said, "Luck is what happens when preparation meets opportunity."

Our experience has been that businesses that have a strategy and know where they are going recognize an opportunity when it presents itself. Although this opportunity may seem like a wild idea to many people, the focused executive can see that it clearly fits into the company's long-term business plan. If an opportunity presented itself to your team today, would they recognize it?

What's Luck Got to Do with It?
September 18, 2012

On February 28, I posted a blog entitled, "Is it better to be smart or to be lucky?" I thought about that question again recently, when I heard Jim Collins speak about his new book, *Great by Choice*.

During his presentation, Collins shared that, during a nine-year study of the most extreme business successes of modern times conducted by his research team, they asked this question: Just what is the role of luck? As you can imagine, this really got my attention. Collins and his team concluded that luck — both good and bad — happens to everyone, whether we like it or not. Really successful people recognize luck and seize it. They grab "luck events" and make much more of them than less successful people manage to do. (Collins and his partner wrote an article in *The New York Times* entitled, "What's Luck Got to Do with It?".)

Now, I am a big believer in having a plan. Many times, I have said, "Without a plan and/or roadmap, you will get nowhere." However, I have also observed that you need to be attuned to, in Collins' words, "luck events." Although these happenings may not fit your strategy or tactics for the next year or two, they could be game changers if you recognize their potential.

I am the same guy who strongly recommends staying focused, but I think this subject is critically important.

So here are few things for you to consider:

1. What is the potential upside of the "luck event" that has shown up at your doorstep? Could it be a winner, a huge success?
2. Does the "luck event" fit with your long-range mission and vision? You may have to be really creative and open-minded in evaluating this, to visualize the full potential and fit.
3. Is your organization in a position to appropriately handle this "luck event"? (i.e., solid leadership team, consistent profitability, strong balance sheet, etc.)
4. As a follow-up question, does your company have the required resources to pursue the "luck event" without crippling the primary business unit?
5. Using the concepts in _Crossing the Chasm_, by Geoffrey Moore, find some "early adopters" in your organization and ask their advice. Then query some "early majority" folks, just to see what they think. Don't be discouraged and be sure to take good notes.
6. The first five steps should go quickly. In my experience, "luck events" have a very short window of opportunity, so you have to think — and move — fast.
7. Assign some of your best people to explore the possibilities, to ensure that you maximize your chance for success.
8. Get the appropriate approvals and go for it.
9. If you suddenly realize it is not a good idea for your company, do not be afraid to pull the plug. Make sure your team has the right perspective and that you are all willing to stop before you get in too deep, if necessary.

Thank you, Jim Collins, for helping me better understand something I have experienced many times in my career. I wish all of you success in dealing with your next "luck event."

Getting Everyone on the Same Page
May 3, 2012

I have been interacting with some folks at Northwood University and have discovered that every semester, the entire faculty and student body reads the same book. Sometimes, the author makes a presentation the following semester to the faculty and students. I'm aware that some company leadership teams follow this practice, too. As I reflected on it, I thought, _what a powerful way to get the entire team on the same page_. You may want to consider this idea for your leadership team, or maybe even all your associates. The book they are currently reading at

Northwood University is *Start With Why: How Great Leaders Inspire Everyone to Take Action,* by Simon Sinek. It's a book that I would highly recommend.

In the past I have endorsed *Drive: The Surprising Truth About What Motivates Us,* by Daniel Pink. One of the three elements of true motivation, according to Pink, is purpose.

I believe Sinek's book is totally focused on knowing your purpose.

 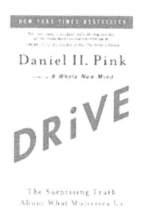

Some obvious examples of how great leaders have inspired our nation include: President John F. Kennedy's challenge to the nation to put a man on the moon; Dr. Martin Luther King's call for others to help him make his dream become reality; the way Apple, under Steve Jobs, changed seven industries; and the way Google, under direction from its leadership, has delivered information to everyone in the world.

A more local example would be Frank Moran, of Plante & Moran, who talked about his firm becoming the Mayo Clinic for businesses.

The key to how these people managed to motivate others to succeed and pursue their dreams and vision is the fact that the leaders themselves could articulate why they wanted to achieve whatever it was they wanted to happen.

The following are a few of my favorite quotes from Sinek's book:

1. "Leading, however, means that others willingly follow you — not because they have to, not because they are paid to, but because they want to."

2. "What all great leaders have in common is the ability to find good fits to join their organizations."
3. "When a team of experts comes together, they often work for themselves and not for the good of the whole."
4. "If you have the discipline to focus on the early adopters (this is a reference to the 1962 book *Diffusion of Innovations* by Everett Rogers), the majority will come along eventually. But it starts with Why."
5. "Volkswagen, translated, means 'people's car.'"
6. "The single greatest challenge any organization will face is success."

In closing, Sinek tells a story about an annual event in Boston called the Gathering of Titans, whose attendees include highly successful entrepreneurs. When participants in GOT were asked how many of them had achieved their financial goals, 80 percent raised their hands. Then they were asked whether they felt successful, and 80 percent of the hands went down. This seemed to demonstrate that even business owners are searching for a purpose, or a "why." I would challenge you to make sure your "why" is clear to everyone in the company.

Same Bed, Different Dream
December 27, 2011 // Tom Doescher //

One day I was talking to a businessman in China who had had a bad experience with a joint venture partner. As he was describing the situation to me, he summed it up by saying, "Same bed, different dream." That says it all. Most joint ventures fail because the partners have different dreams. Are you considering an alliance or a joint venture?

While you are conducting your due diligence, make sure you and your potential partner have the same dream. How can you make this determination? By asking pertinent questions (i.e., What are your long-term goals with this joint venture?). Then, ask deeper follow-up questions.

Are You Focused?
January 31, 2012 // Tom Doescher //

So many good businesses do not reach their full potential because they try to do everything and never become world-class at anything. The other day I went to a new shop to have my car repaired. The owner had a fixed list of services, and fixed hours. He knows what he does, he does it well, and he executes the services flawlessly. If you ask for something that is not on the list, he will cheerfully refer you to someone else.
The result? His parking lot is full of happy, satisfied customers like me. Is your business as clearly focused as this auto-repair shop?

95

Attitudes of 2nd, 3rd, and 4th Generations
February 14, 2012 // Tom Doescher //

If the founder of a business is interested in making sure his life's work continues for many generations down the line, he needs to focus on mentoring the next generation early on, in addition to creating successful products or services. (When I say, "next generation," I mean the next generation of owners and associates.) In my experience, many founders do not take the time to teach the next generation what I call "The essence of the business." In fact, the next generation frequently has different attitudes and opinions about the business than the founder — and these differences need to be discussed and dealt with before younger family members are put in charge.

This is a topic of extreme delicacy, and many businesses fail in the process of making a transition because the founder has not been clear about his vision for the future. If conversations aren't held about the founder's expectations and values, and transition plans aren't put in place while he's still able to coach and nurture younger family members, chances are those left behind won't really understand the critical factors that have made the business successful — and they won't care for the business the way the founder does, either.

Do the key members of your next generation understand why customers buy your products or services? Do they care about each and every detail like you do? Have you started the conversation? If you have not, today is a good day to take that important step.

Create Your Own Path
April 23, 2012 // Tom Doescher //

My wife, Barbara, and I got back into cross-country skiing this year. One day, as we were skiing along a groomed track in beautiful northern Michigan, I thought to myself, "It would be more fun to make my own track through the snow, but it would definitely be more difficult." I think the same is true in business. Too often, I hear discussions where people are analyzing what their competitors are doing versus exploring what their customers and clients want. Is it easier to copy the competition rather than possibly reinventing your product to meet your customers' needs? Of course, it is! Just as in skiing, it is definitely simpler and less risky to follow the track that has already been laid out instead of breaking new ground and trying something different.

A few years ago, I read a really thought-provoking book, *Blue Ocean Strategy*. The authors talked about how most of us operate in the "red" ocean, studying and emulating our competitors.

They went on and gave great examples of companies that operate in the "blue" ocean and have successfully created their own track. Is your team satisfied to glide along in the groomed track, or do you have a mechanism — or, better yet, culture — that encourages breaking out of the mold and trying new things?

What Happens if You Get Hit by a Buick or Bus?
May 28, 2012 // Tom Doescher //

A lot of people seem to think that they are going to live forever. But just in case you don't, do you have a plan? Doescher Advisors has advised so many business owners on this subject, and we have noticed a distinct trend.

Typically, business owners will say, "I don't know whether I want to sell or continue the company." To which I respond, "Either way, you're better off if you have a potential successor in mind." Identifying a successor can be very difficult; in fact, it may take a few tries. But once you find someone, you can focus on what I discussed last week — being involved in creating and developing new products and services.

You will not believe the pressure it will release once you know there is a definite plan for the future. You will lift a huge burden from your shoulders, which means you may even live longer. So, why not take the risk?

He Will Never Make It Being that Focused
May 14, 2012 // Tom Doescher //

On February 21, I posted a blog entitled "The Big Three," in which I named the three traits world-class leaders must possess. The second of those traits was focus.

One of my favorite stories about focus is this: A young CPA moved from New York to Detroit, and he struggled to find a job in his new city. Eventually, in 1981, he started his own firm, which was exclusively focused on turnaround consulting. Most informed professionals predicted there was no way he would survive, being that narrowly focused.

Well, he stayed the course (I am sure there were bumps along the way) and 25 years later, when the firm was sold, public sources put its value at $800 million. Who knows? Maybe that CPA got lucky. All I know is that not many CPA firms are worth that much. Recently it was reported in the local financial news that the firm is for sale again, this time for $1 billion.

Although there are often risks involved, I have observed business after business that has had what many "experts" say is too narrow a focus — yet they have all outperformed their peers. How focused are you?

Do You Personally Invest in New Products and Services?
May 21, 2012 // Tom Doescher //

You are the one who knows your company and its capabilities best. You also probably understand your customers/clients best. So how engaged are you, really, in developing new products or services?

I believe both Steve Jobs and Bob Lutz would say the customer does not know what they want. Of course, neither of them was big on focus groups, either (and that is saying it politely).

What do you think?

I've talked before about Blue Ocean Strategy, and the basic theory behind that concept is this: Don't focus on your competitors; rather, concentrate on what you believe would delight your customers and/or clients (which isn't necessarily easy, and that's why you need to be involved).

If you aren't personally engaged in developing new products/services, consider freeing up some time and helping your team create the next iPhone-type product in your industry.

Will Your Company Be Successful in 20 Years?
October 22, 2012 // Tom Doescher //

Over the years, I have noticed a correlation between successful companies and the average experience level of their leadership team (you may call it your executive or management team). I have worked with companies that, although they are making money, are noticeably slipping.

A common denominator among these companies seems to be that they are not investing in new products or technologies or coming up with innovative concepts; in many respects, they are benefiting from decisions and actions that they — or their predecessors — made years ago. When I attend management meetings at these companies, I feel like one of the youngest people in the room (I know I just stepped over the line with that, but I believe it needs to be said). On the other hand, really successful companies have a blend of seasoned executives and younger members who have fresh ideas and are willing to challenge their elders when they say:

"We do X this way because that's how we've always done it."

If your goal is to be a successful company in 20 years, maybe it is time to take a step back and take a hard look at the composition of your leadership team.

The Ultimate Shoe Dog Story (Nike)

July 15, 2019 // Tom Doescher //

TOM DOESCHER //

Once again, I'm embarrassed to admit a bias I've had for years. I'm not sure exactly when it started, but it may have been when Nike started selling clothing with their name on it — and it wasn't cheap clothing. My reaction was, "I'm not going to pay to advertise for those guys!" And from that and other observations, I developed a negative attitude about what I perceived as arrogance, to the point where I've boycotted Nike shoes and clothing for decades.

I just finished reading the Nike story as chronicled by its founder, Phil Knight, in his book, *Shoe Dog*. I know what you skeptics are thinking: He fell for the story. Well, maybe I did, but I have read a lot of books like this, and I would suggest most tend to eulogize the founder/CEO, and even have a tendency to rewrite history. This book surprised me. If anything, Phil Knight seems to understate his personal impact on Nike and instead praises many others for their unique contributions. Because many of us have observed Nike from its humble beginnings to its current $134 billion market cap, we might draw the conclusion that "it just happened."

Many of you have started your own businesses or have been involved from the beginning, and I found this to be a very real, at times painful, success story. It reminded me of practice units that I was involved in creating and building. Many years later, newer team members had no idea how difficult our journey had been. So, I could relate to Knight.

Some fun facts/stories:

1. Knight ran cross country at the University of Oregon for the famous Coach Bill Bowerman — who was Knight's first business partner, the primary shoe innovator, and a close mentor until his death in 1999.
2. One of Knight's colleagues came up with the name Nike, in honor of the Greek goddess of speed, strength, and victory. Knight did not care for it but had no other option to offer.
3. The famous Nike Swoosh was designed by a young artist at Portland State University for $35.
4. Knight is an introvert who loves his alone time.

5. Knight is a CPA who, while teaching accounting at Portland State University, met his wife, Penny, a student. The couple recently celebrated their 50th wedding anniversary.
6. Due to shoe endorsements, Knight has developed close, personal relationships with many of the greatest athletes of the past five decades.
7. Unlike many other company founders, Knight avoided going public (and cashing out) for years.
8. Knight reported: "Often the problems confronting us were grave, complex, and seemingly insurmountable; and yet we were always laughing."

(Editorial comment: This was my exact experience working with my former partners, Ken Kunkel, and Bruce Berend, in the '70s and '80s — and those are some fond memories.)

Here is a sampling of some of the major obstacles Knight and his team had to overcome in a span of almost 20 years:

1. While Nike had significant profitable growth almost every year, the bad news is that this increased growth and expansion required more inventory, so Nike was always cash poor. Sound familiar?
2. In the early years, Nike Tigers from the Onitsuka shoe company, based in Japan, were the primary shoe sold. Nike was the exclusive distributor for the western U.S. At one point, Onitsuka informed Knight that they were going to change to one U.S. distributor, and it was not going to be Nike. Knight asked, "Why not Nike?" to which Onitsuka answered, "You do not have an East Coast presence." Knight replied, "Yes, we do." Instead of losing their primary shoe source, Nike became the company's exclusive distributor in the U.S. Sound familiar? Just like many of you would do in similar circumstances, Nike quickly opened an East Coast office.
3. To avoid dependency on one source, Nike designed a new shoe and identified a new supplier in Japan. Onitsuka discovered the plan, immediately terminated their agreement with Nike, and filed a lawsuit that went to a full trial. Sound familiar? I know a number of you have spent a lot of money on lawyers defending yourself from unfair, baseless lawsuits.
4. On occasion, athletes whom Nike had under contract would appear in a competitor's shoes (including at the Olympics) because they were offered more money. Sound familiar?
5. One of the greatest runners in modern history, Steve Prefontaine — who wore Nike shoes exclusively — died at age 24. Sound familiar?
6. As Nike grew and cash continued to be tight, the company's primary bank of over 10 years fired Nike and froze their accounts without warning. Sound familiar? It gets worse.

7. The bank suspected fraud, so they notified the FBI. Yeah, more wasted time and money.

If you ever feel these same types of pains, you might want to grab a copy of Phil Knight's book. I promise you will be encouraged.

Fearless
June 16, 2019 // Tom Doescher //

TOM DOESCHER //

is a 2012 book about Adam Brown, a Navy Seal. I thought I was reading it for fun, due to my fetish about Seals over the past decade — but wow, was I wrong. Yes, it was fun and entertaining, but it was way more than that.

I believe Brown is a role model for having a clear mission (he knew his "Why") and for staying laser-beam-focused on it. First, a little background. Brown grew up in a loving, intact Christian family in Arkansas. He was an athlete and well liked in high school. Sadly, he lost his way after graduation and became addicted to drugs. His life got pretty ugly and, near the bottom, he attended a Teen Challenge drug treatment center. Along the way, he decided he wanted to become a Navy Seal and serve his country as a patriot warrior. Before reading *Fearless*, I knew that becoming a Seal was a rigorous process, but it was more complex than I realized. Brown, however, was determined to join their ranks. Here are just a few obstacles he had to overcome:

1. During his dark drug years, Brown was convicted of several felonies and spent time in prison. This was a huge deal-breaker that he miraculously overcame.
2. Near the end of his Seal training, he became blind in his dominant right eye in a training accident, but he was able to train his non-dominant left eye and eventually passed the precision sniper marksmanship tests. More importantly, he convinced the Navy that being blind in one eye would not be a liability to his fellow warriors.
3. During an early deployment in Iraq, he crushed his hand and severed all his fingers in a Humvee IUD accident. His fingers were reattached on his dominant right hand. Still, he learned how to use his left hand and, once again, passed the rigorous marksmanship training.

4. Brown was always the one to volunteer for the toughest assignments and, as the title of the book reflects, he was, indeed, fearless.

If you are struggling with your "Why" or staying on your "Why," I would strongly encourage you read *Fearless* for motivation. I would say that focus is a common challenge for many entrepreneurs, and I think Brown is a poster child for being single-minded.

A postscript: I found Brown's reporting of the ups and downs of his Christian faith and his lifelong struggle with his drug addiction refreshingly candid and realistic.

Some Great Advice Regarding Gossip

April 29, 2019 // Tom Doescher //

 **TOM DOESCHER //**

Recently, Barbara was meeting with a client who shared their gossip policy. In my decades of business experience, I have found that gossip is like cancer in large and small companies alike. The policy below is so well-written that, with our client's permission, I have included it, intact, with only a few editorial comments. If you have not addressed this issue in your workplace, consider adopting a similar policy.

NO-GOSSIP POLICY

In the workplace, gossip is an activity that can drain, distract, and downshift employee job satisfaction. We all have participated in this, yet most of us say we do not like it. In order to create a more professional workplace, we the undersigned are making a commitment to change our atmosphere to be gossip-free.

gossip n. Rumor or talk of a personal, sensational, or intimate nature. A person who habitually spreads intimate or private rumors or facts. Trivial, chatty talk or writing.

You will notice that gossip is a noun — which means it is something you DO. That also means it is something you choose to do — and you can choose NOT to do it. You enter into gossip by choice — you can opt out of the activity at work. In order to end gossip, you must end a particular type of communication — and that can be talk or email communications.

102

Editorial comment: or text messages.

• Gossip always involves a person who is not present.
• Unwelcome and negative gossip involves criticizing another person.
• Gossip often is about conjecture that can injure another person's credibility or reputation.

The persons signed below agree to the following:

In order to have a more professional, gossip-free workplace, we will:

1. Not speak or insinuate another person's name when that person is not present unless it is to compliment or reference regarding (Editorial comment: factual) work matters.
2. Refuse to participate when another mentions a person who is not present in a negative light. I will change the subject or tell them I have agreed not to talk about another.
3. Choose not to respond to negative email or use email (Editorial comment: or text) to pass on private or derogatory information about any person in the agency.
4. While off the job, I will not speak to another co-worker about people at work in a derogatory light. If I have feelings, I will select to talk to someone not at the workplace.
5. If another person in the department does something unethical, incorrect, against procedures, or disruptive I will use the proper channels to report this to the person in authority to take corrective action.
6. I will mind my own business, do good work, be a professional adult and expect the same from others.

Disclaimer: You may want to have an HR consultant, or your labor attorney, review your specific wording.

Are Your Best Successes a Result of Goal-Setting?
June 4, 2018 // Tom Doescher //

TOM DOESCHER //

I will readily admit that mine are not. Goal setting has been on my mind a lot lately, as I recently have been involved in career-planning discussions with twenty-somethings.

As we've talked about their passions — or, sometimes, their lack of passions — I've also spent some time reflecting on my own life (it's true, I didn't feel a strong passion about anything in particular after my football-coaching gig didn't work out).

Any of you who know me realize I am a very serious business and personal goal-setter. I strongly believe in planning and goal setting. Over the years, it is helped me make good choices regarding how to spend my time and money.

That being said, as I have thought about my life, I cannot think of one major thing that has been the direct result of my goal setting. For example, I went to Western Michigan University to become a football coach, but instead I ended up at Plante Moran.

Then there was the time my college roommate and I went to the Lutheran Student Center's dinner one Sunday evening because our dorm did not serve an evening meal. I went simply to get some dinner, but instead I met Barbara (this was over 50 years ago!). Once we were married, Barbara and I had no plans to live in Fenton (long story of how we got here), but today we love it. Finally, it was not my plan to be in business with Barbara, but that is not the way things turned out.

So, here is my current advice:

1. Put your sail up and let the wind blow into it.
2. Do not over-analyze everything.
3. Do not fight gravity. If things are going well, continue — but if you keep bumping your nose, move on.
4. If doors open, go through them.
5. Some of us have to experience a lot of things to find our passion.
6. Do your best wherever you are.
7. Always learn as much as you can, wherever you are. As you go through life, you will be surprised how many of your life experiences will connect years later.
8. If you are in a miserable situation, move on.
9. It is not all about money.

With the advantage of several decades of life, I feel that today I am in my "calling" or "passion," and I love almost every day of it. That being said, it took a lot of experiences for me to realize what I wanted. So, hang in there, put your sail up, and walk through any doors that open, no matter how scary it may seem.

p.s. Give me a call if you want to talk.

Looking for Topics for Your Annual Planning Meeting?

August 20, 2018 // Tom Doescher //

TOM DOESCHER //

I would recommend using *It's Not What You Sell, It's What You Stand For* by Roy M. Spence, Jr., as a resource. If you are like me, after years of attending annual planning meetings you're often looking for something new and fresh. Spence and his colleagues have advised some highly regarded companies, like Southwest Airlines, and have come up with a list of great questions you could use during your leadership team's annual retreat/planning session.

I've written several times about a company's "why" or "purpose." The primary subject of *It's Not What You Sell* is "purpose," and Spence organizes his suggested questions into four categories:

1. Are purpose principles alive and well in your organization?
2. Are you building an organization that makes a difference?
3. Are you a leader of great purpose?
4. Are you bringing your purpose to life in the marketplace?

Each of these categories provides 10 questions that could be used as part of a team building, vision-casting session. In addition, Spence references numerous books and research studies that you may want to obtain as advanced reading material for your team.

Spence and his colleagues assist businesses with marketing services including branding. As I read their client stories, I reflected back upon sitting in company lobbies, reading the plaques on the walls (yes, this was before digital displays). It wasn't uncommon for companies to incorporate Bible verses into their messages (purpose, vision, principles, etc.). On more than one occasion, when I was sitting in a meeting with the company's executives, I had a totally different experience than what I had expected based on the values their lobby displays touted.

So, what's my point? I'm probably playing big brother here, but I believe it would be better to not say certain things if, in fact, they aren't the standards your business (and all its team members) adheres to. The plaques or video displays on the lobby walls should accurately reflect the company's culture. Be careful not to overstate it.

It's All About Jobs

October 8, 2018 // Tom Doescher //

TOM DOESCHER //

I love working with owner-operated businesses competing in the free market. They develop an idea for a new product or service and then take it to the market, where it's either accepted (like the iPhone) or rejected (like the Ford Edsel). Recently I finished reading *Defending The Free Market: The Moral Case for a Free Economy,* by Rev. Robert Sirico. Fr. Robert is a Catholic priest, and he's also the co-founder and president of The Acton Institute.

Before I lose you, bear with me.

From 1998 until 2012, Barbara, my partner, and I led more than 30 humanitarian mission teams all over the world. We visited the continents of Africa, Asia, Central America, Oceania, and South America. Our teams provided medical services, worked on construction projects, offered an educational program, and conducted a children's ministry and marriage enrichment classes. As we looked forward to what we now refer to as our "Last Life Marathon," we decided we were going to invest our time in a combination of work and mission. As follows: "Doescher Advisors was founded to help businesses increase profits and **jobs** through practical and sound advice."

As our economy changes due to innovations, the industrial jobs that once provided wonderful standards of living for so many hourly workers for almost a century no longer exist. Barbara and I are committed to assisting business owners find success so they can provide good jobs to these workers.

To make this point really clear, let me tell you a story. We had a client who found himself in the middle of the perfect storm. As we assessed the situation, we believed we could help "right the ship," so to speak, but we also realized the client was in no position to compensate us for our extra assistance. We decided to help, anyway. I went to the business owner and said, "I think we can help you through this situation. I understand you won't be able to pay us now, but we'll keep track of our time and you can decide what you want to do when we get through it." You can imagine the gratefulness of the client.

I acknowledged his comments, but then I pointed out toward his shop floor and said, "I'm doing this for those 40 families. I cannot effectively help them, but I can help you. And if we're successful, everyone wins."

It's All About Jobs, part 2

October 22, 2018 // Tom Doescher //

 **TOM DOESCHER //**

In my last blog, I discussed the commitment Barbara and I have to helping business owners create good jobs. I mentioned *Defending The Free Market: The Moral Case for a Free Economy,* written by Rev. Robert Sirico, a Catholic priest and co-founder and president of The Acton Institute. Fr. Robert comments on many topics, but here are some takeaways specifically related to jobs:

1. The expression "to make money" is a very good description of the process in a free market. It all begins because people are making things or creating things (it may be a product or a service). Before the taking comes the making.
2. An increasing number of experts from the developing world have come to recognize the pitfalls of government-to-government aid. (Editorial comment: Barbara and I have observed this firsthand in many countries.)
3. The countries that have found ways of unleashing creativity through economic freedom have lifted millions out of poverty.
4. Capitalism is fueled by human creativity in a system that rewards people for serving the wants and needs of others.
5. In summary, the identification of greed with business profits and generosity with not-for-profits is too simplistic. As tempting as it may be, we cannot demonize profit and canonize poverty. (Editorial comment: Fr. Robert does a wonderful job of making this point. I can add that, for years, I've observed business owners do many wonderful acts of kindness for their associates and for the poor in their communities. I will continue this series and share some of my favorites.)
6. The entrepreneur in a free market, far more than the government bureaucrat or central planner under socialism, must submit himself to the wants and needs of the consumer if he is to profit.

7. What tends to make people happier is earned success — in other words, the feeling of accomplishment that comes with a job well done, a job that others find valuable.

Fr. Robert provided many references to credible research studies and wonderfully explained many different dynamics of a "free market" approach versus the alternative.

For those interested in learning more about this subject, I would recommend reading Fr. Robert's book as well as a number of the books he references, such as *The Road to Serfdom* by Friedrich A. Hayek.

Alive at Work

January 7, 2019 // Tom Doescher //

TOM DOESCHER //

Really, is that possible? To be alive at work? I know lots of business owners who wish their associates would share more ideas and be more creative. In fact, I've probably felt that way over the years myself. In his book, *Alive at Work*, author Daniel Cable offers some suggestions for those of us who want to love what we do. Before I get to the main subject, I'd like to offer an observation. Let me start with a story. Probably 20 years ago, I had the privilege of hearing the famous MIT economist, Lester Thurow, speak at an executive forum. He said something that day that I've never forgotten. He stated that he's often asked how he predicts the future. To answer those questions, he said he merely looks at what's already happening, and then extrapolates into the future.

I've noticed in the past year or two that many of the "business" books I read make reference to the brain and how it functions. Cable, for example, quotes Gallup research that I've mentioned before, indicating that 80 percent of workers don't feel they can be their best at work and 70 percent say they aren't engaged at work. According to Cable, the reason for those numbers is the fact that many organizations are deactivating the part of the employee's brain called the "seeking system," which controls an employee's drive and motivation. He suggests that the opposite of the seeking system is the "fear system," which was created by the Industrial Revolution and is a result of the command & control approach to management. Cable goes on to say that when the seeking system is triggered, rather than the fear system, the chemical dopamine is released and employees experience an urge to explore, understand, and contribute.

I'm going to stop there but suffice it to say that treating your associates one way shuts them down and treating them another way causes greater engagement and excitement.

Once again, I'm stepping outside of my area of expertise, but I personally experienced what Cable refers to as the "seeking system" and the related dopamine for most of my 40-year career at Plante Moran.

Cable also offers some great examples of companies that have embraced the seeking system approach. I've talked about many of these types of behaviors before, but I had no idea that doing the right thing can cause a positive reaction in the brain.

If you're interested in this subject, I would recommend Cable's book. To close, I'm going to provide this quote from the book: "To prompt employees' curiosity and learning through experimentation, a leader can start with the humble purpose of serving others and being open to learning from employees. When leaders express feelings of uncertainty and humility, and share their own developmental journeys, they end up encouraging a learning mindset in others." As I've mentioned before, my mentor, Ken Kunkel, has modeled this for the almost 50 years that I've known him, and he continues to have a positive impact on the world today.

What Financial Information Should I Share with My Associates?

September 24, 2018 // Tom Doescher //

TOM DOESCHER //

This was actually a question posed to me by one of my clients. To be perfectly candid, I didn't give him a very good answer. Thinking about how I could have responded better led me to purchase an old book, *Open-Book Management: The Coming Business Revolution* (*Open-Book*), written by John Case in 1995.

I also bought *The Great Game of Business: Unlocking the Power and Profitability of Open-Book Management,* by Jack Stack, and I intend to study the Scanlon plan.

So far, here are my takeaways from *Open-Book*, along with some editorial comments.

1. I would lean toward sharing information. In my experience with all types of businesses, the associates generally seem to think the company is more profitable than it really is. For example, if everyone hears the company has been awarded a million-dollar contract, they may think the owner will get $500,000. But if the company's EBITDA (Earnings Before Interest, Taxes, Depreciation & Amortization) is 10 percent (a pretty common result for a good company), the actual profit is far less.
2. Start out slowly and share just a few metrics, like sales/revenue.
3. Before getting too deep into sharing, think about reporting when you have either a world-class year or a near-bankruptcy year, and anticipate questions. Sharing too much information could become a slippery slope that results in unnecessary concerns or expectations.
4. NEVER FUDGE THE NUMBERS!!!! Rather than fudging numbers, it would be better not to share at all.
5. *Open-Book* appropriately describes the old Industrial Revolution's command & control management style versus today's knowledge workers, even on the factory floor. Have you been on a shop floor recently? Most machines today are computer-controlled, and the operators are required to be very skilled to diagnose issues and/or problems. Command & control would never work.
6. *Open-Book* also recommends that owners view their associates as "partners." I can relate to this because that's how Frank Moran, founding partner of Plante Moran, made me feel from the day I started there as an intern.
7. *Open-Book* suggests rewarding people for making money. In other words, teach them that profit is necessary to maintain a sustainable business.
8. "What gets measured gets done," according to *Open-Book*. Louis Gerstner, former IBM CEO, loved to say, "People do what you inspect, not what you expect."
9. Keep it simple. People don't trust what they don't understand.

The last half of the book provides specific examples of private companies that have adopted some type of open-book management style. When I reflect upon today's workforce, I think some version of open-book management makes a lot of sense.

I would probably suggest reading up on the subject, attending some seminars, and getting outside help to get started. A misstep could be quite painful for you and your associates.

The Great Game of Business

November 12, 2018 // Tom Doescher //

TOM DOESCHER //

In a previous blog, I mentioned I was going to read *The Great Game of Business,* written by Jack Stack. Although it's a book about open-book management (OBM), it was way more than that. Stack details what happened when he and his buddies — non-college-educated, blue-collar people — purchased a failing International Harvester plant where they had worked for years.

In the first third of the book, Stack provides his thoughts on OBM, and shares his leadership philosophies. As my dad would say, "He has a lot of common sense." To whet your appetite for his book, here are a few of my favorite takeaways (of course, with my editorial comments):

1. The best, most efficient, most profitable way to operate a business is to give everybody in the company a voice in saying how the company is run and a stake in the financial outcome, good or bad.
2. Middle managers have the most difficult role in the company because they have to please many masters. (Editorial comment: At my former firm, there's a position called "In-Charge." In my opinion, it was — and probably still is — the hardest job. The In-Charge must supervise the team, keep the client happy, keep the partner happy, and complete the work assignments accurately and within budget.)

3. There's a reason you get paid more when you become a manager. You're taking on more responsibility, and you're giving up some of your freedom. (Editorial comment: Wow, I've never seen this in writing, but I used to say those exact words to our partners. As a leader, in public, you surrender some of your personal points of view or opinions. This was very hard for some, including me, at times.)

4. "That's why I get angry at the loudmouths who talk about winning through intimidation. Not only are they dead wrong, but they are promoting one of the most destructive myths in American business." (Editorial comment: Need I say more?)
5. Tunnel vision is a big problem in business.
6. Too many goals are useless.

7. Bad housekeeping is frequently a sign of trouble. (Editorial comment: Japanese manufacturers have taught us about the importance of adopting the 5S workplace organization method.)
8. No matter how hard you try to be open, people are still intimidated by the title, the door, the desk — all symbols of power. (Editorial comment: This is so true. So, realize it and don't make it worse.)

There are many more great recommendations, but I'll stop there. In the balance of the book, Stack provides practical, detailed ideas for implementing OBM. Just a warning: He also offers some (just a few) political points of view and isn't shy about his support of capitalism. Stack also has a very strong point of view when it comes to his belief that associates should receive stock in the company, and he makes a very good case for his position. I happen to disagree with him and believe you can accomplish the same goal with deferred compensation or phantom stock pegged to the company enterprise value. In this area, I would strongly suggest you seek outside counsel from your advisors, including your attorney and accountants. As always, I'd be happy to discuss my views, if you'd like to talk about it. In my next post, I'll share one last list of rhetorical questions that Stack provided that might be worth asking yourself and your leadership team. The list reminded me of Marcus Buckingham's 12 (now 8) Questions, which I've discussed in the past.

The Stack 9 Hard Questions

December 3, 2018 // Tom Doescher //

 TOM DOESCHER //

In my last post, I summarized highlights from *The Great Game of Business*, written by business owner Jack Stack. In this post, I've listed nine tough rhetorical questions that remind me of Marcus Buckingham's 12 (now 8) Questions. Here goes:

1. What are you personally giving to the people you manage?
2. Do you spend as much time thinking about your team as you spend thinking about customers?
3. Do you share your problems, or do you keep them to yourself?
4. Do you, yourself, operate with an open book? Do you let your people know everything that you know?
5. Are you getting the benefit of your team's intelligence, or do you still think you're responsible for coming up with the answers on your own?

6. Do your people know what to do without being told, or do they wait to get a list from you? Is everybody working toward the same goal? Does everybody know what it is? Do you let people figure out the best way to get there?

7. Do you know what gets your people angriest? Have you ever asked them about their frustrations and their fears? What keeps them awake at night?

8. Have you talked to your team about your own fears and frustrations? Can you let down your guard enough to do that? Are you willing to make yourself vulnerable? Do you have enough self-confidence to take the risk to be transparent with them?

9. Most important, if the answer to any of these questions is no, do you really want to change?

I'm guessing Marcus Buckingham would love this list. Consider doing a self-assessment first. Then, have your leadership team members complete a self-assessment, followed by a company assessment. For those of you who are nervous, I'll quote my dad once again: "It is what it is." Take the risk and, if you're not where you could be, do something about it.

Keep It Simple
February 4, 2013 // Tom Doescher //

My partner, Barbara, and I began to focus on Volkswagen (VW) when our son joined them a few years ago. We quickly discovered that one of their goals was to be the No. 1 automobile manufacturer in the world. We've never understood why companies would set a certain sales level as their goal, and we've watched as two great car companies with this same goal fell on difficult times. To our pleasant surprise, there was more to the story. We had an opportunity to hear a presentation by Tom Loafman, VW Director of USA Purchasing, who referred to VW's four "pillars" (you could call them goals or strategies).

The company's first goal was to be the world leader in **customer satisfaction**, as measured by J.D. Power.

Second on the list was attaining annual vehicle sales of **10,000,000**.

Third (which may be my favorite) was to become the **top employer**; Loafman went on to say that if you were to interview the "man on the street" (say, in Chattanooga), they wanted him to say "VW is the best place to work."

Finally, the fourth pillar was to achieve **earnings before tax of 8 percent**. We thought, "Eureka! Someone is focused on profits!"

The Real Story Behind "Moneyball"

February 25, 2019 // Tom Doescher //

 **TOM DOESCHER //**

The other day I met with a client who shared information about recent discussions he had had with his team about bidding on new work. He believed the team was more focused on landing the project (top-line focused) than on the profitability.

This is a common issue experienced by many businesses, and I was totally following him until he used the word "heuristics." I made him repeat himself three times (he probably thinks I have a hearing problem), and then I asked him to spell it. To my knowledge, I had never seen or heard this word before.

Later he sent me a September 27, 1974, article from the publication *Science* entitled "Judgment Under Uncertainty: Heuristics and Biases," written by Amos Tversky and Daniel Kahneman. (Yes, this was over 40 years ago!)

I started reading the article, which my client said was a "little" heavy. Actually, it was really heavy; in fact, it caused me to relive the pain of my college statistics class. The good news is that he also recommended I read *The Undoing Project* by Michael Lewis, the famous author of three books that became successful movies, including *Moneyball*.

I would be willing to bet that most of my readers are very familiar with the subject explored in *Moneyball*, which is a great story about the phenomenal success of Major League Baseball's Oakland A's that resulted after the cash-poor team changed its selection criteria for baseball players from decades-old traditional methods.

In the introduction of his new book, Lewis cites a very damning book review written by University of Chicago economist Richard Thaler and law professor Cass Sunstein about his original book, and quotes Thaler and Sunstein's assessment: "... the author of *Moneyball* did not seem to realize the deeper reason for the inefficiencies in the market for baseball players: They sprang directly from the inner workings of the human mind." Lewis goes on to explain that the ways in which some baseball experts might misjudge baseball players — the ways in which any expert's judgments might be warped by the expert's own mind — had been described years ago by a pair of Israeli psychologists, Daniel Kahneman and Amos Tversky.

Lewis says: "My book wasn't original. It was simply an illustration of ideas that had been floating around for decades and had yet to be fully appreciated by, among others, me." It reminds me of what King Solomon said in Ecclesiastes: "... there is nothing new under the sun."

I will stop there, and in my next blog, I'll attempt to summarize *The Undoing Project*, which does a wonderful job of explaining and providing practical examples of the dangers of heuristic decision-making.

As I read Lewis's examples, my ears were ringing, recalling situations in the past where I may have made business decisions that weren't grounded in adequate objective data.

"Moneyball," part 2

March 11, 2019 // Tom Doescher //

TOM DOESCHER //

In my last **blog**, I introduced the concept of "heuristics" and promised I would provide more insight from *The Undoing Project*, the latest book by Michael Lewis.

So, here's a brief overview: In the 1950s, Nobel Prize-winning psychologist Herbert Simon suggested that while people strive to make rational choices, human judgment is subject to cognitive limitations, and people are limited by the amount of time they have to make choices/decisions.

In the 1970s, Amos Tversky and Daniel Kahneman introduced and labeled the specific ways of thinking people rely on to simplify decision-making.

As I mentioned in my previous blog, this topic is quite technical, but it's very important for business owners and senior executives to be aware of the practical implications present in the decisions they make every day. For that reason, I would highly recommend reading *The Undoing Project*.

To whet your appetite, I'll share two basic examples of the impact of heuristic biases from the book.

Belief in the Law of Small Numbers

The power of this belief can be seen in the way people think of totally random patterns — like, say, those created by a flipped coin. People know that a flipped coin is as equally likely to come up heads as it is tails, but they also think the tendency for a coin that's flipped a great many times to land on heads half the time would also express itself if it were flipped only a few times — an error known as "the gambler's fallacy."

If I flipped a coin a few times in a row and it landed on heads every time, what do you think it would land on the next flip? Most people would say it will land on tails, as if the coin itself could even things out. Tversky and Kahneman would say this is a glitch in human behavior. In reality, if you were to flip a coin a thousand times, you would be more likely to end up with heads or tails roughly half the time than you would if you only flipped it 10 times.

Framing Sensitivity to Negative Outcomes

If I gave you $1,000 and then gave you a choice between another gift of $500 and a 50/50 shot at winning $1,000, what would you pick? Most people pick $500, because it's the sure thing. Now, how about if I gave you $2,000 and then gave you a choice between losing $500 for sure and a 50/50 risk of losing $1,000? Most people would take the bet. The bottom line is that the two questions are effectively identical. In both cases, if you decide to gamble, you'd wind up with a 50/50 shot at being worth $2,000. And in both cases, if you chose the sure thing, you'd wind up being worth $1,500. When the sure thing is framed as a loss, people choose the gamble. However, when you frame it as a gain, people choose the sure thing.

Hopefully these two examples give you a brief glimpse into heuristics. When you reflect on your business, think about those times when you're quoting on new work or evaluating your team members. Are you basing your conclusions on objective data, or intuition? As a seasoned businessman, I realize more and more each day how many biases, rules of thumb, and gut feelings I have that are wrong. Give the book a chance.

Please, No More Surveys

September 2, 2013 // Tom Doescher //

I don't know about you, but I find the plethora of feedback surveys extremely annoying. Part of the reason is that I don't get a warm and fuzzy feeling that assures me that anyone has really read my answers. A few years ago, my wife and I stayed at an exclusive hotel and reported more than 10 significant complaints. No one ever followed up with us — so why should we take the time to fill out another customer feedback form?

Here's what I'd recommend. If you're compelled to send out a survey, ask just two questions: 1.) What did you really like about us? (And encourage them to fill in a little more detail.) 2.) How could we make your experience with us even better?

After your clients/customers have responded, acknowledge the thoughtful feedback they provided with a personalized note. That way, even if they have a complaint or a suggestion for improvement, you're almost guaranteed to win them over.

As the Business World has Truly Become Global,

July 29, 2019 // Tom Doescher //

TOM DOESCHER //

even fairly small, privately owned businesses have become globally active. Therefore, it's important that they're tuned in to cultural differences in those countries where they do business. To save money (or make more), it's critical that they avoid the mistakes made by many multinational companies — and me. In his book, *Driven by Difference*, David Livermore provides practical tips for companies with diverse customers and/or a diverse workforce, or what he calls "cultural intelligence." He refers to a Google internal employment survey that discovered teams that were both diverse and inclusive were also the best at innovation. When I purchased the book, I thought it would be about diversity in the workplace, which it is. But it's much more. If you're looking to improve innovation and even marketing in your company, I would highly recommend *Driven by Difference*.

As I've done with other books, I'll whet your appetite with several excerpts:

1. "Priming" is the process of presenting a particular stimulus to make people feel and act in a certain way. For example, in supermarkets around the world, freshly cut flowers are the first thing you see, priming you to think freshness from the moment you enter the store.
2. There's insufficient evidence to support any conclusion that one national culture is consistently more innovative than another.

117

3. The gut can be a shockingly reliable mechanism for decision-making, but it's subject to enormous error when the cultural context changes.
4. Most of us start life with a pretty insulated view of the world.
5. Most innovators are intense observers.
6. Mark Zuckerberg has Facebook engineers prove that what they're coding works on old, low-end flip phones to simulate the conditions in most of the world.
7. There's evidence that many people do their best independent thinking outside the office.
8. Culturally intelligent innovation comes from a climate of trust, where differences are perceived as an asset rather than a liability.
9. A.G. Lafley, CEO of P&G, which is considered a very innovative company, insists on in-home visits with consumers when he travels internationally. He doesn't want to make decisions based solely on market research done by consultants or his R&D teams.

Those are some highlights, but Livermore presents lots of really interesting, practical stories. Again, the underpinnings of the book are diversity, but there are some great reminders of the importance of really listening to and understanding our customers.

Please, No More Rules
May 27, 2013 // Tom Doescher //

My partner used to work in an office of 10 people. When someone would step out of line, instead of the boss confronting this person, they would establish a new rule. Needless to say, there were an awful lot of controls and restrictions in place for such a small staff.

First of all, Level 5 leaders (i.e., the best leaders, according to Jim Collins in his book *Good to Great*) should wisely confront associates who are exhibiting bad behavior. Second, remember that job seekers would rather work for a company that doesn't burden its associates with hundreds of unnecessary rules. If they're considering several offers, they'll choose the business that seems to respect its employees most.

The fewer the rules, the better — "Speaking the truth in love" equals higher profits and, as Jim Collins would say, a business built to last.

I Make My Money During Bad Times
March 2, 2012

During one of the recessions prior to 2008-2009, I was meeting with a business owner who said to me, "You know, now is when I make most of my money" — and then he smiled at me.

He went on to say, "The key decisions made during an economic downturn are what really drive my profitability post-recession ... we get sloppy during the good times."

His closing comments reminded me of Seneca, who, in 65 B.C., said, "Luck is what happens when preparation meets opportunity." Laying the groundwork for success takes place during bad times.

As I listen to and read all the positive economic forecasts (trust me, I like good news), I'm getting progressively more nervous about companies ramping up too quickly and too much. (For example, if you add up the 15 automotive companies' projected U.S. sales, you get 14.5 million units — which is 1.8 million vehicles higher than the number sold in 2011 and 700,000 higher than the estimates of all the forecasters.) Every day I read about companies looking for *thousands* of new employees. Really?

So, my challenge is to try to understand why you're adding team members. Are you slipping back into pre-recession bad habits? Are you adding people based on *booked* business or *hoped-for* business? In Jonathan Byrnes' book, *Islands of Profit in a Sea of Red Ink*, he states that 40 percent of every business is unprofitable. Instead of hiring additional people, should you be shutting down an unprofitable division and redeploying the associates to your expanding business segment?

The other day I heard an economist say, "We usually overreact to a bad economy (i.e., it will never come back), and we overreact to a good economy (i.e., this is going to last forever)."

Before you make any drastic moves, remember this: Try not to lose all the money you made during the recession.

Business and Businesspeople Are Not Evil
July 10, 2012

That was the title of a speech I recently gave. Having read five books on the financial crisis of 2008-2009, I understand why some people may believe that business and businesspeople are, in fact, evil. But implying that all businesspeople are greedy, based on the behaviors of a relative few, is quite irritating.

As businesspeople ourselves, my partner and I have been alarmed by the hostility that has been shown to business owners and businesspeople. We've made a vow to be more outspoken on behalf of business owners — especially those who operate small and medium-sized enterprises (SMEs), which are defined as firms with fewer than 500 employees. (Most such businesses, by the way, are owner operated.)

SMEs employ half of all private sector employees, generate 60 to 80 percent of net new jobs annually, and employ more than 40 percent of high-tech workers such as scientists, engineers, and computer specialists.

In 2001, I gave a presentation at the Plante Moran Manufacturing & Distribution Practice Workshop entitled, "Who Are Our Clients?" My opening comments were as follows: "Our clients are men and women who risk their wealth every day to make stuff. Most of them work quietly behind the scenes, providing great jobs and career opportunities for millions. They serve on nonprofit and school boards, and city councils. They seem to be the ones driving much of the charitable activity in their communities."

These don't sound like evil people to me. Most of them sincerely care about their customers, associates, and suppliers. If you talk to them, they'll say 2008-2009 was the worst period of their lives — not because of the losses, but because of the tough decisions they were required to make to stay in business (i.e., layoffs). They worked harder than they'd ever worked before, and very few went the route of Chapter 11.

There are some people who believe the best way to eradicate poverty in the world is through creating sustainable, for-profit jobs. You can read more (or, in summary, accept that a pretty compelling case can be made for jobs being the answer to poverty) about this subject in the article "MIT Essay Competition" on the Resource page of our website.

If you're a business owner or executive, we at Doescher Advisors would like to encourage you to keep going. Ignore the media. You know who you are and what you do. Keep on keeping on.

Doescher Advisors — *Champions for Owner-Operated Businesses!*

Talent Is Overrated — So We All Can Win
July 21, 2014 // Tom Doescher //

The title for this post is from Geoff Colvin's book, *Talent is Overrated.* As you would imagine, the title really grabbed my attention. Based on significant research, Colvin concludes that having talent is helpful, but what distinguishes the good performers from the great is what he labels "Deliberate Practice." In other words, you want to get to the point where you're good at something, then practice the right stuff with the guidance of a knowledgeable coach.

Unfortunately, Colvin uses mostly accomplished athletes — like Tiger Woods — to demonstrate his point. Tiger may have some natural talent, but he started playing golf at age 2 — and, since he has been a professional golfer, he's changed his swing three times as he has worked to get even better.

As I read the book, two Plante Moran partners came to mind almost immediately: Ed Parks and John Sirhal. Many would describe them as being really smart, and they probably are. But I think the secret to their amazing client service is the "Deliberate Practice" Colvin referred to. Both men are voracious readers. When they meet with a client, they're prepared. They know what's going to be discussed, and they do their homework. They anticipate different scenarios. They are very client-focused and look at the issues from many different angles. I've always thought, "Can you imagine what it feels like to be their client?" So why am I talking about this subject? I'm currently assisting a few young executives and helping them to improve certain leadership skills. I believe — and I've told them — that they can, in fact, be better if they want to and if they're willing to put in the "Deliberate Practice."

Here's the challenge. Do you have associates whom you would like to see improve in a particular skill? Think about what Tiger, Ed, or John would do, then design some specific activities for your associates to practice (i.e., conducting the next important meeting with your key customer). Make sure they have an opportunity to practice these activities in a situation where you or others will be able to give them feedback — and watch for the results!

New Scientific Discoveries About Talent
April 23, 2018 // Tom Doescher //

TOM DOESCHER //

I've commented on the importance of "deliberate practice" in other posts, including on July 21, 2014. Many of us want to say, "Well, I could never do that because I'm not as talented as he or she is." According to a number of authors and studies, however, that's just not true. The fact is that with a reasonable amount of talent, you can become outstanding — but understand that it will take a lot of hard work and practice (unfortunately, there's no supplement you can take). On the front cover of *The Talent Code,* by Daniel Coyle, there's a quote from *In Search of Excellence* author Tom Peters: *"I am willing to guarantee that you will not read a more important and useful book in this or any other year."* Wow, what an endorsement!

In his book, Coyle focuses on what are termed "talent hotbeds." Talent hotbeds are tiny places that produce disproportionate, "Everest-size amounts" of talent — examples include Brazilian footballers or Korean women golfers — and the book provides a wide variety of impressive examples. The key theme of the book is that these talent hotbeds aren't random occurrences but are places that share the same skill acquisition and success. Each hotbed has certain characteristics and patterns of targeted, deep practice that builds skill, and the result is accelerated learning.

What was fascinating to me were recent studies of the brain that support the premise that practice — as Coyle calls it, "deep practice"— makes Tom a better (insert whatever you want to be better at). Coyle uses a lot of medical terms, including "myelin," to make his case, and his conclusions are supported by the work of other scientists.

I believe the most important takeaway is this: If you want to get better at something, find others who are perceived as the best, learn from them, and then practice, practice, practice.

Finally, a Positive Story About Corporate America

March 19, 2018 // Tom Doescher //

TOM DOESCHER //

If you're like me, you're probably getting sick of reading and listening to negative stories about corporate America. Even hearing those two words together can be a turnoff.

Well, the other day I was with a client who shared a very positive story.

In his industry, there's a growing shortage of independent installers for their product — and, you guessed it, installers are very critical if the manufacturer and the distributor are going to be successful. A huge problem is that fewer workers are entering this field, since it's so physically taxing, and most installers burn out at a relatively young age.

My client shared how the manufacturer has responded to these concerns by developing a new product that's less complex and easier to install. Since its introduction, the new product has resulted in a 50 percent increase in productivity. To the customer, the changes have no effect whatsoever on the look, functionality, or pricing of the product. Environmentally sensitive customers, meanwhile, have been happy to discover the new product is manufactured from fully recyclable materials.

To my client's surprise — and mine, too — the manufacturer's representative, who is promoting this product, says, "We recommend the installers continue to charge the same price to install the product." As a result, younger, stronger installers are able to increase their income by 50 percent, while older, experienced installers can keep earning the same income with significantly less wear and tear on their bodies.

Wow, I just got re-recruited — here's a business that truly cares about its workers. I hear and read a lot of similar stories indicating there's a shortage of skilled manual laborers. Are you in one of those industries? Is there an innovation in your industry that would be customer-neutral, but would improve your workers' lives?

Do You Have a Uniquely Better Product?

October 2, 2017 // Tom Doescher //

TOM DOESCHER //

In a recent presentation, Andy Stanley, author of *Next Generation Leader*, which is on my Top Picks Leadership Book list, shared some of his recent thinking related to his 20-year-old church. It may seem like an odd source for business strategy advice, but I found his thoughts to be exceptional and very applicable to businesses that have been around for a while.

Stanley and his leadership team asked the following rhetorical questions: If we had to do it again, what would we do over again? Why were we so successful? Why did we grow so fast? In Stanley's case, his team concluded that when they launched North Point Community Church, it was the only church with its type of format in Atlanta. In other words (as we hope for in business!), they had no competition. As Stanley would say, "We had a uniquely better product." Today, churchgoers in Atlanta have many similar choices. As we know from Clayton Christensen and his disruptive innovation work at the Harvard Business School, it's very difficult to change almost anything in a successful organization/business.

To help those of us with 20-plus year successful businesses who want to continue to thrive, Stanley offered the following tips:

123

1. Be a student, not a critic. As Steven Covey would say, "Seek to understand why others are providing a new approach to their product or service." For you old-timers, remember what IBM said when the first Apple computer came out?
2. Keep your eyes wide open. What trends may be going on that will affect your uniquely better product?
3. Replace "How?" with "WOW!" Let me explain this one. Have you ever heard a young associate suggest a fresh, new idea and some old-timer says, "How can they do that?" Do you think that young associate will ever dare bring up a new, fresh idea again? On the other hand, what if the old-timer, like my mentor Ken Kunkel, would say, "Wow, I never thought of that. Maybe we should investigate and try it." Actually, Kunkel had the following rule: If someone on the team had an idea, he would try his best to utilize or implement it in some way and give lots of public praise to the person who had come up with the idea. Do you think Kunkel received more ideas using that approach? What about you? Do you say "How?" or "WOW!"?
4. Finally, ask uniquely better questions and be open-minded to the answers.

Barbara and I are in our sixth year of Doescher Advisors. We plan to ask ourselves, and maybe some of you, this question: Do we have a uniquely better product? We would encourage you to do the same.

Do You Listen to Your Team and Get the "Right" Strategy?

July 7, 2014 // Tom Doescher //

I've added *Multipliers: How the Best Leaders Make Everyone Smarter*, by Liz Wiseman, to my list of Top Picks, and would highly encourage you to read it. You may wonder why I've classified this blog as Strategy and Focus. Well, that's a good question. As I was reading the book, I began to reminisce back to a strategic planning meeting where my successor and I had designed an agenda for the annual strategic planning session of our industry leadership team. Both of us believed quite strongly that there was no need to spend any time on one subject in particular. We added it to the agenda, but our plan was to spend just a few minutes on it. When the item came up during the meeting, we expressed our thoughts — and assumed everyone would then move on to the next matter on the agenda.

To our surprise, a number of younger colleagues dug in and expressed their concern that this area needed more resources and attention, not less. For once, I was able to keep my defensiveness to myself and listen. Their points of view were compelling. They were right. Wow, we had missed it. So, we changed our position and allocated more resources to this initiative.

Are you a multiplier or a diminisher with your team when you're setting the direction of the company? What would your team say? BTW, I often wonder how many times I didn't "hear" my team and ended up heading in the wrong direction.

Why Don't They Read My Email?

September 18, 2017 // Tom Doescher //

TOM DOESCHER //

This is a common complaint I hear from senior executives. Over the years, I've received well-written communications (I'll use this label to include emails, memos, texts, tweets, letters, and all other written messages), as well as poorly composed ones. I notice that I always read the good ones and often skip the others. Here are a few tips I've accumulated over the years to help improve readership:

1. First of all, why am I sending this communication? Should I? Often, I decide not to send the message after all.
2. Pace your communications — or, maybe I should say, limit your communications. Avoid the "*another* email from Tom" reaction.
3. Would I read my own communication?
4. Make sure the subject line or the opening sentence is intriguing and/or catchy.
5. Be brief and be succinct. So many people seem to think longer is better, but that's not the case. It often takes more time to be precise, but your readership will go up.
6. Use bullets, headings, and a lot of white space, so readers can scan the material more easily.
7. Re-read your draft communication multiple times, to make sure it's clear.
8. Create an environment where your readers get something. Give them a tip, or some nugget of information that will help them be more successful.
9. If you're asking a question, make sure the reader(s) know you're looking for a response.
10. When appropriate, slip in a little humor (this is tricky; using sarcasm and/or referring to inside jokes can backfire and go horribly wrong).
11. Assume your communication may be forwarded. I always ask the question, "What if my communication ended up in *the WSJ*?"

Hopefully, these suggestions will improve your readership. As you know, we're all being bombarded with so many communications on myriad devices — and much of it is, indeed, junk mail. When your name appears, you want your readers to give your message priority status. I believe they will if you invest the time before hitting "send."

How Good is Your Company at Solving Problems?

June 19, 2017 // Tom Doescher //

TOM DOESCHER //

How good is your company at solving problems?

That's the rhetorical question addressed in a *Harvard Business Review* article entitled "Are You Solving the Right Problems?"

The authors believe managers, spurred by a penchant for action, tend to switch quickly into solution mode without first making sure they really understand the problem.

Can you relate?

I know I'm guilty as charged. The article offers what the authors believe are the seven best practices for effectively reframing problems:

1. Establish legitimacy — get agreement to utilize the reframing method.
2. Bring outsiders into the discussion — choose someone who will speak freely.
3. Get people's definitions in writing — have you ever left a meeting thinking everyone agrees with the loose oral description, and found out later that they don't?
4. Ask what's missing — make sure you ask explicitly what has not been captured or mentioned.
5. Consider multiple categories — identify specifically what category of problem (i.e., incentive, expectation, attitude, etc.) the group is facing.
6. Analyze positive expectations — what's different about this situation?
7. Question the objective — pay attention to the objectives of each party involved, first clarifying, and then challenging them.

Although this article may seem a little academic, I would highly recommend reading it. As I've already admitted, I love jumping in and solving the problem — and, at times, I've missed the mark.

This article provided advice that would have saved me time and embarrassment in the past.

What Is One of the Hardest Jobs to Perform Today?

May 22, 2017 // Tom Doescher //

TOM DOESCHER //

According to a *Harvard Business Review* article entitled "Kick-A Customer Service – Consumers Want Results – Not Sympathy," **81 percent** of customers across all industries attempt to take care of matters themselves before reaching out to a live representative. The investment in self-service technologies has been enormously effective at removing low-complexity issues from the live service queue. According to the article's authors, 84 percent of customers prefer a straightforward solution to their problem. When they do call for assistance, they're knowledgeable and very demanding.

The authors conclude that customer service representatives fall into seven profiles, which they outline in the article. The big "aha" is focused around two profile types: Empathizers, who enjoy solving others' problems, seek to understand behaviors and motives, and listen sympathetically; and Controllers, who are outspoken and opinionated, and like demonstrating their expertise and directing the customer interaction.

Intuitively, I would think Empathizers would be the best reps — and so do customer service rep managers, since Empathizers represent 32 percent of all representatives (the largest category).

As it turns out, we're wrong! The trouble is, the messaging that managers use in recruiting service reps is often stereotypical of yesterday's customer service workers, and tends to repel rather than attract Controllers, who represent only 15 percent of all reps. Controllers want flexibility to express their personality and handle issues as they think best.
They are keen problem-solvers with a unique ability to think on their feet and are self-starters who are comfortable taking the initiative.

If you're part of a company that provides customer service reps who assist clients by phone (and probably face-to-face, too), I would highly recommend reading the HBR article.

Our old, well-established "best practices" no longer work in this tech-savvy world.

By the way, according to the authors' research, the best reps, Controllers, are paid the same as other reps and are satisfied with it.

What One Trait Do You Want in a Chief Marketing Officer?

April 24, 2017 // Tom Doescher //

TOM DOESCHER //

I'm probably going to offend someone, and I'm sorry.

Recently, a client asked me for marketing assistance. At Doescher Advisors, one of our values is that if we believe someone else is more qualified to advise the client, we refer that client to them.

In this case, we arranged meetings with two extremely successful chief marketing officers who were in businesses that were similar to that of this particular client.

The next time I met with the client, he told me the two CMOs were very impressive and helpful, and he said they both offered to respond to any questions he may have in the future.

To his surprise, when he asked them what traits, experience, and knowledge he should look for in a CMO, they both said exactly the same thing: The best CMOs they had ever worked with had been personally successful selling a product or service.

Neither my client nor I were expecting that, but the more we thought about it, it makes great sense. The next time you're hiring a CMO, you may want to consider this advice.

Where Was Erin Back Then?

January 9, 2017 // Tom Doescher //

TOM DOESCHER //

Barbara and I have had the privilege of traveling to more than 30 countries on six continents for business and humanitarian trips. Speaking for myself, I've made many mistakes attempting to build relationships in other places, from the Rift Valley of Kenya to the Highlands in Papua New Guinea to Pudong, Shanghai.

Hopefully, I've learned from my faux pas, but they were usually painful experiences, nonetheless. This past year, I had the pleasure of hearing Erin Meyer, a professor at INSEAD, speak and then read from her book, *The Culture Map — Breaking Through the Invisible Boundaries of Global Business*.

Meyer could have saved me a lot of wasted time, energy, and blunders. She provides a field-tested model for decoding how cultural differences impact international business, and she combines a smart analytical framework with practical, actionable advice for succeeding in a global world.

If you have team members from different countries (Barbara and I worked with a team in Brazil that included people from more than 10 different countries including the Netherlands, Korea, Malaysia and, of course, Brazil), offices/plants located in other countries, or if you're pursuing business cross-culturally for the first time, I would highly recommend Meyer's book.

In addition, if you go to the Tools section of her website, *erinmeyer.com*, she provides a Self-Assessment Cultural Profile and a tool you can use to compare how two (or more) cultures build trust, give negative feedback, and make decisions. If your company has cross-cultural dealings, how are you doing with your associates, customers, and vendors from other cultures? My guess is Meyer has a few practical tips that you'll find valuable.

Footnote: I could share hundreds of stories, but this one comes to mind.

One of my Japanese partners asked me to attend a seminar where he was the presenter. He wanted to introduce me to several Japanese business

129

executives and was excited that I would be sitting through his presentation (even though it was all in Japanese).

Although I knew no Japanese words, my partner had a clock built into his presentation and I could tell, as time went on, that he was significantly over the allotted time — probably by 25 percent.

After the presentation, he asked for feedback, so I courageously offered my observation of his running over the scheduled time (a fatal mistake in U.S. business).

He thanked me for my feedback and then went on to say, "In the Japanese culture, the participants' reaction to the speaker who exceeds the allotted time is to be happy that they received more than they paid for." All I could say was, "Really?"

All Lives Have Equal Value
December 19, 2016 // Tom Doescher //

TOM DOESCHER //

In the past year, I had the good fortune of watching an interview with Melinda Gates. WOW!!! The title of this blog is her and Bill's mantra, and it's what drives the Bill & Melinda Gates Foundation. Melinda, who refers to herself as an introvert, is making an enormous impact worldwide. (By the way, she grew up in a strong, faith-based middle-class home in Dallas, attended an all-girls Catholic high school, and then went to Duke and received a bachelor's degree in computer science and an MBA.) She left Duke to join Microsoft, where she was leading a large team, but elected to leave after 10 years to be home with the couple's three children. She was very refreshing to listen to.

In addition to caring for the children, she runs the foundation, which employs 1,400 people. Another Wow. What they do all over the world is amazing, and I'm sure overseeing such a large enterprise creates a lot of pressure and stress. However, if I were her, my biggest stress would be caused by the responsibility of appropriately utilizing Warren Buffet's fortune, most of which has been pledged to the Bill & Melinda Gates Foundation.
That's a Wow, Wow, Wow. I'm sorry, I just needed to get her story out there. So now to the business idea. When Melinda and Bill got involved

with various causes, she said they were surprised to find out that very little accurate data — or even the measurement of important issues — was available. She then went on to recite a list of the data she receives regularly and uses to determine the impact of their philanthropic investment; one example is that she gets a monthly report on the status of polio outbreaks around the world (one of Bill's passions is to eradicate polio from the earth).

As I was listening to her, I thought of many companies whose leaders make decisions without good data. Money is spent based on anecdotal information, personal opinions, what a couple of customers said, and myriad other subjective sources. If Melinda can get data on polio from some remote African village, I'm sure companies can retrieve useful data. It's not easy, but it is possible. Are you collecting the key data and metrics that will enable you to give your clients/customers what they "really" want, and then providing it in a profitable way?

Culture Change

October 3, 2016 // Tom Doescher //

TOM DOESCHER //

I'm sure I'll offend someone with this post, but here goes. For years, I have seriously questioned whether you can change a culture. To me, the culture is the culture. Even so, there are lots of consultants who make good money advising clients on how to change their culture (by the way, some of these consultants are good friends of mine).

On March 21, 2016, I posted "How the Mighty Fall," about Arthur Andersen, a company that for decades had an amazing culture, but still failed. AA, as we called them, had a great culture. What happened? Well, I recently read *"Culture is Not the Culprit"* in the April 2016 *Harvard Business Review* and had an epiphany. The authors, Jay Lorsch (whom I had the privilege of interacting with at a Harvard Executive Program) and Emily McTague, said: "... culture is not something you 'fix.' Rather ... cultural change is what you get after you've put new processes or structures in place ..."

I know what you're thinking. This sounds like consultant mumbo jumbo, but it's exactly what Alan Mulally did at Ford Motor Co., which the authors explain. In one of his first management meetings at Ford, Mulally found

131

that all his direct reports brought their assistants to the meeting (picture two huge circles with the direct reports in the inner circle and their No. 2 in the outer circle). When a question came up, the direct reports would defer the answer to their No. 2. At the conclusion of the meeting, Mulally excused the assistants and then told the direct reports that, in the future, they needed to answer the questions — and the No. 2s were no longer invited.

Often, we want to make business more glamorous sounding, but it's a lot about accountability, taking responsibility, focusing on the customer/client, treating team members with respect, and what I like to call just basic blocking and tackling.

So, in simple English, don't focus on the culture. Focus on doing the basics right. Take good care of the customer and your team members. Are you thinking you need a culture change? If your answer is yes, are your basic processes working well? Really? As I've said to many of you, it ain't easy running a company.

Is Your Business Designed to Give Your Customers What They Want?
April 28, 2014 // Tom Doescher //

In my April 23, 2012, post, "Create Your Own Path," I encouraged business owners to focus on their customers' needs, not on what their competitors were doing. You can be in what appears to be the same business as someone else, but chances are you have totally different clients/customers.

In my community, there's just such a situation occurring with two fitness clubs/gyms. I'll attempt to contrast the features of each gym without promoting one over the other. Gym No. 1 has significantly more members, extended operating hours, many cardio machines, free weights and exercise machines, amenities like tanning booths and massage chairs, limited group training, and an attractive low monthly fee. Gym No. 2 has fewer members, some machines, and free weights, and lots of group training options — some included in the monthly fee and others offered for an additional fee. Gym No. 2 is affiliated with a physical therapy (PT) clinic, which refers many members to the gym to participate in classes designed to promote an active lifestyle for life. Gym No. 2 refers its members to the PT clinic, too. I don't have official demographics, but the average age of Gym No. 2's members would appear to be higher. I haven't seen any financial data on either gym, but it seems as though both are successful, even though they have two entirely different approaches.
Is your business designed to give your clients/customers what they want? Do you *know* what they want — or are you copying one of your competitors?

Wow, 240-Year-Old Company Was Able to Change!

June 10, 2013 // Tom Doescher //

I'm on a roll with the value of the *Harvard Business Review*. In the March 2013 issue, Jorge Cauz, president of Encyclopedia Britannica, tells an encouraging story about why his company stopped producing the iconic encyclopedia and how they became a successful provider of online K-12 educational services.

I've read about or observed so many companies that aren't willing to modify their product to keep up with a changing marketplace and, as a result, die. Encyclopedia Britannica understood and met its challenges head-on, which is why I found this story refreshing. I learned a number of things from Britannica's experience:

- They recognized the need to change at their sales peak.
- They experimented with many different business models (i.e., spent money to do this). Most concepts failed, but they weren't deterred.
- They realized their greatest strength/uniqueness was their editorial staff of researchers and scholars (i.e., high-quality content).
- They resisted the urge to reduce their editorial team when sales plummeted.
- They eliminated their 2,000-plus door-to-door sales force (I would assume they were a very powerful and influential internal voice at the time).

Cauz concluded his article by saying, "We don't want to be like an old actor trying to hold onto his youth." (Or, as I would say, be like Brett Favre!) Are you in a situation like Britannica's?

Do you need to change?

Is It Better to Buy at the Top of the Market or at the Bottom?

April 14, 2014 // Tom Doescher //

This isn't a trick question. At a recent automotive trade group meeting, two warm-up questions were posed to the participants. They were: What sales revenue do you expect for next year? and, Are you planning to make any equipment or facility investments this year?

As you would expect, the answers were all — except for my responses, that is — very optimistic. Not that I'm a pessimist, but for years I've watched the shrewd operators know when to buy and when to wait. I don't know if we're at the top or near the end of the cycle, but modern economic history has shown that we don't stay at the top forever.

The smart operators are very calculating, independent thinkers who don't follow the herd. For example, Warren Buffet invested $5 billion in Goldman Sachs on September 24, 2008, (while most of us were running for cover) and made a very handsome return on his investment.

I'm not saying not to invest; what I'm saying is that you should base your decision on hard data (i.e., booked business with realistic, predicted volumes), not emotions and hype.

By the way, remember that the goal is long-term profitable growth, not increased sales. Are you absolutely certain you should build that new facility or purchase that new press now?

p.s. I know successful business is all about guessing right, so I encourage you to base your decisions on as many facts as you can.

Love? Are You Kidding Me?

May 30, 2016 // Tom Doescher //

TOM DOESCHER //

Is there a place for love in the workplace? Some people would answer with a resounding "Yes!" During the last decade of my first career, I spent a lot of time on airplanes. Because I lived in Detroit, Delta was the most convenient and sensible airline to fly, but I have to say I was intrigued by how many times highly respected business consultants speaking about great companies would use Southwest Airlines as an example. They would rave about their experience with Southwest (in a good way).

So, I decided to read *Lead with Luv: A Different Way to Create Real Success*, by Ken Blanchard and Colleen Barrett. Wow, what a story. First of all, Southwest leads the airline industry in all important metrics, and they've been profitable every year since their founding in 1971. I realize you probably already know this, but most, if not all, major airlines went bankrupt during that same period — some more than once.
Of all the things that could be discussed when it comes to a successful company like Southwest Airlines, what did former Southwest President Colleen Barrett select to talk about in her book? Love.

A short time after I had finished reading *Lead with Luv*, I was at the gym and a friend who knows I read a lot said, "Hey, I read a book you would like. It's called *Love Works,* by Joel Manby." There it was again: love. What my friend didn't know is that I knew Manby back when he was the Saab North American CEO. Needless to say, based on the title and the author, I read the book. Joel Manby is now CEO of Herschend Family Entertainment (HFE). I wasn't familiar with the company, but according to his comments, it's a very successful Disney park-type business. Just like Colleen Barrett, Manby credits HFE's founders, Jack, and Peter Herschend, with creating a very special culture focused on their love of the park guests *and* their love for the HFE team members. Manby concludes that as a result of that philosophy, the HFE venture has been a huge success, and he offers many specific examples of making difficult business decisions that involved balancing "profits" and "love." (My mentor, Frank Moran, was fond of using the tightrope as a metaphor for making decisions.)

I would strongly suggest that you read both books. For some of you, it will be very encouraging; for others, it may cause some discomfort — but that's OK. If I were to anonymously interview some of your team members about "love" at your company, what would they tell me?

How the Mighty Fall
March 21, 2016 // Tom Doescher //

TOM DOESCHER //

One of my former partners suggested that I read *Final Accounting: Ambition, Greed, and the Fall of Arthur Andersen,* by Barbara Toffler and Jennifer Reingold. Let me start by saying I believed — and still believe — Arthur Andersen was one of the greatest professional services firms of all time. My brother came very close to going to work for them back in the '70s. They were high-quality, client-focused, and very innovative (e.g., their technology practice started in the '50s).

I still grieve their demise in 2002. Even all these years later, it's so hard for me to acknowledge that Andersen is gone.
I always looked forward to their latest service or discovery. In my humble opinion, they were the best for decades.

That said, who should read *Final Accounting*? I would recommend it to anyone who's leading an organization that, for years/generations, has been considered "the best" in whatever industry you're in.

Are you considered the best in your industry? Are you sure you're *still* the best?

Pixar's Braintrust

February 22, 2016 // Tom Doescher //

TOM DOESCHER //

In Ed Catmull's book *Creativity, Inc.*, he describes the "Braintrust," which he says is one of the most important traditions at Pixar.

For those of you who may not know, Pixar made the first computer-animated movie, "Toy Story"— and it took Catmull, John Lasseter, and Steve Jobs 20 years to accomplish that task (I'll save that story for another blog).

Catmull describes Pixar's Braintrust as follows:

1. It was a group of executives who met every few months to assess movies.
2. The group would provide candid feedback on developing movies. According to Catmull, "Candor is forthrightness or frankness — not so different from honesty, really. And yet, in common usage, the word communicates not just truth-telling, but a lack of reserve."
3. Members of the group were funny, focused, smart, and relentlessly candid with each other.
4. Catmull says the group went against common boardroom principles. "Societal conditioning discourages telling the truth to those perceived to be in higher positions," he says.
5. I know nothing about making movies, but Catmull has this to say about the profession: "Candor could not be more crucial to our creative process. Why? Because early on, all of our movies *suck*."

I've talked about this before. Do you have a way to get the truth?
Can you imagine how crushed a director/producer would be if, after all their time and effort, they discovered their creation completely missed the mark? Many industrial and service businesses have experienced the same result, and it's called **FAILURE.**

Do you have a Braintrust?

The Impact of Private Equity Groups

September 23, 2019 // Tom Doescher //

TOM DOESCHER //

As I reflect back on my decades in the workforce, I can't think of anything that has affected and impacted businesses, especially middle market businesses, more than private equity groups (PEGs). Most of you know this, but for those who may not, in its simplest form the sponsors of a PEG raise investment monies from pension funds, insurance companies, wealthy individuals, and others. The money is pooled and then invested in the purchase of companies, many owned by their founders. If you own a business, this has created a great avenue for liquidating your investment in your business. Some PEGs will do partial purchases, and a few will even invest without gaining voting control (under 50 percent ownership). For private company owners, it provides another type of buyer in addition to individuals, companies, or going public, which has its pitfalls.

In this blog, I would like to point out one change in commerce that's a direct result of PEGs: the concept of subscriptions (customer commitments to regular monthly payments, often automatically renewed annually). Obviously, subscriptions existed before PEGs, but if you look at different business sectors, there are many new versions of "subscriptions" that exist today. Some are obvious, others are not.

1. Many IT product companies have transitioned from selling you their product for $1 million to effectively leasing their product for $20k per month forever.
2. My partner's dentist sold out to a dental roll-up group owned by a PEG, and they now offer an annual fee that includes basic cleaning, X-rays, etc., which is automatically charged to a patient's credit card.
3. There are a number of businesses that already had an annual, multiyear, or automatic renewal provision — so they already had a subscription.
   For example, I work with a security firm that provides home and business security alarms and cameras that are in this category.
4. There are businesses that are attempting to transform what I might call a service into a product that can be sold as a subscription with a monthly fee.
5. One of my personal favorites has to do with my lifelong passion for alpine skiing. Two companies have created a partnership through the

outright purchase of multiple ski resorts or some other "arrangement." They offer "season lift passes" that allow you to ski at many different major ski resorts throughout North America. The price point is such that with only two trips, it's worth the investment. So, me being me, I'm trying to figure out what's going on. They've taken a weather-dependent business, snow skiing, and solidified and made the revenue stream less variable and more predictable. Skiers need to purchase the season pass before Thanksgiving. (How's that for cash management?) In addition, they've substantially increased the price of daily lift passes, which makes the season pass even more valuable; they get premium prices from those who opt for daily passes. Brilliant!!!

Why are the PEGs so focused on subscriptions? The simple answer is that they're reducing variability in revenues and increasing profit predictability for the purpose of reselling their investment as quickly as possible for as much as possible.

Maybe you should take this concept and apply it to your business. If you do, I'm confident your company will be more valuable.

Jobs, Jobs, Jobs

October 7, 2019 // Tom Doescher //

TOM DOESCHER //

Part of our mission statement says: "Doescher Advisors was founded to help businesses increase profits and **jobs** ..." After enjoying a very rewarding career at Plante Moran and having the privilege of leading more than 30 global mission teams (and achieving Delta Airlines' Diamond status by logging over 150,000 Frequent Flyer miles annually), I decided to spend my "next season" advising local business owners. As a free market advocate, I believed the best way to help the world was to help business owners create "great jobs," especially for the less-skilled workforce. I know you're thinking "That sounds pretty corny," but it's the truth — and, eight years later, I could tell you some great stories.

When I recently read *The Coming Jobs War* by Jim Clifton, CEO of Gallup, I was encouraged and motivated to continue in this line of work. As you probably know, Gallup is a 75-plus-year-old, highly regarded global polling organization. Clifton's book supports my decision to combine my business and philanthropic activities into Doescher Advisors.

The following are some fascinating excerpts from his book, with a few editorial comments:

1. "If you were to ask me, from all the world polling Gallup has done for more than 75 years, what would fix the world ... I would say the immediate appearance of 1.8 billion jobs." (Editorial comment: I know you're reading this at a time when the U.S. unemployment rate is at a 50-year low but think about what he didn't suggest — like peace, democracy, or the alleviation of world hunger.)
2. Gallup also looks at underemployment, which is at nearly 20 percent. (Editorial comment: We also know that many people have dropped out of the workforce, resulting in a labor participation rate that's 63 percent down from its peak at 67 percent.)
3. Very few Americans are aware that small- and medium-sized businesses are responsible for most of the jobs in America.
4. Don't allow your local constituencies to look to Washington for support. Free money eventually makes you more dependent. (Editorial comment: I've observed this phenomenon all over the world.)
5. All prosperous cities have a self-organized, unelected group of talented people influencing and guiding them — call them local tribal leaders. These leaders are loyal, highly successful, usually wealthy, respected, well-known people. (Editorial comment: In Detroit, I think of Dan Gilbert, and in Flint, Phil Hagerman.)
6. Innovation itself doesn't create sales. Entrepreneurship is the driving phenomenon within the city supercollider. (Editorial comment: In other words, sometimes the innovator can successfully commercialize their idea, but other times, the inventor needs help from someone who can build a business — Clifton calls this person an entrepreneur — around the idea. It takes both.)
7. Entrepreneurs are the most valuable people in the world, at least as far as the pursuit of economic development, GDP growth, and job creation.
8. Approximately 20 percent of workers in the U.S. are actively disengaged. (Editorial comment: I find this statistic very sad, and I actively work with my clients to reduce this phenomenon.)
9. According to Gallup economic estimates, nearly one in five U.S. managers are dangerously lousy. (Editorial comment: This is another area in which Doescher Advisors spends time assisting our clients.)

Because I work with so many businesses, I'm aware that many of you are struggling to fill openings due to the lack of qualified candidates. Please don't give up. Hang in there; it's important that you continue to grow. There are many initiatives to work on this problem, but I'll save that for another blog.

For those of you who have trusted Doescher Advisors to partner with you, thank you. I promise we'll continue to do our best!

The Business Roundtable Joins Owner-Operated Businesses

October 21, 2019 // Tom Doescher //

TOM DOESCHER //

The August 20, 2019, *Wall Street Journal* reported that the Business Roundtable, consisting of 188 of the largest corporations in the U.S. including GM and Ford, and led by JPMorgan Chase CEO Jamie Dimon, has changed its statement of purpose.

For decades, the Business Roundtable adopted the position Milton Friedman took in his 1970 article entitled "The Social Responsibility of Business is to Increase its Profits" — or, simply stated, The Social Responsibility of Business is to Yield Higher Profits for Shareholders. Of the Business Roundtable's 188 members — Mary Barra and Jim Hackett are part of the group — 181 CEOs endorsed a new proposal.

The new position includes the following statements concerning the responsibilities of businesses:

1. To deliver value to customers.
2. To invest in our employees.
3. To deal fairly and ethically with our suppliers.
4. To support the communities in which we work.
5. To generate long-term value for shareholders.

I believe these 181 large global corporations are catching up to the owner-operated companies I've worked with for the past five decades. I could provide so many examples of where they've already embraced these principles for years.
Here are just a few:

1. I had a $10 million auto supplier client who solved a critical air bag problem for a Ford Motor Co. vehicle, avoiding an expensive delayed launch.
2. There are many stories where owners have helped team members and their families. Recently, I experienced an owner who went above and

beyond to console an associate whose young wife died in a tragic auto accident.

3. Many owner-operated businesses are really good with their suppliers. Some pay them very timely — and, as a result, they often receive priority treatment.

4. With regard to community involvement, I retrieved excerpts from comments I made at a 2001 Plante Moran Manufacturing Practice presentation to our team:

"Who are our clients? They are men and women who risk their wealth every day to make stuff. Most of them work quietly behind the scenes, providing jobs and career opportunities for millions. They serve on not-for-profit and school boards, and on city councils. They seem to be the ones driving many charitable fundraisers in our communities."

So, what's my point? Simply stated, owner-operated companies have been holistic in their approach to business forever. I'm delighted that Jamie Dimon and the Business Roundtable have joined them.

The Corruption of Capitalism in America

November 18, 2019 // Tom Doescher //

 **TOM DOESCHER //**

is the subtitle of David Stockman's book, *The Great Deformation*. Some of you more seasoned readers may recall the young Grand Rapids congressman who served as President Reagan's budget director.

I remember it clearly because we lost a very senior Plante Moran staff member, who joined Stockman's staff.

Those of you who know me well have often heard me say that I'm a fan of the free market. Well, in this 700-plus-page book, Stockman rocked my world.

It continued a theme in my life where I'm realizing that much of what I've believed to be factual may not be. Again, my seasoned readers probably get it. Here are a few of my thoughts:

1. First of all, this could be a college-level economics textbook; it pushed me to the limits of my personal knowledge.

2. Stockman has an enormous vocabulary or a Ph.D.-level thesaurus.

141

3. Best I can tell, he isn't aligned with either the Democratic or Republican party.
4. The interconnections between the big banks and investment banks and our government are spooky. Just one example: How did Hank Paulson, former Goldman Sachs CEO, happen to be available to serve as the Secretary of the Treasury just as the Great Recession began? Patriotism?

Learnings from Stockman:

1. He provides a fairly detailed history of 20th and 21st century U.S. economics, with relevant details about countries like China and Japan.
2. He explains and provides details about the Keynesian monetary theory and application and gives his views about its negative impact over the past 50 years.
3. As a capitalist, he is opposed to deficit spending and would say that Presidents Reagan and George W. Bush significantly increased the federal deficits to an alarming level.
4. He reminds us that President Eisenhower warned the nation that we must guard against the influence of the military-industrial complex.
5. President Eisenhower reduced the defense budget and did *not* reduce taxes, against his party's wishes.
6. Based on their actions and policies, both political parties support Big Government.
7. According to Stockman, who was in the Reagan White House, the trickle-down theory of economics, or the Laffer curve, did not and does not work.
8. He provides some very interesting, detailed insights regarding the causes for and the remedies of the Great Recession.
9. He is a true capitalist and his criticisms in the book are of crony capitalism, where the government intercedes in the free market on behalf of a special group, like bailing out Wall Street or the auto industry. He believes the Republican Party has really drifted away from true free market capitalism, and his book provides many solid examples to support his view.

As I've already stated, over the years I've made assumptions that later turned out to be myths. Throughout this book, I once again felt that way. If you consider yourself a capitalist/free market person, I would highly recommend you take the time to read it.
Unfortunately, politics have twisted some truths to fit positions or platforms.

Closing comment: For any automotive suppliers who are reading this blog, yes, this is the same guy who created, founded, presided over as CEO, and took Collins & Aikman bankrupt, and he also covers that in the book. Honestly, I was a little disappointed with his lack of remorse for his failure.

The Everything Store

February 26, 2020 // Tom Doescher //

TOM DOESCHER //

is the story of Jeff Bezos and Amazon, the highest market capitalization company in the world. For some reason, I didn't know too much about Bezos, and I'm glad I read the book.

Here are my takeaways:

1. Bezos is very smart (summa cum laude from Princeton majoring in electrical engineering and computer science), hard-working, and driven/competitive.
2. Right from the beginning, he hired intelligent, well-educated people at low salaries, with the promise that they would participate in changing the world — and maybe become wealthy.
3. Like Steve Jobs, he's very customer-focused and gets the product or service right, including delaying launches (like the Kindle) if necessary.
4. He outlawed PowerPoint presentations and instead required his associates to describe their ideas in a narrative (maybe six pages at most).
5. Like Jobs, he's very demanding and, at times, demeaning to his team members.
6. To my surprise, he's very frugal (at least at Amazon).
7. He was quick to meet with executives from other tech or retail companies that he perceived to be world-class, and he wasn't too proud to learn from them.
8. The story of the evolution of his fulfillment centers (warehouses or distribution centers) was fascinating — they're a combination of technology, Dr. W. Edwards Deming thinking, and manual processes. It's very interesting, especially for those of you who are manufacturers or distributors.
9. Like Jobs, Bezos was adopted.

If you're an entrepreneur or working in a startup business, I recommend reading *The Everything Store* to get a reality check.

Often, companies like Amazon or Nike are glamorized — but in truth, the path to success isn't very pretty. Although it requires a lot of hard work and luck, there are no guarantees.

Why Isn't Your Team More Creative?

March 3, 2020 // Tom Doescher //

TOM DOESCHER //

If I have to admit one more time that I was wrong about someone, I'm going to go crazy.

I have to confess; I've been on the skeptical bandwagon related to Jim Hackett leading Ford Motor Co. The jury is still out, but recently I learned more through a friend who was applying for a job in a new group inside Ford. As I spoke with my friend, he started using words like "creative design" and "human-centered design." After listening patiently, I couldn't take it any longer and said, "I have no idea what you're talking about." Then I asked, "Where did you learn about this subject?" He told me about IDEO, a company with more than 700 consultants working all over the world that was founded in 1991 by David Kelley. That led me to purchase *Creative Confidence: Unleashing the Creative Potential Within Us All*. On page 145, the authors — David and Tom Kelley — write, "Many years ago, our longtime strategic partner Jim Hackett, CEO of Steelcase ..." I'm getting a lot of practice in being wrong.

In addition to providing some great suggestions on increasing the creativity of your team, *Creative Confidence* challenges us to refocus on our customers/clients.

As I reflect on the book, one of the most significant takeaways for me is the concept of "failure." Do you allow yourself to fail? More importantly, do you give your teammates permission to fail? I won't recite how many times Edison, Lincoln, and so many other famous people failed along the way, but never gave up.
Instead, I'll quote Uncle Dan. (For my new readers, he's my little bro — but more importantly, he's an amazing dreamer. And very successful, I might add.)

Here's what he told me several months ago:

144

"In my world, there are no failures. Life is one great laboratory full of experiments providing opportunity for many learning experiences."

I've decided not to summarize highlights from *Creative Confidence;* instead, I'd like you to ponder a few questions:

1. Would you say your company is really creative? What would your customers/clients say?
2. Would you say you really understand your customers'/clients' needs? What would they say?
3. How many of your teammates would agree with Uncle Dan's quote? If I asked them, would they tell me they have permission to experiment and fail?

If you don't like your answers to any of these questions, I would highly recommend you read David and Tom Kelley's book.

News Flash: COVID-19
March 19, 2020 // Tom Doescher //

TOM DOESCHER //

As it relates to COVID-19, for months I had a conspiracy theory going on inside my head, and I finally realized I was in denial. I still may be right about the conspiracy theory, but either way, we have a global crisis. So, I'll keep this simple.

1. If you are like I was, get over it and face reality.
2. Who knows how long this is going to last? On March 19, my business networking group thought it would last four weeks to three months longer. To be conservative, let's assume it will be six months, or until the end of 2020.
3. Develop a contingency plan for your business and your personal finances for 2020, assuming it lasts all year.
4. Execute on your plan!

Based on my observations during the Great Recession, the companies that reacted the quickest were hurt the least, and some of those that waited didn't make it.

I have a question for you: So far, how does this crisis feel compared to the Great Recession?

COVID-19 Contingency Planning

March 23, 2020 // Tom Doescher //

TOM DOESCHER //

Who knows how long this coronavirus (COVID-19) pandemic is going to last? As I mentioned in my last post, at a recent meeting of businesses owners the estimates ranged from four weeks to three months, but it could go on even longer. With that in mind, I'm recommending that you develop a contingency plan with markers at different points and create a list of actions for both your business and personal finances. I would suggest reviewing your plans on the following dates: Immediately; April 1; May 1; June 1; and July 1. I'd also suggest that you think about what drastic measures you'll need to take if this pandemic goes on beyond July.

The economy has been growing since mid-2009, when the Great Recession technically ended, and it's now the longest expansion on record. We have had it pretty good for more than a decade.

As I was reflecting, I thought of the following story, which I previously shared in my March 2, 2012, post:

During one of the recessions prior to 2008-2009, I was meeting with a business owner who said to me, "You know, now is when I make most of my money" — and then he smiled at me.
He went on to say, "The key decisions made during an economic downturn are what really drive my profitability post-recession ... we get sloppy during the good times." His closing comments reminded me of Seneca, who, in 65 B.C., said, "Luck is what happens when preparation meets opportunity." Laying the groundwork for success takes place during bad times.

I'm not saying you got sloppy, but I'd be willing to bet that many of you have added costs over the past decade. Now, as the tide goes out and the rocks (or additional costs) become exposed, it's a great time to execute some course corrections. Here is another idea I've been thinking about: Since many of us are working remotely from our homes, are there expenses we can do without in the future, and not hurt the customer or our team?

Being a risk-taker, I'm going to volunteer to collect nonproprietary cost-reduction suggestions you and your team have identified — big and small alike. I'll compile the ideas I receive from my 350 subscribers, and then post a blog (the source of anything I post will remain anonymous). Even if you have ideas you're not going to implement, I'd like to see them.

All you have to do is hit "**Reply**" to the blog email notification and send me your ideas. Assuming I receive any suggestions, I'll periodically (i.e., weekly) share the **COVID-19 Contingency Plan Cost Reduction** list with all of you. As one of my partners used to say, no idea is too small or insignificant — so please hit "**Reply**" and share what's on your mind.

COVID-19 Contingency Ideas

April 6, 2020 // Tom Doescher //

TOM DOESCHER //

I promised I would share COVID-19 survival tips I received from subscribers. One of my observations from this crisis is that, unlike the Great Recession, some companies are thriving (i.e., those that provide essential services), while others are closed (i.e., no revenue). So, although the following suggestions may or may not apply to your business, I hope you get at least one or two good thoughts.

The authors haven't been identified, but their ideas are verbatim (i.e., in other words, I pretty much left what you sent to me intact).

As it turns out, the list includes cost-reduction ideas plus many other items to consider during these unusual times.

1. Two items came up immediately from a professional services standpoint. One can have a long-term cost benefit and the other pertains to staff development. The first is the forced efficiencies of **Zoom meetings.**
   While clunky in the first stages, as those who work from home adjust, we're seeing quick improvements. Another idea is the **power of delegation.** When things need to happen fast, allowing colleagues to step up and take ownership with the proper amount of authority is providing huge personal growth and allowing leaders to continue to lead.

2. Remote work presents unique obstacles for teams and projects. For some helpful tools, go to *Project Manager.com* and check out Coronavirus: Work From Home Software & Tips.
3. This may be the time to deal with underperformers.
4. As your team works remotely, identify normal recurring expenses that could be reduced, like office space.
5. Can you or should you draw down on your line of credit, like Ford and GM have?
6. Consider reducing or canceling noncritical outside services and have your employees perform them.
7. Renegotiate communications services (i.e., phone and internet).
8. Consider a temporary layoff of salaried staff, including engineers (for two to three weeks).
9. Reduce the workweek to 32 hours, with a 20 percent reduction in salaries.
10. Eliminate 401k matches.
11. Renegotiate building leases before they expire.
12. Terminate leases of unused or partially used facilities.
13. Consolidate the use of facilities.
14. Negotiate to stop monthly lease payments on hi-lo equipment or other rental equipment that's not being used until it's needed again (i.e., pay when you use it).
15. Conduct virtual happy hours with your team to save travel time and costs.
16. Reduce compensation now and repay when the crisis is over.
17. Is this the time to do a reset? Make some long-overdue changes.
18. Institute face-to-face meetings via the computer and *Zoom.com*. This was an application we had used in the past, but it has quickly become a daily part of our world.
19. We reviewed our current client base and the receivables for each. We went through and "rated" clients based on our knowledge as to which would continue/shut down due to the crisis, or which might cut back services or increase services. We also discussed and set credit limits for each client.
20. We instituted a significant increase in our rates for new work.
21. This week we added the caveat that all new work must pay one week in advance, and we'll continue that practice moving forward. We've become very selective with new work, for fears of getting the necessary manpower.
22. This crisis will someday end, and we need to make sure we come out on the other side with positive feelings from our current clients.
23. We looked at all our support positions and have put "check points" in place to stay proactive with layoffs. At this point we haven't laid anyone off, but we will continue to monitor.

24. We moved/converted our hiring and employee orientation during this crisis, to be done online. Interviews are conducted via an HR software package and orientations are completed via Zoom and other media.
25. We implemented an attestation questionnaire for entrance to our offices and are currently taking the temperatures of all employees and visitors prior to entering the secured area of the building.
26. We're sending weekly memos to our staff and frontline folks expressing our gratitude for their efforts, along with reiterating CDC standards for controlling the virus. We have also communicated regularly with our clients and kept them informed of our status.
27. At this point, we have continued to pay our bills as normal; however, that appears to be against the grain. (Editorial comment: I've spoken to this issue before. Being appropriately good to your suppliers pays huge dividends in the long run.)
28. Being a Michigan resident, the original feel to this was like hunkering down for a blizzard. The thought was we would all be locked in for a few days, the storm would pass, and we would return to business as usual. Well, that will not be the case. This "blizzard" is more like an early return to winter. We'll have a whole season ahead of us with many adjustments before we get back to "normal."
29. Apply for a Paycheck Protection Program loan/grant.
30. Apply for other loans related to the virus.
31. Maximize unemployment benefits.
32. From an insurance standpoint, this is a good time to review sales and payroll projections and ask your agent to lower to match projections.

    Put unused vehicles in storage (comprehensive coverage only) and if you need help with premiums contact your agent, as many carriers will work with you to avoid cancellation and defer payments.

I'm not sure whether I'll republish the list, but if you have some ideas that aren't on the list above, please hit "Reply" and send them to me.

4 SHARPENING YOUR PERSONAL LEADERSHIP SKILLS

<u>Leadership and Personal Development</u>

Doescher Advisors Executives Health Check-up

April 4, 2017

Over several decades, I've gleaned a lot of health-related information from books, conferences, and various health experts. Actually, two of my mentors — Frank Moran and Ken Kunkel — were ahead of their time with their focus on executive health.

Based on my observations, I've come to realize that most great leaders understand the impact of their overall health on their leadership, and they pay close attention to it.

Since my original **Executives Health Check-up "Food For Thought," posted on April 21, 2015,** I've had the pleasure of speaking with William Malarkey, M.D., a professor at Ohio State University and author of *Take Control of Your Aging* and *Finding Joy*. In his books, Dr. Malarkey describes the check-up that he refers to as the PIERS Model. It includes relational health, which I've now added to my own check-up.

During our conversation, I asked him if he thought financial health might also be a significant category, and his response was, "Absolutely!" Based on that, I added it to my process.

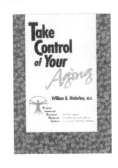

Take Control of Your Aging

by William Malarkey, M.D.

Purchase book from Amazon.

Finding J.O.Y.

by William Malarkey, M.D.

Purchase book from Amazon.

Borrowing from many sources, including Dr. William Malarkey, I've developed the Doescher Advisors Executives Health Check-up, using the acronym **SMERPF** to represent the following six:

S (Spiritual); **M** (Mental); **E** (Emotional); **R** (Relational). **P**(Physical); and **F** (Financial)

In a person's life experience, all attributes are interconnected and affect how that individual behaves.

Often, my mentors would say, "The whole person goes to work." They were right; that's exactly what I've observed.

Spiritual Health

Don't get nervous. I'm not going to get religious on you. But, based on my personal experience and what I've seen in studying many great leaders, here is my observation.
I believe at the inner core of all of us is a spirit, or a soul — or whatever you want to call it. I believe it's the "command center"

that drives our behaviors and causes us to do this and not do that. It is at the root of our actions.

Over the years, I've shared my Christian beliefs with people all over the world. Often, I would say, "This is what I believe and base my life on; what do you believe?"

My first challenge to you is this: Get in touch with your spiritual life. Take some time to think about the following questions: What do I believe, and why? Do my actions match what I say I believe?

Mental Health

By mental health, I mean the types of thoughts and ideas you're putting into your mind. To figure out what your mental focus is, I would suggest asking yourself several questions:

1. What do I look at?
2. What do I watch?
3. What do I read?
4. To what and to whom do I listen?

Because all my readers are mature adults, I'm not going to give a bunch of examples. Instead, I encourage you to privately assess your answers to the four questions. I'm pretty sure the answers will have a huge impact on you.

Here's one silly example, but it gives you an idea of what I mean. If you read the obituaries every day, it impacts you in some way — maybe good, maybe bad. My advice is to know which it is because it makes an incredible difference in how you approach issues that arise in both your business and personal life.

Emotional Health

My epiphany with this trait came more than 25 years ago. There was — and is — a very well-known leader whom I consider to be a long-distance mentor through his books and conferences. At one of his presentations, he shared what he had learned in dealing with a bout of clinical depression. During his talk he said that prior to his illness, he had a daily routine of assessing his physical and spiritual health (he knew, like many of us, that he was going at it pretty hard, and he didn't want to get derailed).

What he discovered during his illness was that he needed to monitor his emotional health as well as what was going on physically and spiritually.

These are my takeaways from his talk:

1. All of us have a fixed amount of emotional energy.
2. Just like not eating will cause physical problems, negative emotional energy can do the same.
3. Some people give you emotional energy.
4. Other people drain you of emotional energy.
5. Know who those people are.
6. Limit your time with the drainers.

Like this leader, I would recommend assessing your emotional energy daily, and I suggest that you monitor your time with drainers. This may sound harsh but remember that you're the leader of the whole team, not just that one person(s).

Relational Health

If I ask you this — Is there someone from whom you need to ask forgiveness, or is there someone you need to forgive? — does a particular name come to mind?

Over 20 years ago, I heard a pastor teaching on this subject, and I still remember his message, entitled "Repair Ruptured Relationships." Do you have a relationship that you need to repair? If you're married, this is a huge area. Even after spending decades with Barbara, I'm still trying to get it right. Here are a few tips from others:

1. If you have unkind thoughts/words (or have made up a story in your mind per *Crucial Conversations*), do something about it.
2. If you feel divided, do something about it; counseling could be helpful.
3. Fatigue is often the enemy. Reschedule difficult conversations for a time when you both have more energy.
4. Are you being prideful (i.e., it's his or her fault)?
5. Be patient. Yes, I said be patient.
(*Editorial comment: I know what to do; I just can't always do it.*)

6. Remember that marriage is hard, but worth it!

Physical Health

If you're reading this post, chances are you probably know plenty about your physical health.

Things to ask when evaluating your physical health include:

1. Is there something that's been bothering me for a while? Don't ignore pains/symptoms, like I have done. They won't go away.
2. Am I getting regular feedback from my doctor? Get an annual physical and follow your doctor's advice or get a new doctor.
3. Am I getting enough sleep? Most experts would recommend seven to eight hours per night. I've found that some of us need more.
4. How much do I weigh? Do your best to stay within your recommended body weight.
5. Am I giving my body the fuel it needs? Eat regular, balanced, healthy meals.
6. Am I moving enough? Exercise regularly. I suggest having a trainer design an exercise program that meets your specific needs.

Financial Health

I've spoken about this subject in my blog post, **It's All About the Expenses, Not the Income.** Now I would add to those comments the concept of "financial independence."

Here's one definition: **It means you can do whatever you want without having to worry about money. Work would be an option and you become a master of your destiny, at least financially.** It's a worthwhile goal to shoot for.

In my practice, I've encountered a number of very successful executives who have failed in this category. My suggestion is to get a good financial planner.

Conclusion

Based on my experience, if you're not doing well in your spiritual, mental, emotional, relational, physical, and financial life, it will directly impact your overall health. Where you have cracks, they will be exposed.

My mother-in-law is 98 years old and has excellent health and no pain. Her secret weapon is moderation.

Finally, in my conversation with Dr. Malarkey, he emphasized the importance of **gratitude**. Do you feel grateful?

So, now you have it — the complete program known as the Doescher Advisors Executives Health Check-up. Sad to say, I've known too many talented leaders who have ignored one of these aspects of their health and have fallen short of their full potential. That's why I recommend periodically performing a gut check and asking, "How am I doing spiritually, mentally, emotionally, relationally, physically, and financially?"

Level 5 Leaders Are "Really Good" at Crucial Conversations
February 10, 2015

Crucial Conversations by Kerry Patterson, Joseph Grenny, Ron McMillan, and Al Switzler is a groundbreaking book that was published in 2002, and somehow, I missed it at the time. This book is so practical and applicable, I've decided to memorialize the key points. In case you don't have the time to read the book, you'll at least get the main takeaways — with, of course, some editorial comments.

Here goes ...

1. A crucial conversation is a discussion between two or more people where the stakes are high, opinions vary, and emotions run strong. (Editorial comment: Most people have several every week.)
2. We usually handle crucial conversations one of three ways: we avoid them, we face them and handle them poorly, or we face them and handle them well.
3. The negative feelings we hold in, the emotional pain we suffer, and the constant battering we endure as we stumble our way through unhealthy conversations slowly eats away at our **health.**
4. At the core of every successful conversation is the free flow of relevant information, or a **dialogue.**
5. Each of us enters conversations with our own opinions, feelings, theories, and experiences about the topic at hand.

6. Remember that the only person you can directly control is yourself.
7. Focus on what you really want for yourself, for others, and for the relationship. What is the **mutual purpose** of the conversation?
8. Wanting to win or seeking revenge is a dialogue-killer.
9. Stay alert for the moment a conversation turns from a routine or harmless discussion into a crucial one. As you anticipate engaging in a tough conversation, pay heed to the fact that you're about to enter the danger zone.
10. When others start forcing their opinions into the pool of meaning, it's often because they figure that you're trying to win (versus having a healthy dialogue), and they believe they need to do the same.
11. The instant people perceive disrespect in a conversation, the interaction is no longer about the original purpose — it's now about defending dignity. (Editorial comment: No matter what, we need to behave like healthy adults.)
12. When you've made a mistake that has hurt someone, **start with an apology.**
13. As previously mentioned, both parties are often trying to force their view. Say to the other person, "**I commit to stay in this discussion** until we have a solution both of us are happy with."
14. Other people don't make you angry; you and only you create your strong emotions. You either find a way to master them or you fall hostage to them.
15. Just after we observe what others do and just before we feel some emotion about it, we **tell ourselves a story.** We add meaning, motive, and judgment to the action we observed (i.e., he doesn't trust me, she thinks I'm weak, etc.). Then we respond with emotion. **Don't confuse stories with facts.** (Editorial comment: This point is huge. Has anyone ever said to you, "I know what he's thinking"? How do they know?)
16. The three most common unhealthy stories: Victim Stories — "It's not my fault"; Villain Stories — "It's all your fault"; and Helpless Stories — "There's nothing else I can do."
17. Am I pretending not to notice my role in the problem?
18. Why would a reasonable, rational, and decent person do this?
19. We should make sure we tell our story as a story, rather than disguising it as a fact (i.e., "I was wondering why ...").
20. Most arguments consist of battles over the 5 to 10 percent of the facts and stories about which people disagree.
21. Decide how to decide. The four methods of decision-making are: command, consult, vote, and consensus.
    To determine which method you're using, ask these four questions: Who cares? Who knows? Who must agree? How many people is it worth involving? (Editorial comment: My mentor used to say, "Be careful what you ask for.")

22. Consult with others regarding a decision when: Many people will be affected; You can gather information relatively easily; People care about the decision; and There are many options, some of them controversial.
23. To avoid common decision-making traps, make sure you consider the following four elements: Who? Does what? By when? How will you follow up?

I would still highly recommend reading the book, unless you live in a cave by yourself and have no contact with other people. When I reflect on the really great leaders I personally know, I realize they're all experts at effectively handling crucial conversations.

Let's all commit to improving our crucial conversation skills.

What's Limiting Healthy Communication in Many Businesses?

January 22, 2018 // Tom Doescher //

 **TOM DOESCHER //**

Once again, I'm out of my area of professional expertise, but I would suggest the answer to the title question is "passive-aggressive behavior." My partner, Barbara, will write more on this subject later, but I wanted to at least introduce it.

Based on reading *8 Keys to Eliminating Passive-Aggressiveness,* by Andrea Brandt, and my own experience and observations over the decades, I believe most of us could do better. Here are my takeaways from Brandt's book:

1. Unlike extrovert/introvert, passive-aggressive is a learned behavior developed during our formative years. Brandt would say that if one parent is dominant and the other is subservient, children will almost inevitably develop some passive-aggressive tendencies.
2. Unrealistic standards can cause a child, who becomes an adult, to develop passive-aggressive tendencies.
3. Brandt would say that we don't express our feelings because we leap to the conclusion that any difference of opinion will lead to a quarrel, which in turn will threaten our relationships.
4. She would also say that if you don't ask for what you need, the odds of getting it are greatly reduced.

5. The best thing we can do for our children is to raise them in an environment where it's safe to express our feelings and speak the truth to each other.
6. People with passive-aggressive behavior will say "yes" when they really mean "no."
7. According to Brandt, conflict — even if it's occasionally uncomfortable — can help create good, enriching relationships. (Editorial comment: this is very counterintuitive.)
8. Don't assume the other person knows what you're thinking and feeling.

Hopefully, this list whets your appetite for reading Brandt's book. It's not an easy read, but I believe that for any leader or senior executive, it's worth the effort. Two closing comments:

1. Since it's a behavior learned as a child, many of us may not realize we have passive-aggressive leanings. I would encourage you to ask your mentor, supervisor, coach, spouse, or someone who really cares for you what they think.
2. In reading the book and self-diagnosing myself, I don't believe I'm passive-aggressive. However, as I reflect on my interactions, I would say that, at times, I've behaved in a passive-aggressive manner. This has generally resulted in confusion, miscommunication, and bad results.

Dealing with this subject could be a game-changer for your team. I encourage you to read this book in order to better understand the impact this very common situation may be having on your company.

Anger: A Secondary Emotion
November 13, 2017 // Tom Doescher //

TOM DOESCHER //

OK, I'm a little out of my field of expertise, but I believe I can speak as someone who has received some great professional counseling.
Years ago, when I was promoted to a new job that resulted in more responsibility, I noticed that I would become angry more often. I wasn't the happy-go-lucky Tommy of the past, and there were times when my reaction was disproportionate to the situation/problem at hand.

To be honest, I blew up. Fortunately, before I caused too much damage and embarrassment, I received some really wise counsel: Anger is usually your second emotion. For me, I discovered the primary issue behind my anger is often frustration. Here's a wonderful one-page write-up and chart that I found to be extremely helpful.

Anger: A Secondary Emotion

 ## Anger Iceberg

Anger is often called a secondary emotion because we tend to resort to anger in order to protect ourselves from or cover up other vulnerable feelings. A primary feeling is what is felt immediately before we feel anger. We almost always feel something else first before we get angry. We might first feel afraid, attacked, offended, disrespected, forced, trapped, or pressured. If any of these feelings are intense enough, we think of the emotion as anger.

As the drawing below illustrates, anger is like an iceberg in that only some of the emotions are visible. The other emotions exist "below the water line" where they are not obvious to outside observers.

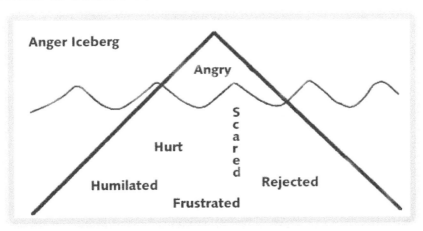

I keep this chart in my daily journal and refer to it often. If you can relate to my story, I would recommend you do the same.

Once I understood what was going on, the counselor suggested that I deal with issues — usually people — along the way, to avoid escalation. Here's an example: Say someone on your team has an annoying habit or practice that bothers you and the team. Too often, no one tells that team member how they're feeling about the habit or practice until it becomes a monumental issue, at which point the team member becomes the target of an angry outburst. I learned — and am still refining — the practice of healthy confrontation or speaking the truth in love.

Over the years, I've discovered that if I keep short accounts — in other words, deal with little things before they become big things — I avoid the atomic explosion. How about you? Can you relate?

The Power of Introverts

November 10, 2014 // Tom Doescher //

TOM DOESCHER //

Earlier this year, I had the privilege of hearing Susan Cain, an author and former corporate attorney, speak. As I reported in LinkedIn, I had a major epiphany while listening to her comments regarding introverted people. It was a great reminder of a simple fact: If your goal is to be the best leader you can be, you must be a lifelong learner *and* be open to new points of view. Cain's observations and revelations, which were supported by years of research, were eye-opening.

I found a 17-minute TED Talk featuring Cain, and it speaks for itself. If you want to be a Jim Collins "Level 5 Leader," I encourage you to invest the time to **listen to it.** TED Talk 2012 – The Power of Introverts by Susan Cain.

You can learn more about these ideas in Cain's book, *Quiet: The Power of Introverts in a World That Can't Stop Talking.*

Do you have introverts in your company who you have been encouraging to become more outgoing?

Does your company have a bias toward extraverts?

Have I Modified My Behaviors After Listening to Susan Cain?

May 27, 2019 // Tom Doescher //

TOM DOESCHER //

I shared the epiphany I had after listening to Susan Cain's landmark (at least to me) TED Talk. Well, it's almost five years later, and I continue to observe and read about innovative new workspace, collaboration, and brainstorming ideas. Something I've noticed, though, is that almost all of them totally ignore introverts. This stuff is written by very successful business executives and consultants who get paid a lot of money, so it's a bit disappointing to me to see this group completely overlooked. Maybe I get it more because I'm an ambivert who leans slightly toward extrovert. Maybe because I can understand both personality types, I feel the pain of the introverts. As a result, I want to share two very practical suggestions:

Office Space. I know the latest rage is open-landscape office designs. While this may be great for extroverts, I'd suggest that before you make a change to your office setup, you select a few of your high-performing introverts and meet with them privately. Let them know ahead of time, in writing, that you want their candid input on office design, specifically as it relates to privacy. Maybe list some possible solutions and ask them to add any ideas they have to your list. You can also encourage them to bring their list of suggestions to you one-on-one.

Brainstorming Meetings. Next time you conduct a brainstorming meeting, instead of sending a brief note stating the topic, send a more detailed write-up of the goal of the meeting and explain, in detail, what will occur during the session. Encourage the recipients to spend some (company) time thinking about the subject and recording their ideas. This will give the introverts a chance to think about the subject and write down their thoughts, rather than being put on the spot in the meeting.

When the team arrives, collect the sheets and record the ideas on the white board. The super extroverts may not hand in a list, but they'll be pleased to share their ideas as the session proceeds.

Following the session, send out another communication, this time summarizing the meeting. Again, ask the team members — especially the introverts — whether they have any additional thoughts they'd like to share after spending the day together and having a few days to think about the conversation. Basically, half the population consists of extroverts and the other half are introverts, with a few token ambiverts thrown into the mix. If you want to get creative, innovative ideas from your introverts — who definitely have some great ideas — then converse with them in their own language, so to speak. I apologize for being so direct, but I hear so much about the need for new ideas and I sincerely believe this is a way to double them at no extra cost.

What Is the Key to Leading a Healthy and Happy Life?

February 4, 2019 // Tom Doescher //

TOM DOESCHER //

Believe it or not, for 80 years Harvard researchers have studied the question of what is key to a healthy and happy life. In 1938, scientists began tracking 268 Harvard students to try to determine the answer, and today the Harvard Study of Adult Development is still working on the project with the remaining 19 students, who are now well into their 90s. I'll let the current study director, Robert Waldinger, share with you their surprising findings. Go to TED Talk – What makes a good life? Lessons from the longest study on happiness.

What Is the Key to a Happier Life?

May 21, 2018 // Tom Doescher //

TOM DOESCHER //

Rhonda Byrne, in her book *The Magic*, claims the answer is gratitude. This reminded me of a conversation I had last spring with Dr. William Malarkey. He espoused the importance of gratitude in a healthy life.

Byrne, a television and film producer, quotes many diverse sources to support her position, including Einstein, Isaac Newton, John F. Kennedy, the Holy Bible, the Quran, and Buddha. It's impossible to prove with absolute certainty that she's right, but her advice is very practical, so I thought I would summarize her key points — and, of course, add a few editorial comments:

1. Give to others, rather than taking (Byrne believes merely taking is a sign of ungratefulness).
2. Say "thank you" often.
3. Make lists of the things for which you're grateful.
4. At the end of each day, journal the best thing that happened to you. (Editorial comment: I'm going to incorporate this one into my daily routine.)
5. For every complaint you have about another person, whether in thought or word, there have to be 10 blessings for the relationship to flourish. (Editorial comment: John Gottman says it's five to one, but whether it's five or 10, I think you get the point about negativity.)
6. When you're grateful for your job, you will automatically give more to your work.
7. The way to receive your dream job is by first being grateful for the job you have.
8. Lucky breaks don't happen by accident. (Editorial comment: Luck is what happens when preparation meets opportunity.)
9. Taking things for granted is a major cause of negativity.
10. Be kind, for everyone you meet is fighting some kind of battle.
11. There's no room for harmful, negative thoughts when your mind is focused on looking for things to be grateful for.
12. Everyone has received help, support, or guidance from others when we needed it most. (Editorial comment: Make your list and make sure you've thanked people for their help.)
13. Holding onto anger is like grasping a hot coal with the intent of throwing it at someone else; you're the one who gets burned.
14. There's gold in every relationship, even the difficult ones. To bring riches to all your relationships, you have to find the gold.

Again, these are Byrne's opinions, but I found the list to be very practical and applicable to my life.

The "Big Three"
February 21, 2012 // Tom Doescher //

After years of observing leaders, reading about pathfinders and trailblazers, and being a leader myself, here are the top three traits I attribute to world-class leaders.
First, they have a high degree of self-knowledge. Socrates knew what he was talking about when he said, "Know thyself." Second, they manage to stay focused.

Most companies and leaders never reach their full potential because they spread themselves too thin and attempt to do too much.

Finally, great leaders are able to have hard conversations with their fellow owners, associates, customers/clients, and others. Speaking the truth in love is a huge leadership differentiator. Which of these traits do you think you already possess? What do you think you need to work on?

The "Big Four"
July 16, 2012 // Tom Doescher //

On February 21, I posted a blog entitled "The Big Three," which listed the top three traits of great leaders. Shortly thereafter, I realized I had missed an important ingredient. In my March 29, 2012, Food for Thought article, I referenced an article entitled "Three Profiles in Organizational Humility," by Patrick Lencioni. In this article, I included comments about Brady Hoke and Tom Izzo. That got me thinking, and I'm officially adding humility to the list of the top traits all great leaders possess. In fact, one of my colleagues suggested it might even be the foundation for the other three. But whether it's the underpinning of the original three traits I listed or whether it's the first of four traits isn't important. What is important is that every great leader I've personally known for an extended time (i.e., decades) checks their ego at the door.

Jim Collins, the business expert, and author says Level 5 leaders channel their ego needs away from themselves and into the larger goal of building a great company. And that most definitely requires a sense of humility.

Check Your Ego at the Door
January 10, 2012 // Tom Doescher //

The other day, I was talking with my mentor of 40 years. He said with a sense of disbelief, "It's surprising ... the older I get, the more famous I am." In other words, he was saying his legend is becoming bigger than life.

I like to say it another way: "There is no room for hubris." The reason my mentor's reputation is so strong is because of the great things he has helped others accomplish, both personally and in their business. And he's successful because he doesn't dwell on the legends that have sprung up about him and his efforts. Rather, he lets the work speak for itself. It's one thing when your associates compliment you about how you've been able to lead the organization — but don't become absorbed by what's written in the press, and don't pat your own back. Stay focused. Stay hungry. Check your ego at the door.

Haven't We Learned Anything?

April 17, 2012 // Tom Doescher //

Recently I met the son of one of the Detroit 3 executives. (Just to give you a little background, his father is at a senior level with the same company, and the son is an up-and-coming, manager-level engineer.) Back to my encounter. The son, like his dad, displayed a fair amount of hubris. He was quick to criticize the engineers in country X. This same country is home to the fastest-growing OEM in the U.S.

In business, there are a lot of emotions. Jim Collins talks about hubris being the first stage of how mighty companies fall. Do you base your decisions and views on facts and data, or emotions (I don't like XXXXX)?

Was Steve Jobs a Great — or Even a Good — Leader?

August 21, 2012

Earlier this year I read the biography *Steve Jobs*, by Walter Isaacson. I have to say it was one of the most challenging books I've ever read — not because of the length (although, in my opinion, it was too long, with lots of repetition), but because Jobs violated almost every leadership principle in which I believe. As I read, I felt like my brain was being stretched in ways it had never before experienced. I kept telling myself, "Hang in there, absorb, and seek to understand." For those of you who haven't read the book, Isaacson was recruited by Jobs to write it, and much of the biography is based on interviews with and comments made by Jobs. My point is that this book seemed objective, and Jobs himself had a hand in it — so it's by no means a character assassination.

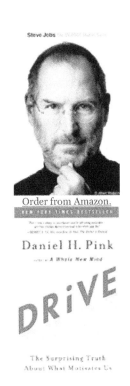

Order from Amazon.

Besides the influence of Frank Moran and all the other great leaders at Plante Moran, what principles have I based my view of a great leader on? The list would be long but would include Tom Peters, Jim Collins,

Steve Samples, Patrick Lencioni, Daniel Pink, Marcus Buckingham, Coach K, Bo Schembechler, Brady Hoke, and Tom Izzo. Obviously, I'm not the only one who thinks highly of these individuals and their ability; most of them receive thousands of dollars for every speech they make on leadership.

You could also add Presidents Lincoln, Washington, and Mandela, plus Mother Teresa, to my list of great leaders and role models.

Not to be judgmental, but according to Isaacson, Jobs was a "jerk." (Isaacson didn't actually use that word; it's my interpretation of the behavior he reported that Jobs exhibited.)

In fact, Jobs' team came up with a description for his behavior. They called it "Reality Distortion Field." Some members of the team would explain that the label was just a clever way to say that Jobs tended to lie, and to unfairly mistreat people. He would tell an associate who suggested something new that their idea was bad, and he would even belittle the individual in front of his colleagues. Then Jobs would come in the next day and propose the same idea, as if it were his own. Another example is that although Jobs said he had wonderful adoptive parents; he was known to treat them disrespectfully.

The example I find most troubling, however, is that before Apple officially became a company, Jobs took advantage of the actual inventor of the Apple — his partner, Steve Wozniak.

All that being said, Jobs built and rebuilt the most valuable company in the world today. The Apple market capitalization (based on

current values) is approximately $500 billion. Compare that with the numbers for the following companies: Microsoft, $250 billion; Exxon Mobil, $400 billion; IBM, $230 billion; Wal-Mart, $230 billion; and GE, $200 billion.

I decided to run Apple and Steve Jobs through the three elements Daniel Pink describes in his book *Drive: The Surprising Truth About What Motivates Us.*

The first element is purpose, which is defined as a desire to be involved in a cause larger than oneself. Can you imagine working at Apple on the teams that developed the Mac, iPhone, iPod, iTunes, and iPad? Isaacson interviewed associates from these teams. Many of them said something like, "Despite how Steve treated me, I would do it all over again."

The second element is mastery, which is defined as the desire to get better and better at something that matters. Jobs exemplified this trait with his obsession for the perfect device (defined by the customer, by the way, not the techies).

The final element is autonomy, which involves behaving with a full sense of volition and choice. This one is a mixed bag. If you had the courage to stand up to Jobs, like the associate who ignored Jobs when he ordered him not to use a certain supplier, you would be demonstrating your autonomy. This particular associate was worried about the ability of Jobs' chosen vendor to deliver on time, so he secretly worked with another vendor. Sure enough, in the end, Jobs' vendor failed, and the alternate was used.
At first, Jobs demeaned the associate for what he did — but eventually, he praised

him for his initiative.

I'm going to leave it up to you to decide whether Steve Jobs was a great leader. Whether he was or he wasn't, he certainly built a great company — although the jury is still out on that, too.
For example, in his book *Built to Last*, author Jim Collins determined that an organization had to be more than 100 years old to be included in his study. Based on that criterion, Apple has a way to go.

Maybe the real question should be: Are you building an organization that's valuable today, or are you building a valuable organization that will last forever?

Levels of Leaders: Is He or She a Leader?
June 12, 2012

Over the past several years, I've been part of many discussions centered on this question: Is he or she a leader? I've heard more than one person whom I sincerely respect say, "We are all leaders," and I've struggled with that premise. Then my partner (who also happens to be my wife) told me, "I'm not a leader" — to which I responded, "Well, you're certainly not a follower, so I think you must be a leader."

According to management expert Peter Drucker, a leader is someone with followers. Author John Maxwell says leadership is influence — nothing more, nothing less. Unfortunately, it seems to me that the words "leader" and "leadership" have become overused and in-vogue terms, just like "robust" and "paradigm." Confusion results when someone who is clearly not a leader is given a leadership role, or when someone who has the potential to be a leader is not qualified to lead in their current position. In fact, I can see how this applies to me — I think I am a leader, but I realize I would not do well in many types of leadership roles.

My beliefs about leaders and leadership are:

- Leaders are born (i.e., not everyone is a leader).
- My partner and I believe and have dedicated the rest of our lives to discovering, encouraging, and mentoring what we call "dormant"

leaders. For whatever reason, many born leaders haven't had the good fortune of having a mentor to help them develop their gift of leadership.
- Great leaders are a work in progress. They're lifelong learners, continually developing and honing their leadership skills. The best leaders get better every year.
- Some leaders are better at leading a small platoon than a whole army, and other leaders are better at leading the army.
- Not all leaders can lead everything. Call it capacity. Not everyone could lead GE like Jack Welsh or Jeff Immelt.

I'd like to expand on my fifth point, and directly address leaders of leaders, or someone trying to figure out if they're a leader. ("Capacity" may or may not be the right word, but I'll use it to explain my theory.)

Different leaders have different capacities for leading. To illustrate this point of view, I'll use a manufacturing company to make my point, drawing on more than 20 years of experience in that industry.

If you know anything about manufacturing, you realize a lot of money is made or lost on the shop floor by machine operators. They need a team leader/coach — or, as they call them, production supervisors. When you observe a great supervisor, it's like listening to a jazz quartet. When the supervisor is a great leader, the operators are measurably more productive, and they love their jobs.

At the same time, most production supervisors — even great ones — wouldn't be able to function as the plant manager. The leadership skills the plant manager must possess are substantially different than what is required of the production supervisor; the plant manager is like an orchestra's conductor, while the production supervisor is more akin to a first-chair musician.

Finally, the owner/CEO/general manager of the company is like the president/CEO of an orchestra. They sit (helplessly) in the audience, while the conductor and the musicians perform.

As mentioned above, leaders who can lead an entire army may not be as gifted when it comes to leading a smaller platoon. The challenge is to figure out what type of leader you are. If you're a leader of leaders, your job is to help each leader grow, reach their fullest potential, and operate in a role that fits their capacity and giftedness.

Note: I saw an interesting article, written by Michael Watkins, entitled "The Big Shift — How Managers Become Leaders," in the June 2012 Harvard Business Review. *As you know, I'm not a big fan of labeling people as "managers." However, I still found Watkins' article to be very thought-provoking.*

Do You Know Your "Why"?

August 8, 2016 // Tom Doescher //

TOM DOESCHER //

Recently I read *The Art of Why,* written by Steve Luckenbach. It reminded me a lot of *Start with Why,* by Simon Sinek, which I wrote about in a Food for Thought. Words, words, words — like vision, mission, purpose, and others. Why not just use "Why"?

Many people have mentioned how upbeat, cheerful, and joyful Barbara and I are. I now know how come we're perceived that way: We've figured out our "why."

After 40 years at Plante Moran and 30-plus mission trips, Barbara and I know our "why," or "calling." According to Luckenbach, your "calling" is what you believe, down deep, you were put on this earth to do. According to Louis Nizer, "A man who works with his hands is a laborer; a man who works with his hands and his brain is a craftsman; but a man who works with his hands and his brain and his heart is an artist."

At Doescher Advisors, we have a "why." Our mission statement, which appears on our website, says, "Doescher Advisors was founded to help businesses increase profits & jobs through practical and sound advice." We want our clients to be extremely successful, so they're able to hire lots of associates and pay them great wages. Do you know your "why"?

A Tribute to My New Hero: Mary Kate Bryant

October 27, 2014 // Tom Doescher //

In March, I had a life-changing experience. I attended the funeral of Mary Kate Bryant (grandmother of my former partner Paul), who died just shy of her 97th birthday. Due to her age, I anticipated a small crowd, mostly family members. When I arrived at the church, the parking lot was full.

To my surprise, the place was packed with people who Mary Kate had helped throughout her life. At one point in the service, participants were allowed to say a few words. The line was long, and the stories were touching.

Mary Kate was truly an impact player. So what? Here's the "So what": I carry Mary Kate's picture, along with my "Last Life Marathon" goals, in my wallet. Looking at her face challenges me to invest in people, like she did, all the way until the very end.

Here's my challenge for you. Consider this question: Ultimately, why does your company exist? Once you've done that, spend some time contemplating whether there's a picture/visual that you and your team could rally around, like my photo of Mary Kate.

LifeMission: Do You Know Where You're Going?

October 30, 2017 // Tom Doescher //

TOM DOESCHER //

Successful executives know where they're going, stay focused, and have an uncanny ability to know when to say "**NO.**"

They may not use these exact words, but they're operating off a **LifeMission**. They've discovered there's limited unscheduled time and know their current "Season of Life."

The following thoughts are meant to help you develop your own unique game plan:

Step 1 — What's Your Destination?

Reflect on these rhetorical questions:

1. How do you know you're on the right road if you don't know where you're going?
2. When you're sitting in your rocking chair in the twilight of your life, what would you like to look back at?
3. If you were writing your own eulogy, what would you like it to say?

Step 2 — Realize That Time is a Limited Resource

Many resources can be increased through hard work, good investing, inheritance, and even luck — but time is a finite resource. We all get 24 hours each day. Have you ever thought about how you spend your time?

If you go to the Resource section of our Doescher Advisors website, you can download a tool entitled "How I Spend My Time," which will provide a simple way to reflect upon your time commitments (you don't need to fill it out!).

Step 3 — What "Season of Life" are You In?

Reflect on the following questions:

1. Are you still in school? Are you going back to school?
2. Are you married? Do you have children? Are your children still minors? Do your children live with you? Are you a single parent? If so, what's your support system? Are you coaching sports teams, or do you have some other commitment related to your children (i.e., PTA)?
3. If you're married with children, do both spouses work outside of the home?
4. How demanding is your job? Is it 24/7? Does your work require travel outside of your home city?
5. Are you involved in outside organizations (i.e., charities, service clubs, a neighborhood association)?
6. Do you attend church? Do you have other commitments/responsibilities related to church? Do you belong to a social or athletic club? Are you involved on the board or on a

committee? What other responsibilities, hobbies, or activities do you have? Do you travel recreationally?

7. Do you have responsibilities for aging parents, adult children, or others?
8. Do you have a regular exercise program and/or participate in golf, tennis, fishing, hunting, etc.?

In developing your LifeMission, you need to consider what's important to you now — and realize that may change over the years.

LifeMission Summary

In a survey of 95-year-olds, Dr. Tony Campolo, a professor of sociology, asked them: What would you do differently with your life if you could live it over? Many responded: **"We would reflect more, risk more, and invest more in people."** With their advice in mind, begin the process of developing your LifeMission:

- Think about "How I Spend My Time" and reflect upon your current "Season of Life."
- If you've ever used any assessment tools, consider and incorporate your identified strengths.
- Brainstorm key words, thoughts, and themes.
- Format isn't important. We've evolved from words to a graphical representation of our LifeMission.
- Like strategic planning, your LifeMission is an ongoing process.
- Be accountable to someone.
- Just do it!

Leaning In Is Harder Than You Think
September 5, 2016 // Tom Doescher //

TOM DOESCHER //

I had the good fortune of being influenced by a visionary. Frank Moran was a champion for women executives back when author Sheryl Sandberg was in elementary school. In the 1970s, he asked a very successful Plante Moran partner, who happened to be a woman, to help the firm figure out how to best recruit, develop, and encourage young women executives.
The firm did a lot of things right — and I'm sure we did a few things wrong — but our intent was always pure.

I found Sandberg's book, *Lean In*, refreshing. So often, people try to portray themselves as super-human, but I found Sandberg to be very transparent, and I think her book is a must-read for businesswomen *and* men. I thought Chapter 7, "Don't Leave Before You Leave," was especially relevant.

I have several very successful executive clients who are women, and I've encouraged each one of them not to say, "I'm not interested in being CEO (or whatever)." You never know where you might climb, and why exclude yourself from consideration some day? You can always say "No, thank you," if you're not interested when an offer is made, but why would you drop out prematurely?

Sandberg does a very nice job of discussing mentoring in Chapter 5 and talking about giving and receiving developmental feedback in Chapter 6. She offers terrific advice to both women and men. If you're a leader and you have female executives, do you really understand their special challenges? What would they say if I asked them?

If You Liked "Lean In," This Is a Must-Read

May 7, 2018 // Tom Doescher //

TOM DOESCHER //

If you've been reading my blogs for a while, you know I've recommended *Lean In* — and I still do. I thought the author, Sheryl Sandberg, was very transparent about being a woman executive, and she offered some great tips.

That being said, I would also highly recommend reading *The Confidence Code: The Science and Art of Self-Assurance — What Women Should Know,* by Katty Kay and Claire Shipman. It reminded me of a Daniel Pink book, filled with references to substantial research from many sources.

If I were to attempt to summarize the main topic, it would be that there's a difference in perceived confidence between men and women.

If you're a business leader, man, or woman, this is a must-read. As I've already mentioned, the book is rich in objective research. In addition, the authors have interviewed successful women executives and

174

they weave their own stories into the book, too.

To whet your appetite, I'll offer some of my favorite takeaways/quotes:

1. We see it everywhere: Bright women with ideas to contribute who don't raise their hands in meetings.
2. Yes, there is evidence that confidence is more important than ability when it comes to getting ahead.
3. In studies with business school students, men initiate salary negotiations four times as often as women.
4. Confidence is the stuff that turns thoughts into action.
5. Confidence is life's enabler — professionally, intellectually, athletically, socially, and even amorously.
6. So, is confidence encoded in our genes? Yes — at least in part.
7. It's the effect of nurture on nature that really matters and makes us who we are.
8. There's a direct link between playing sports in high school and earning a higher salary later in life.
9. When a man walks into a room, he's assumed to be competent until he proves otherwise. For women, it's the other way around.
10. Women are judged more harshly at work and in life on their physical appearance than men.
11. An unhelpful habit most women have is overthinking.
12. Of all the warped things women do to themselves to undermine their confidence, the pursuit of perfection is the most crippling.
13. Confidence comes from stepping out of your comfort zone and working toward goals that come from your own values and needs — goals that aren't determined by society.
14. Nothing builds confidence like taking action, especially when the action involves risk and failure.

This book is based on extensive research, and I believe it offers some very practical advice.

p.s. Here's a closing idea for those of you who are dads with daughters. I have a friend who read the book with his 20-something daughter and had a discussion after each chapter. What a special gift — for both of them!

It's All About the Expenses, Not the Income

January 23, 2017 // Tom Doescher //

TOM DOESCHER //

Not long ago, I thought I should read *The Millionaire Next Door,* by Thomas J. Stanley and William D. Danko. To my surprise, it wasn't what I expected. It offered very practical, common-sense financial advice.

Then I read *Rich Habits,* written by Thomas C. Corley — a CPA who watched a lot of clients squander millions of dollars, and worked with a few who became financially independent.

Finally, I read *The Behavior Gap,* by Carl Richards. It seems to me that many people are looking for the shortcut to everything.

For example, they spend millions of dollars on diet products and elaborate exercise equipment that produce limited or no results, rather than making a concerted effort to change bad habits and make actual lifestyle changes.

It wasn't until I arrived in my "seasoned" years that I realized the financial habits my dad taught me were quite profound. One day I was meeting with a very successful senior executive who was about my age.

In the course of our conversation, he said, "Well, I'm not financially independent like you." I was shocked by his comment. He was a very accomplished executive and still going strong.

Later, as I thought about his comment, I realized that although his income was — and is — very high, his standard of living was — and is — probably higher.

So, what's the point? No matter how much you make, if you spend more than what you bring in, you'll never get there. I remember hearing my mentor, Frank Moran, suggesting to us recent college graduates: "Spend less than you make and invest the difference wisely."

It sounds easy, but few achieve it. *The Millionaire Next Door, Rich Habits*, and *The Behavior Gap* provide some very simple, useful guidance.

(By the way, I think the same principles apply to businesses, too.)

Common-Sense Spending Advice

February 19, 2018 // Tom Doescher //

TOM DOESCHER //

For most of my adult life, I've considered myself "cheap." For example, I've been known to say things like: Why buy something new when the old one still works? or Why pay more when I can get essentially the same thing for less?

In Chapter 6 of *Your Money or Your Life,* by Vicki Robin, the author states: "Frugality is enjoying the virtue of getting good value for every minute of your life energy and from everything you have the use of."

After all these years, Robin helped me understand me. There are times where I *will* spend/invest money — a lot of money, in fact — and feel good about it, but I've never understood why. So, using her words, I've realized that I'll buy/invest if I believe I'm getting good value.

That being said, Robin provides a common-sense list for helping us save money:

1. Stop trying to impress other people.
2. Don't go shopping.
3. Live within your means.
4. Take care of what you have.
5. Wear it out.
6. Do it yourself.
7. Anticipate your needs.
8. Buy it for less.

It's not rocket science, but I'm guessing these are the habits of the Millionaire Next Door.

Are We Having Fun Yet?

June 4, 2012 // Tom Doescher //

Most people have no idea what kinds of pressures business owners have to deal with every day. From the outside, the idea of being in charge and owning a business looks pretty cool — yet we've all heard it said that it's lonely at the top.

I had an experience with a business owner one day that brought home that point. I was at a business meeting at the Birmingham Country Club; from the conference room windows, those of us who were in the meeting could see the club entrance and the valet parking attendants.

During one of the breaks, only the owner of the business and I were in the room. We were idly looking out the window, and not saying much of anything. All of a sudden, he said, "Now, there's a good job." To which I replied, "Excuse me?" I had no idea what he was talking about. He responded, "The valet parking attendant job. Most customers are very polite to you, and they usually smile and pay you cash." He was serious, and obviously dealing with some tough customers.

I felt honored that he felt safe enough with me to be so transparent.

On those days when your job as the boss leaves you feeling rather lonely — because, no doubt, there will be some days like that — I hope you have someone to support you.

Making Your Bed Is Important? Are You Kidding Me?
September 10, 2018 // Tom Doescher //

 **TOM DOESCHER //**

Recently I finished *The School of Greatness* by Lewis Howes, a former All-American who is currently on the USA men's national handball team. He's also a motivational speaker, author, and executive coach. His book was similar to many others I've read and, halfway through the book, I concluded I wouldn't blog about it.

Then I got to Chapter 6, where Howes recommends making your bed every morning. As support for his position, he references the 2014 commencement address at the University of Texas, which was delivered by Adm. William McRaven, a retired Navy Seal.

I had listened to McRaven's address a few years ago, and I highly recommend it to you.

Go to YouTube August 17, 2017, "If you want to change the world, start off by making your bed" by Adm. McRaven.

Howes also quotes from *The Happiness Project* by New York Times best-selling author and blogger Gretchen Rubin.

I'm sure you'll be skeptical, but Rubin reports that many of the readers who have communicated with her in response to her happiness project report that making their beds had the biggest impact on their happiness. Paraphrasing Rubin, "Making your bed is a step that's quick and easy yet makes a big difference. Everything looks neater. It's easier to find your shoes. Your bedroom is a more peaceful environment." She goes on to say, "Because making my bed is one of the first things I do in the morning, I start the day feeling efficient, productive, and disciplined."

Wow, very interesting. I'll leave it up to you whether you decide to read the Howes or Rubin books, but if you haven't heard Adm. McRaven's address, I would definitely recommend listening to it.

Hopefully, you'll accept this post in the spirit it is offered.

All I Want Is to Blend In
August 6, 2018 // Tom Doescher //

TOM DOESCHER //

One of my Flint business colleagues gave me a copy of *Imperfect: An Improbable Life*, an autobiography of Jim Abbott. Because he grew up in my new hometown, I found the book to be very educational. For those of you who don't know of him, Abbott is a famous baseball player who got his start as a star pitcher at Flint Central High School and the University of Michigan. He was a starting pitcher on the 1980 U.S. Olympic gold medal-winning baseball team, and he pitched a no-hitter for the New York Yankees at Yankee Stadium.

After finishing the book and reflecting on Abbott's life, I pondered what I could tell you about this remarkable man. I could focus on his mom and dad, who were teenage parents, or the cutthroat nature of professional baseball, or the painful process of determining when to end a professional career, or what it's like to be the spouse of a professional athlete in the crosshairs of the media, or what a great job his young parents did raising him.

Oh, yeah, did I mention that Abbott was born without a right hand?

After a great deal of thought, I decided to share two lessons I learned from reading about Abbott's life.

The first deals with his desire not to be thought of as different. If you see pictures of him in street clothes, he always has his right (hand) in his pocket and looks like any other person you might walk past. He tells a story about a time he was being introduced as the speaker at an event.

In his introductory comments, the well-intentioned master of ceremonies mentioned that Abbott was missing his right hand. As Abbott listened, he thought to himself, Why? Just let my accomplishments of a gold medal and a no-hitter stand for themselves.

The takeaway, for me, is that it's important to be more sensitive to any labels or adjectives I use when telling my many stories. Is it really necessary to say things about a person's height, or where they're from, or what ethnic group they belong to, or to make observations that sound more like stereotypes? I felt convicted.

My hero on the subject of avoiding labels is my youngest son, Joey. He had a new roommate who I had not yet had a chance to meet. Joey often spoke about his roommate and, from everything he said, they seemed to really be a good match.

Well, one day I finally met the roommate. Based on things my son had said when describing his roommate, I had been expecting that this young man was going to look a lot like our family.

To my surprise, he wasn't like us at all. I was proud of Joey's ability to overlook the *stereotypes* that might have been placed on his roommate, and to instead focus on the *person* his roommate is.

The second lesson I gleaned from Abbott's life is "deliberate practice," a concept with which I'm obsessed. Starting at 4 years old, Abbott would throw baseballs against a wall in his backyard for hours and hours.

It was there, in his backyard, that he taught himself to switch his glove to his right arm so he could throw, and then return it to his left hand to catch the rebound.

(The book includes some really cool stories of how Abbott overcame adversity and was able to field balls, including bunts, in the majors.)

Do you want to be successful at something? If you didn't have a right hand, would you dare to set a goal of pitching a no-hitter against the Cleveland Indians in Yankee Stadium?

It's Not Fair

July 23, 2018 // Tom Doescher //

TOM DOESCHER //

After reading *The Capitalist Comeback*, by Andrew Puzder, I debated blogging about it. I'm still not sure what the exact angle is, but I decided to offer a few sound bites and leave it up to you.

Even though I spent the first 15 years of my professional career advising (financially, that is) local governments — where I experienced some really nasty politics at times — I was shocked by this book. To reinforce his comments and views, Puzder provides more than 500 references to other books, articles, studies, and speeches to support his findings. (Editorial comment: As you know, I prefer authors who reference credible sources versus those with "just" strong personal opinions.) Puzder was a successful commercial trial lawyer who joined the parent company of Hardee's Restaurant. After five years, he became CEO — a job he successfully held for 16 years.

President Trump nominated Puzder to serve as his Secretary of Labor but, after a long and contentious confirmation hearing process, he withdrew his name from consideration. What happened is very sad to me, although I'm sure it happens to members of both political parties.

Based on the positions presented in his book, I think Puzder would have been a refreshing addition to the cabinet. (And, just so you're not confused, he was actually in favor of increasing the minimum wage. You need to read the book to get more details on his position.)

Although he doesn't say it this way, Puzder seems to believe that for more than 100 years, the U.S. has been drifting away from its roots. Prior to the industrial revolution, most Americans were business owners. Many were farmers and the rest had businesses that provided products or services to the farmers, like blacksmiths. Daniel Pink refers to them as "free agents" in his book, *Free Agent Nation*. Puzder doesn't get into this subject in his book, but Pink and others are excited that we once again seem to have more self-employed workers.

Probably to the surprise of many, Puzder is a champion of what he refers to as entry-level jobs. He's also really focused on income inequality.

I guess I would say that if you want to hear a side of the story that's rarely told, I recommend reading Puzder's book. I found him to be a guy who cares about his family, his business, his employees and, most of all, his country.

Switch On Your Brain

July 9, 2018 // Tom Doescher //

TOM DOESCHER //

Switch On Your Brain is actually the title of a fascinating book written by Dr. Caroline Leaf, a neuroscientist with more than 20 years of clinical experiences. Since the '80s, she has intensely studied the brain.

Caution: I want to mention, upfront, that she's a practicing Christian who incorporates her faith and scripture into her practice (which I believe only strengthens her scientific positions). With or without the scripture references, the plethora of brain research over the last 20-plus years is quite convincing.

I'm out of my area of professional expertise when it comes to discussing the brain, but I'll take that risk. Today, we all experience and observe so many situations that seem hopeless and have the potential to drag us down. I found that Dr. Leaf offers some very practical and worthwhile advice for many of us.

For over 100 years, learned students, brain experts, and conventional wisdom believed that the brain was hardwired, or fixed. However, based on volumes of brain research over the past 20 years, Dr. Leaf and colleagues from prominent medical research institutions have come to recognize that the mind can reprogram the brain.

The scientific word describing how the brain changes as a result of mental activity is called *neuroplasticity*. This means the brain is malleable and adaptable, changing moment by moment every day. Additionally, the research indicates that DNA changes shape according to our thoughts.

Dr. Leaf would say, "You are not a victim. You can control your reactions. You do have a choice." She would also say neuroplasticity can operate for us — as well as against us — because whatever we think about the most will grow (this applies to both the positive and negative ends of the spectrum).

Dr. Leaf provides a 21-day detox plan, which I decided to personally apply to a 15-year-old issue in my life. Just the idea that there may be light at the end of the tunnel was encouraging for me. So far, it has actually worked. I don't want to take the space here to explain it, but I would be happy to share my issue with you if you're interested.

Most of you who know me will probably say that I'm pretty solid, stable, and fact-based. That being said, if you are, or have for some time, struggled with an issue — even something as debilitating as posttraumatic stress disorder, for example — consider at least taking the time to read Dr. Leaf's book. I found her life views very uplifting and inspiring, and I hope you do, too.

p.s. In previous posts, I've referenced *Mindset,* by Carol Dweck, who coined the terms "fixed" and "growth" mindsets. Her studies support the position that with the proper instruction/coaching and lots of correct practice (deliberate practice), you can get better. I like both Dr. Leaf and Dweck's views because they provide hope.

Trust Your Gut
June 18, 2018 // Tom Doescher //

TOM DOESCHER //

Over the past few years, I have worked with business owners who, when relating a situation in their business, would say something like, "I knew I should have done this or that." I can relate. Based on my self-diagnosis, I would say that I am not naturally intuitive. This conclusion is the result of working with a number of partners and clients who really *are* intuitive. To me, it seems like they have a sixth sense.

What I have discovered later in my business career is that although I may not be intuitive, I have experienced a lot — both good and bad — and I've tried to learn from these situations. As I reflected on the subject, I recalled a February 2001 *Harvard Business Review* article entitled "When to Trust Your Gut," written by Alden M. Hayashi. The reason I remembered the article is that the author highlights a story about Bob Lutz, who at the time was a member of the Lee Iacocca Chrysler Dream Team, and who many consider to be one of the greatest auto executives of all time. I will not spoil the article, but it details Lutz's conceptualizing and then launching the very

183

successful Dodge Viper with no market research, just his gut instinct, to support him. The article quotes Herbert Simon, of Carnegie Mellon, who came to the conclusion that experience enables people to "chunk" information so they can store and retrieve it easily.

In a November 16, 2017, article in *Psychology Today*, titled "When Should You Trust Your Gut? Here's What the Science Says," Al Pittampalli states, "In order to trust our intuition, we need to have had enough practice. Our intuitions are only as good as the database of patterns that we draw them from. So, we need to have had sufficient experience noticing and revising patterns in order to have built up a database that is both robust and refined."

In the HBR article, the author says, "Executives like Lutz and Eisner (former Disney CEO) will be the first to admit that their instincts are often plain wrong. Don't fall in love with your decisions. They warn against overconfidence, and they suggest routinely soliciting the opinions of others when faced with tough choices."

So, here is my advice to "seasoned leaders," based on my own experience and my observations of some awesome leaders:

1. Do not ignore your gut, especially if it is related to a subject you know really well.
2. Make sure you are not emotionally too close to or attached to the subject.
3. Seek the counsel of others.
4. Listen carefully; try to understand their views and the basis of their opinions.
5. Do not ignore your gut!

p.s. If you are just beginning your career, be careful — unless you're Steve Jobs, Elon Musk, Thomas Edison, or Herb Kelleher of Southwest Airlines.

To "Type A" Executives: You Might Think You Can Do It All, But ...

September 4, 2017 // Tom Doescher //

TOM DOESCHER //

One of my favorite Frank Moran stories occurred when I was in my early 40s and Frank was in his 70s. Both of us were members of the Birmingham Athletic Club (actually, Frank was one of the founding members).

One evening I was standing in front of my locker after a long day, having a debate with myself about whether or not to exercise. Out of the corner of my eye, I saw a flash go by. It dawned on me that it was Frank. His appearance put an end to my debate. After I was dressed but before going into the gym, I went over to Frank's locker to say hello. As always, a huge Irish smile lit up his face and he greeted me warmly.

I said to him, "Frank, where do you get all the energy?" Without thinking about it, he looked me straight in the eyes and responded, "What makes you think I have a lot of energy?"

That few-second exchange made a lasting impact on me. I am venturing out of my professional field here (I admit I'm not a psychologist!), but I'm telling you what I and others have experienced. Some of us are so driven, and our minds think we're still 18 years old. Unfortunately, both physically and emotionally, we're much older than that. After so many years, sometimes our "young" minds drive us to exhaustion and/or burnout.

Having been burned out more than once, my advice to you is to give some serious thought as to what you can realistically accomplish/achieve in a healthy way. I'm not saying you should lower the bar, but I am suggesting that you try to be honest with yourself. It will save you from a lot of pain, as well as possible embarrassment and regrets.

I think the saying "Act your age" may fit here.

Integrity? Who Are You Kidding?
September 16, 2013 // Tom Doescher //

Back in 2002, I attended David Cole's annual Automotive Management Briefing in Traverse City. The prior year, several nonautomotive companies (like Enron, WorldCom, and Tyco) had been embroiled in scandals that led to their collapse. During the briefing, one automotive executive presenter after another gloated about the high level of integrity found in the automotive industry.

I did everything I could to keep from getting visibly sick. These were the leaders of my clients' customers, and their dealings with my clients could be labeled anything but scrupulous or inspired by integrity. In my thinking, the word that comes to mind is "hypocrisy." The reason I'm discussing this subject now is that I've just read Dr. Henry Cloud's book, *Integrity – the Courage to Meet the Demands of Reality*, which I would highly recommend. Dr. Cloud sets the bar pretty high but has lots of practical advice. Do you walk your talk?

Is It Better to Be Efficient or Effective?
July 10, 2017 // Tom Doescher //

TOM DOESCHER //

Those of you who know me well can testify to how obsessed I am with efficiency. When I observe wasted time, it drives me crazy.
I've come to realize, though, that often you can achieve both — efficiency *and* effectiveness.

That being said, there are times when it may take longer to handle an item/issue properly. When you're dealing with a more complicated issue, it's better to speak in person with someone rather than communicating via an email or a text.

A few years back, I was meeting with a client and, when I asked how his day was going, his response was, "I have spent most of the day mopping up messes/misunderstandings caused by emails that should **NEVER** have been sent."

That's a great example of an instance where it may have been more efficient and less stressful if the people communicating by email had spoken with their colleague directly.

Many of you are probably not aware of it, but before emails and texting, there used to be a document referred to as a memo (yes, paper) that was delivered through inter-office mail (you may not know about that, either).

Back then, my mentor, Frank Moran, would instruct his team members that if their communication had any emotion involved, they should speak with the colleague or client as soon as possible.

His directives were clear then and still make sense today: Do not send a memo, email, or text, or leave a voicemail message, if some level of emotion might be involved; all of those forms of communication can easily be misinterpreted.

I'm guessing that most of you have experienced this unpleasant situation. My advice is to learn from your painful experience and, next time you're dealing with something that's really important, challenging, or difficult, resist sending an email or text.

Be Careful What You Say

May 8, 2017 // Tom Doescher //

TOM DOESCHER //

I was recently working with a client and, during our interaction, I was reminded of an experience that impacted my entire career. The scene was the celebration of new partners at my former firm. It was — and still is — a tradition to have newly elected partners (new owners in the firm) give an acceptance speech at an all-partner and staff conference. It has always been the highlight of the year.

Years ago, a new partner — I'm guessing this individual may have been very nervous — made some very colorful, off-the-wall, hard to believe comments. Those of us in the audience were stunned and kept waiting for the punch line, which never came. The room became very quiet. I don't remember anything after his speech; we were all in shock. The next day, everyone received a memo (yes, a paper memo in our mailbox; for those of you who have never experienced this, please ask someone more senior than you to explain). There was a brief cover memo from the firm's HR partner, and then an apology memo from the newly elected partner. The cover memo said, "Let us not judge one another by the dumbest thing someone has ever done or said." Wow. It was perfect. I will resist getting into a philosophical or theological discourse, but suffice it to say that, in a few words, our HR partner got us all back to work and prevented days, weeks, and months of gossip and speculation (i.e., a lot of wasted time).

What is the application for you? Today, things move so fast and sometimes, under severe duress in trying to serve customers, we lose it in some way. I'm not talking about chronic road-ragers, but those of us who drop our guard and say something out of character that we soon regret. Let's learn to apologize and to forgive.

p.s. This new partner went on to have a very successful career and was loved by his clients and colleagues alike.

The Lenses of Leadership
December 5, 2016 // Tom Doescher //

TOM DOESCHER //

Once again, this past year, I had the privilege of hearing Bill Hybels speak at the Willow Creek Global Leadership Summit. This time, he talked about the four leadership lenses and the important role they play in leading your team "from here to there" (Hybels loves to use this metaphor).

The following are my takeaways:

1. **Passion Lens** — Find and fill your passion bucket. Are you excited about the future and where you're going? Is your dream as big as ever? How full is your passion bucket? Here are a couple of suggestions of things you can do to fill the bucket: Hang around or meet passionate people/leaders, and read books written by or about passionate leaders.

2. **People Lens** — How are you doing with your team? Hybels said if there's a high level of trust among team members, there will be high levels of performance. (Editorial comment: I talk about this subject frequently in my blogs, so I'll only say that there's a lot of value in his strong suggestion to have an outside firm measure your team's "health.")

3. **Performance Lens** — Hybels' main point here was that it makes a real difference when you have clear, achievable goals for your team members, and it's important to let them know how they're doing. They want to know, and they deserve to know. He also recommended using a color-coded system that many of you are already aware of, which he labels as follows: Green — Thriving; Yellow — Healthy; Red — Underperforming.

4. **Legacy Lens** — What is your legacy? What will people say about you when you're gone? If you perceive that it's not what you want, then do something about it and make some course corrections.

You may want to reflect on this list and set a few personal/business goals. Hybels closed by saying, "Leadership matters and we should never stop getting better!"

When Is Helping NOT Helping? And When Feedback Hurts.

November 14, 2016 // Tom Doescher //

TOM DOESCHER //

After helping launch Plante Moran Global Services (PMGS) in China, I would visit twice a year and spend time with clients, suppliers, and our Shanghai-based team. On the last evening of each visit, as a way of expressing my thanks to the team, I would host a dinner for the team members, their spouses, and their children. So far, so good.

Several years after the tradition began, I was traveling with one of the Shanghai team members to a supplier's location. We began our journey in a taxi heading to the subway that took us to the high-speed bullet train to the Pudong Airport. There, we boarded a flight to a coastal city. When we arrived, my colleague had a distressed look. The plan had been to take a passenger vehicle to the supplier's town, but a severe rainstorm was in progress and my colleague thought it would be safer to take a bus. My colleague was trying to figure out how to politely ask me if it was OK. I agreed to the revised plan, and we continued our adventure on a bus filled with local people, animals, and lots of luggage (like something you would see in the movies).

When we finally arrived at our destination, my colleague had that distressed look again — this time because there were no taxi cabs at the bus station. There were, however, bicycle rickshaws. Finally, the colleague summed up the courage to ask, "Would it be OK if we rode in this?" My answer? "I would love to!" The supplier was waiting for us when we arrived at the rickshaw station and drove us safely to the plant. (Editor's note: I have been wanting to tell that story for years.)

As you might imagine, I had a lot of questions for the colleague during our lengthy journey. Most of what I was trying to find out was how the team was doing, and how they thought we were doing supporting the Shanghai team, 8,000 miles away from Plante Moran's office.

During the course of our seven modes of transportation, and after I had asked the same question various different ways, my Shanghai colleague finally had the courage to tell me that the traditional team dinners were "nice."

However, since we went to a Western/American restaurant, the team had experienced sticker shock (my translation) and, to make matters worse, they didn't especially care for the food. The crowning blow was when my colleague said, "It seems like a poor use of PMGS monies."

I swallowed hard and changed the venue for all future team dinners. And I wondered, What else are we doing that is stupid?

Hopefully, this story motivates you to get feedback from your team. But can you beat my personal record of seven modes of transportation in just one day?

Consider the Facts, but Don't Forget to Listen

May 16, 2016 // Tom Doescher //

 **TOM DOESCHER //**

Over the past several years, I've advised several clients who have found themselves working with challenging boards of directors. In each case, the CEO was very competent and successful, but struggled with certain board members who had contrarian points of view.

As I reflected on their situations and attempted my best to offer advice, I was reminded of books about two great leaders. The first is *Tough Choices*, written by Carly Fiorina about her time as CEO of HP; the second is *Three and Out: Rich Rodriguez and the Michigan Wolverines in the Crucible of College Football*, written by John U. Bacon.

(I'm not crazy; I know those subjects sound like they're worlds apart!)

Let me try and connect the dots. In both books, commissioned and endorsed by Fiorina and Rodriguez, I made the following observation (and I repeat that all I know is what was in "their" books):

Obviously, facts are important — but often, there's more to consider.

In my opinion, both Fiorina and Rodriguez were out of touch or acted as if they "didn't care" what key stakeholders thought. I'm not recommending being political. What I am recommending is using your common sense and listening — **actively listening**, asking clarifying questions, and attempting to understand other points of view, especially those of your board members.

In both situations, I'm sure there were other factors involved.

But as I advise executives, especially those leaning toward "right is right" attitudes, I encourage them to leave their ego at the door and work hard to understand from where the board member is coming. They may actually have a good point, but perhaps they're doing a poor job of expressing it.

To summarily dismiss the board member's point of view is suicide.

Ask Carly Fiorina and Rich Rodriguez.

Humble Inquiry

April 4, 2016 // Tom Doescher //

TOM DOESCHER //

Over the years, many people have told me that I'm a good listener. Recently, I discovered that I'm not as good as I would like to be.

One behavior that I've identified and that I don't like in myself is that sometimes, when someone describes a business problem that I've experienced many times, I jump to a conclusion and offer my advice without asking many questions about the individual's specific concern.

In Edgar H. Schein's book, *Humble Inquiry: The Gentle Art of Asking Instead of Telling*, he says, "We must become better at asking and do less telling in a culture that overvalues telling." Ouch!

He also says, "Humble inquiry is the fine art of drawing someone out, of asking questions to which you do not already know the answer, of building a relationship based on curiosity and interest in the other person."

He suggests thinking about what we ask, how we ask it, where we ask it, and when we ask it.

Even for those of you who are "great listeners," I would suggest reading this short little book because it's filled with many very practical suggestions.

So, you say you're a good listener.

What would your subordinates say?

The Johari Window

April 18, 2016 // Tom Doescher //

TOM DOESCHER //

In Edgar H. Schein's book, *Humble Inquiry: The Gentle Art of Asking Instead of Telling*, he mentions the Johari Window tool, which was invented by two American psychologists — Joe Luft and Harry Ingham — in 1955.

Instead of me trying to explain it, I would highly recommend watching a two-minute video. Go to Mind Tools – The Johari Window to view. I have written before about the importance of leaders being transparent with their team. I had the good fortune of experiencing my longtime mentor, Ken Kunkel, model the behaviors that are discussed in the video.

Are you the Marlboro Man (or whatever the equivalent is for a woman)? Would your team say they know you really well?

As a Leader, Do You Feel All Alone? That's How I Felt.

February 8, 2016 // Tom Doescher //

TOM DOESCHER //

I must admit that I stumbled into the use of a leadership team (LT). I wish I could tell you that I followed a more thoughtful, strategic process, but that wouldn't be the truth.

(If you want more details, let me know.)

That being said, the result turned out to be more — and even better — than I anticipated. If you go to the Resource section of our website, there's a Leadership Team Checklist that was created for our clients who are setting up leadership teams.

I won't take the time here to summarize everything that's on this comprehensive list.

However, I'll point out a few items and offer some editorial comments:

1. I find that LT meetings, if properly organized (i.e., the right agenda), provide practical, relevant "leadership development" for everyone involved (senior *and* junior executives).
2. If you have the right LT and you behave (i.e., you keep your mouth shut and listen), you'll get immediate feedback on the decisions or initiatives that you're considering.
3. I felt like I wasn't all alone because others had skin in the game.
4. Communications regarding new initiatives or significant decisions came from the LT, rather than me (although, obviously, there are times they should come from the leader).
5. It's a great way to find out if there's an issue that needs attention.
6. In between meetings, you have others who are looking at the big picture of the organization.
7. I would evaluate the LT based on the number of contrarian views expressed (you want to avoid groupthink).

I would strongly recommend that most companies take the time and effort to put a LT in place. I'm so passionate about it, in fact, that I would be happy to discuss the value of leadership teams with you, at no cost.

The Five Intangibles of Leadership

January 11, 2016 // Tom Doescher //

TOM DOESCHER //

Last year I heard Bill Hybels, of the Willow Creek Association, speak on the subject of leadership. He gave the appropriate acknowledgements to Richard Davis, author of *The Intangibles of Leadership: The 10 Qualities of Superior Executive Performance*, which he used as a basis for his comments.

Here's a list of the five intangibles:
1. **Grit — Passion & Perseverance** The best leaders never quit. They say, "I think I can do this." Often, they're the same people who challenge themselves physically with marathons, mountain climbing, etc. They over-deliver to their customers/clients. Their followers notice this intensity and respond positively to it.
2. **Self-Awareness** The best leaders know two things. First, they understand what they're tethered to.

This was Bill Hybels' way of expressing that we're all a product of our past, both the good and the bad. What are you tethered to? Second, they recognize that we all have blind spots. Hybels quoted some research that concluded that leaders have, on average, 3.4 blind spots. Do you know your blind spots? Your team does. Do you have the courage to ask them?

3. **Resourcefulness** Bill Hybels says good leaders have a "high learning agility." In other words, they figure it out. They identify what's broken in their company and they either fix it themselves or ask someone to help them solve the problem/s.

4. **Self-Sacrificing Love** Hybels says that because there are so many celebrity, narcissistic leaders today (I'm sure you have your list), people are confused. He quotes the Gallup Organization, which has done extensive research on this subject, and he says he has come to the conclusion that if you want to be the best leader possible, you must love your team. He quotes a Bible verse: "Love never fails." Does your team believe you love them?

5. **Sense of Meaning** I've written on this subject before, quoting Simon Sinek, Daniel Pink, and others. Is the "why" or the "purpose" clear to your team? For example, Doescher Advisors exists to help business owners and executives achieve profitable growth that results in the creation of good jobs. This "why" motivates us every day. What is your "why"?

Another Boss Story (Sorry!)

July 20, 2015 // Tom Doescher //

TOM DOESCHER //

Marcus Buckingham told us in *First Break All the Rules* that the manager — not pay, benefits, perks, or a charismatic corporate leader — was the critical player in building a strong workplace. The manager, he said, was the key.

I recently read a story (maybe you could call it a confession) written by a leader I've closely studied for more than 25 years. By any measure, his organization would be considered successful, and many leaders ask for advice from this leader. So, what did he confess? Based on some feedback, he decided to retain a consulting firm to determine his staff's job satisfaction. He was shocked, almost derailed, and spent many sleepless nights as he read the responses from his team.

More than one team member said things like, "My supervisor is crazy." By crazy, they meant controlling, inattentive, uninspiring, uncaring or, worse yet, mean-spirited.

One of his conclusions was, "People join organizations, but they leave managers." Do you really know how you're viewed by your team members? Do you really know how they feel about your company? How do you know? As you have experienced significant growth, have your team members suffered?

p.s. Over several years, this leader took the input from his team seriously and made changes, including removing some of the supervisors/bosses.

After reviewing the results of the company's most recent independently administered satisfaction survey, their consulting firm labeled the company "elite" — they have made dramatic improvements since the first survey, and the environment is much more positive than it used to be.

Leading Up
July 6, 2015 // Tom Doescher //

TOM DOESCHER //

One of the most common topics I've covered with my clients has been what I call "Leading Up." Consider these examples:

1. A CEO/president needs to help her board of directors advise her, especially if they don't agree. It's tricky, but absolutely necessary for survival.
2. A non-owner CEO/president gives the entrepreneurial owner a positive method/approach for providing and getting input.
3. A COO enables a narcissistic CEO to be successful while still building a great team.
4. The CEO of a North American subsidiary facilitates an appropriate information exchange with their foreign parent to provide a degree of comfort.

You can probably come up with your own scenario, but the point is that the subordinate needs to help their supervisor lead them.

Why, you ask?

Because I've seen too many disasters occur when there's no communication or poor communication from the supervisor (Could be a Board of Directors) — which almost always leads to the subordinate finding another job. My advice to those of you who are in this situation is to very surgically offer a structure to help you and your supervisor be successful.

Here are a few tips:
1. Set up regular, periodic meetings to update your supervisor.
2. Provide summarized updates of your activities/goals.
3. If they don't ask for goals, create some — and get their buy-in.
4. Utilize every interaction with your supervisor as a chance to enhance your relationship.
5. This may sound weird but treat your supervisor like your best customer/client.
6. Never upstage your supervisor; rather, provide them opportunities to shine in front of customers/clients and the team.
7. Harry Truman said, "It's amazing how much we can do if we don't care who gets the credit." Don't be insincere or unnecessarily flattering but give your supervisor credit for new ideas if they were involved in any way.

Hopefully, you're getting the point. I've observed some very strong, successful subordinates (i.e., CEOs, presidents, COOs) do this really well. If I can help you with your specific situation, please let me know.

Give and Take: Why Helping Others Drives Our Success

June 22, 2015 // Tom Doescher //

TOM DOESCHER //

Adam Grant is the youngest full professor and a top-rated teacher at the University of Pennsylvania's Wharton School. I found his book, *Give and Take: Why Helping Others Drives Our Success*, to be very inspiring and somewhat counterintuitive. Here are my takeaways:
1. Givers prefer to give more than they get; Takers like to get more than they give; and Matchers effectively give to get.
2. Givers get lucky.
3. Givers show respect for the people who speak up, rather than belittling them.
4. When star performers move to a different firm without the rest of their team, their performance drops.

5. When Givers put the group's interests ahead of their own, they signal that their primary goal is to benefit the group.
6. Show up, work hard, be kind, and take the high road.
7. Even well-intentioned people tend to overvalue their own contributions and undervalue those of others.
8. Students (people) perform better when their teacher (leader) believes in them and expresses that they have really high potential.
9. Givers will avoid the escalation of commitment to a losing course of action (sunk cost fallacy) to protect their image of looking good.

How are Givers, Takers, and Matchers affecting your team?

Stepping It Up In Your Next Third

June 8, 2015 // Barbara Doescher //

 **BARBARA DOESCHER //**

As a baby boomer, I was saddened to read a Gallop research study indicating that boomers are no more likely to use their unique strengths than Generation X'ers and millennials.

After decades of work and life experiences in which we've honed our skills, talents, and expertise, I would have hoped more of us would love what we do.

I'm encouraging my fellow boomers to first find and then live out your passions. According to the actuaries, many of us in our 60s will live for another 30 years — that's a long time, and we can still make plenty of significant contributions to the world.

Whether you plan to stay in the marketplace or serve in other ways, I would suggest you find an enriching way to utilize your strengths — or, if you've never thought about it before, I would suggest you read my November 24, 2014, blog.

If you're looking for ideas, you may want to read my Thoughts for the Next Season. We all have something special to offer. Please don't just sit in the bleachers. Get into the game, and I guarantee you'll experience fun and fulfillment along the way.

Simplify. (Replenishing Your Energy Reserves.)

May 25, 2015 // Tom Doescher //

 **TOM DOESCHER //**

As you know from reading my blogs, I'm a huge fan of being focused as a leader. It's one of the "Big Four" traits of world-class leaders.

Bill Hybels' recent book, *Simplify*, provides some fresh, clear advice to us super-busy leaders who often feel overwhelmed, over-scheduled, and exhausted, and who become irritated by small things and often feel resentful.

I would recommend the book and, to whet your appetite, the following is a brief summary of the main topics Hybels explores:

1. Assess your energy level — have you snapped at someone close to you for no apparent reason?
2. Are you in control of your schedule? Does your calendar reflect your stated life priorities?
3. Do you have mastery over your finances or are you overextended? (Editorial comment: I think financial independence is more a function of spending than of income.)
4. Are you passionate about your work/vocation? If the answer is no, do something about it.
5. Do you have an unresolved relational issue where you've refused to forgive the other person? Consider dealing with it, since it definitely affects your effectiveness.
6. Do you have a destructive fear (phobia)? This can consume a lot of energy.
7. Do you have friendships that are energizing?
8. What season of life are you in? Do your goals and activities match your season?
9. Is your life focused on what matters most to you? Simplify.

Disclaimer: Bill Hybels is the leader of a major Christian organization and sprinkled throughout the book are Christian references.

That being said, he arguably is one of the best leaders in the world today, and I've learned a lot from him. Whether you're a Christian or not, you can substitute your belief system and still gain some great advice.

15 Leadership Lessons from the All Blacks

May 11, 2015 // Tom Doescher //

TOM DOESCHER //

The "All Blacks" is the nickname of the New Zealand national rugby union team, current holders of the Rugby World Cup, and the winningest rugby team of all time.

As many of you know, I love to use sports teams as examples for great leadership and teamwork.

James Kerr, author of *Legacy*, was embedded in the team and summarizes the following 15 leadership lessons he learned from his time with them:

1. Sweep the Sheds — Never be too big to do the small things that need to be done.
2. Go for the Gap — When you're on top of your game, change your game.
3. Play with Purpose — Ask "Why?"
4. Pass the Ball — Leaders create leaders.
5. Create a Learning Environment — Leaders are teachers.
6. No Jerks — Follow the spearhead.
7. Embrace Expectations — Aim for the highest cloud.
8. Train to Win — Practice under pressure.
9. Keep a Blue Head — Control your attention.
10. Know Thyself — Keep it real.
11. Sacrifice — Find something you would die for and give your life to it.
12. Invent a Language — Sing your world into existence.
13. Ritualize to Actualize — Create a culture.
14. Be a Good Ancestor — Plant trees you'll never see.
15. Write Your Legacy — This is your time.

The list includes some great points, but my favorites are No. 4 and No. 14.

Are you and your company creating "Leaders," and are you planting trees you'll never see?

Is a Narcissistic Leader a Bad Leader?
February 3, 2014 // Tom Doescher //

In my last blog, I suggested that in an effort to grow and develop as a leader, it's important to read books and listen to folks who have different points of view.

My latest example comes from reading *Narcissistic Leaders* by Michael Maccoby. He presents a pretty compelling case and explains why what he calls "productive narcissistic leaders" have made significant contributions to the world. Maccoby, a psychoanalyst born in 1933, would label the following individuals as productive narcissistic leaders: Abraham Lincoln, Henry Ford, John D. Rockefeller, Herb Kelleher, Steve Jobs, Bill Gates, and Jack Welch, among others.

He calls them "change the world" personalities, and says they have the following strengths: a vision for changing the world, independent thinking, a willingness to take risks, passion, and charisma. They are/were also voracious learners, knew how to persevere, were alert to threats, and possessed a sense of humor.

Probably what most of us observe are their weaknesses, which Maccoby would list as: not listening, oversensitivity to criticism, paranoia, anger, putting down others, a sense of over-competitiveness, over-control, isolation, exaggeration, lying, lack of self-knowledge, and grandiosity.

In my August 21, 2012, Food for Thought article entitled "Was Steve Jobs a Great – or Even Good Leader?", I discussed many of these weaknesses. I also pointed out that Jobs changed six industries, including personal computers, phones, tablet computing, music, digital publishing, and animated movies.

For those of you who are working with a productive narcissistic leader, I would highly recommend that you take a look at Maccoby's book. In my next blog, I'll consider his tips for successfully working with a productive narcissistic leader.

How to Be Successful Working with a Productive Narcissistic Leader
February 17, 2014 // Tom Doescher //

This is a continuation of my discussion regarding narcissistic leaders. Author Michael Maccoby, in his book *Narcissistic Leaders*, offers five principles for working with these types of individuals: know yourself and your type (in the book he gets into the other personality types, which include erotic, obsessive, and marketing); acquire deep knowledge in your field (using Steve Jobs as an example, you'd better know a lot about technology); learn how to partner effectively; don't invest your own ego (or I would say "check your ego at the door"); and protect the narcissist's image. In the book, Maccoby provides some examples of other leaders who have been successful in dealing with a narcissist. Many of them served as COO-types: Henry Ford had Harry Bennett, Herb Kelleher had Colleen Barrett, and Bill Gates had Steve Ballmer.

For those of you who are working with a productive narcissistic leader, I would highly recommend reading Maccoby's book. In my next blog, I'll discuss tips for those of you who may be a productive narcissistic leader.

If You Are a Productive Narcissistic Leader, Keep Reading

March 3, 2014 // Tom Doescher //

This is a continuation of my three-blog series regarding narcissistic leaders. Michael Maccoby, author of *Narcissistic Leaders*— a book that definitely broadened my thinking related to leaders — includes in his book an 80-question assessment that you can take to determine your personality type.

If you're a productive narcissistic leader and you want to maximize your impact on the world, I would strongly recommend you find a partner, or what Maccoby calls a "trusted sidekick."

This person needs to understand you, and not want to change you. They need to be strong (sure of themselves, but not arrogant) and, as they say, they must be comfortable in their own skin. They need to share your dream and be very knowledgeable about your business. They need to be able to tell you the truth (and be good at timing this discussion), even when you don't want to hear it.

If it turns out that you're a productive narcissistic leader, don't let it intimidate you. You're in pretty good company with Henry Ford, Herb Kelleher, and Bill Gates.

Just follow their examples.

Do You Listen to or Read Points of View Different Than Yours?

January 20, 2014 // Tom Doescher //

I recently read a book written by an author whose economic positions are diametrically opposite from mine. I read it because there's one aspect to my position that bothers me, and I wanted to find out what he had to say on that point.

Although the author didn't offer a solution I would endorse, I gained a much better understanding of where he's coming from — and that solidified and deepened my commitment to my original position.

Too often I observe leaders who just parrot their mentor or hero, as it may be, and don't have as deep a knowledge of the subject matter as I believe they should. I think such a lack of knowledge and understanding hurts these leaders' effectiveness with their team members.

When is the last time you read a book or listened to a speaker who has a viewpoint that's different than yours?

Leading with the Heart
June 24, 2013 // Tom Doescher //

As my wife and I sat and watched Duke become Louisville's latest victim during the NCAA Elite Eight, it reminded us of one of our favorite leadership books, *Leading with the Heart*, written by Coach Mike Krzyzewski.

Here are just a few of Coach K's thoughts on leadership:

- People want to be on a team. They want to be part of something bigger than themselves. They want to be in a situation where they feel they are doing something for the greater good.
- Too many rules get in the way of leadership. Rules put you in a box. Sometimes, people set rules just to keep from making tough decisions.
- Luck seems to favor teams where the members trust one another. As a leader, when you make a mistake, admit you're wrong. Apologize in front of the whole team.
- If you put a plant in a jar, it will take the shape of the jar. But if you allow the plant to grow freely, 20 jars might not be able to hold it.

After reading the book, it became obvious why Coach K has been so successful. How do you and your company stack up against his common-sense advice for leaders?

"Not All Readers Are Leaders, but All Leaders Are Readers."
April 29, 2013 // Tom Doescher //

This quote is from President Harry Truman. I made it until age 30 before I developed the discipline of reading (i.e., other than *Sports Illustrated* and the sports section of the local newspapers). One of my running buddies was always talking about the most recent book he had read, and his enthusiasm was contagious. Before long, I had become a "real" reader, too.

I highly recommend incorporating a reading program into your daily routine. It's amazing what a difference it can make in expanding your knowledge base and broadening your view. I'm currently reading a book about the pre- and post-Depression eras, called *Forgotten Man*. The similarities between FDR and President Obama are amazing. I've come to realize that there may, in fact, be nothing new under the sun. I would recommend starting by reading about something you're interested in. There are some really cool books on leadership, written by great coaches, for example. Just do it!

You Either Are or You Are Not an Entrepreneur

April 1, 2013 // Tom Doescher //

I have two clients who just get it. When I first met each of them, I asked the following question: What was your first business? They both smiled and enjoyed telling me how, when they were in their early teens, they would go down to the corner store to purchase candy and then resell it to their classmates.

This past summer I was in Guatemala, staying at a mission house. After a week of building houses for widows, my work boots were pretty dirty. The locals told me there was a young man (actually a young boy) who could clean them up for me. At the designated time, he arrived at the house and gave me a great shine. As he was working on my boots, I couldn't help but think, "This guy is a 10-year-old businessman."

So, what's the point? In the past, I've encouraged you to hire "owners." As you build your teams, look for clues to each individual's personality and attributes, and strive to develop associates who have entrepreneurial skills.

Some of them may leave to start their own companies, but if you treat them right, most will stay.

Is It Possible to Have Too Many Advisors?

February 18, 2013 // Tom Doescher //

Over the years, I've observed that the most successful business owners have carefully selected advisors, and these advisors may change from time to time. I've also noted that other owners have, in my view, too many advisors.

The most successful business owners assess where they're strong and where they need help, and they identify potential advisors based on those factors. Many owners get advice from way too many people.

Receiving a lot of advice may sound like a good thing, but someone explained the result this way: "Too many voices creates confusion."

Do you have advisors (the right number, the right people) who complement your skills and knowledge, or do you suffer from "advice overload"?

What Did I Say?
January 21, 2013 // Tom Doescher //

During the past decade, I've spent a lot of time in airports. I'm sure everyone has their own stories on what they do to pass the time. One of my favorite activities is to listen to other people's conversations (I know, it's pretty tacky, but after long delays you get awfully bored). While listening in, I've learned something. Conversations generally go like this: The first-person comments on the weather. In response, the second person mentions something about a sports team. The banter continues to go back and forth in the same fashion. Both people are talking, but no one is really listening (except for me).

I recently discovered in Bill Ury's book, *Getting to Yes* (which I would highly recommend), that this is a common problem in business. Let's say we have a disagreement. While you're expressing your position, I'm crafting my rebuttal — not listening carefully to what you're actually saying. Needless to say, the chances of us resolving our differences are pretty slim.

My question to you is: How good are your listening skills? I believe to be a Level 5 leader; you must be a great listener. You may want to ask one or two of your senior team members, who you believe will tell you the truth, what they think of your listening skills.

Can You Admit Your Mistakes?*
January 7, 2013 // Tom Doescher //

I recently read an article about Lance Armstrong in which the writer said, "NBC's 'Rock Center' recently covered Lance Armstrong's fall from grace, and they show that the scandal is much worse than merely doping.

The lengths that Armstrong went to in order to cover up his misdeeds were much worse than the doping itself."

Some of you either remember the Watergate scandal or have read about it. Most would say that it was the elaborate cover-up that caused President Nixon's resignation, not the break-in itself.

So, what's the business application? It's simple: Tell the truth. We all make mistakes and bad decisions, we say things we regret, and so on.

If you want to build credibility with your team, admit it when you're wrong. Avoid sugar-coating problems and making excuses.

Recently I experienced a great example of this ideal. I have a client who's an Air Force major reservist pilot. She invited me to go on a KC-135 refueling exercise (someone had to go with her, might as well be me), and I sat in the cockpit right behind her and her boss. I had my own set of headphones, so I could listen to their communications. They were taking turns at the controls and, at one point, my client determined the aircraft was off course. Her boss, a colonel, was quick to admit it was his fault.

So, there I was, listening in, and I heard a military superior telling his subordinate he had made a mistake. Wow! Later, my client told me the colonel is a great boss and leader.

My question to you is this: Do you admit your mistakes? Do you have a culture where your team members take responsibility for their mistakes? This is a trait I observe in the best companies.

p.s. For those of you with children, I would say this is one of the best things you can do to build a strong relationship with them.

*Disclaimer: We aren't picking on someone when they're down!

Second in Command
April 27, 2015 // Tom Doescher //

TOM DOESCHER //

One of the most impactful areas of my client work has been identifying the need for, and then finding and retaining, a second-in-command — or what I call a COO. I just finished reading Larry G. Linne's book, *Make the Noise Go Away*, and found it to be extremely on the mark and very practical (I wish he'd written it years ago).

The easy-to-read, 100-page book is written in parable style, and it's a great reference tool for both first- and second-in-commands. In addition to providing a wealth of solid ideas, it includes several handy and valuable checklists.

I believe Linne hits all the sensitive, "elephant in the room" issues head-on.

The following are just a few thoughts from the book, to whet your appetite:

1. Recognize the importance of continuous, open, candid communication that travels both ways. This sounds obvious, but seemingly small concerns often go unstated, are not dealt with, and grow into big problems over time.
2. Identify what's keeping the first-in-command awake at night. That person needs to tell the second-in-command, who needs to listen. If you're the first-in-command, don't assume the second already knows what issues are of concern to you.
3. One of the biggest reasons for failure is that the second doesn't understand the "values" of the first and makes decisions that are out of alignment with those values.
4. The second-in-command should find ways to make the company and the first-in-command look good.
5. The second needs to spend time with clients/customers, and with prospective new clients/customers, too. My translation of this suggestion is that the second has to really understand the business deeply, or the first will not trust (or respect) the second's opinions.
6. When proposing new ideas (which is really important to the first), the second should not oversell, but should try to be balanced and present both the pros and the cons. I've seen far too many executives lose their credibility by understating or not mentioning the downsides.

Let's stop there. If you're an owner or CEO considering hiring a No. 2, or if you're a No. 2 and you want to be the best you can be, I would highly recommend reading this book. Actually, I would suggest using it as a guide during the interview process; this isn't a place where either party can afford to make a mistake. Never forget that hiring mistakes can be very embarrassing and costly.

Should You Hire a COO?

April 8, 2019 // Tom Doescher //

TOM DOESCHER //

Probably one of the more common topics discussed with clients involves whether or not they should consider hiring a COO.

Actually, just yesterday, one of my clients said, "I've built this company to a size where I need help managing it."

A few years ago, I read *Make the Noise Go Away: The Power of An*

Effective Second-in-Command, by Larry G. Linne. Since then, I've recommended it to several clients. Just recently, I read *Riding Shotgun: The Role of the COO,* by Nathan Bennett and Stephen A. Miles. In their 2006 book, they observe that not much has been written about the role played by the COO.

Although I've been involved for years with hiring and working with COOs, I found the book to be a deep dive into the subject. Bennett and Miles appropriately point out that COOs are hired for different reasons.

Unlike other positions, such as CFO or CIO, the COO's role needs to be tailored to the situation.

For example:

1. Is the COO's role to put an organization together around a young founder with a unique product/service who has innovative-type technical skills and is a successful new-business developer and client-server?
2. Is the COO brought in to run the organization (inside leader) while the CEO is more focused on strategy and new acquisitions?
3. Will the COO become the next CEO?
4. Is there a transition underway from one generation to the next, and is the COO responsible for grooming/developing the next generation so someone is prepared to lead the company as CEO?
5. In anticipation of the sale of a company, is the team bringing in a COO who would be qualified to lead/run the company after the sale?
6. Is a COO needed to assist a tired founder/CEO who would like to go on vacation and not have to spend a lot of time dealing with problems back home?

The authors offer some challenges faced by COOs in their jobs and provide Q&A interviews with successful CEOs and COOs. Here are some of the topics they address:

1. Developing a trusting relationship with the CEO. (Editorial comment: When advising clients, I've often said the CEO-COO relationship is similar to a marriage.)
2. Developing a workable meeting and communication cadence that works for both executives. (Editorial comment: In this case, they'll probably need more touchpoints early on.)
3. The importance of clearly defining the COO's authority and making it clear to the other executives. The authors offer some practical warnings for those instances where the COO position is new and the other executives, who previously reported to the CEO, now report to the COO. This poses a distinct risk of the executives going around the

COO and continuing to report directly to the CEO. (Editorial comment: In my experience, this is extremely difficult, and the CEO and COO will need to work closely together to achieve the optimal situation.)

4. Establishing boundaries to avoid micromanaging by the CEO, whose behavior needs to change.
5. The fact that the COO will need to keep their ego in check.

This may sound self-serving, but I think getting outside help in hiring and onboarding the first COO will increase the chances for success.

In my experience, it's very emotional for the CEO, especially if that individual is also the company's founder, and the outside advisor can help the CEO work through it. Obviously, Doescher Advisors would love to help!

More On the "R" Word, Which Makes You Irrelevant

October 31, 2016 // Tom Doescher //

TOM DOESCHER //

In the June 2016 *Harvard Business Review* article, "Next Generation Retirement," the authors offer some thoughts about what I call the "Next Season." The suggestions aren't bad, but most of the people offering advice haven't yet experienced that phase of life, and really don't get it.

I would suggest reading this short article, but I highly encourage those who are in the "Next Season" — or people advising those in the "Next Season" — to read my Food for Thought in the Resource Section of my website, which includes input from more than 20 executives who have successfully navigated the "Next Season." Enjoy!

The Final Quest

June 17, 2019 // Tom Doescher //

 **TOM DOESCHER //**

is a fascinating little book that has significantly impacted me for the past several months.

First, a disclaimer: It's written by a Christian pastor about a series of dreams (visions) he had about the spiritual world. For that reason, you may want to skip this post.

Secondly, again as a Christian, he's writing from his point of view of the Bible. Again, if that's not something that's to your taste, you may want to skip this post.

For those of you who are still with me, I would highly recommend this book, written by Rick Joyner. It's a short, easy read. Whether the author's vision of the spiritual world is "real" or whether he just has a vivid imagination, he's able to paint a very realistic picture. In my three decades of being a Bible student, I've had limited exposure to the dark side of scripture. Joyner's version of what could be or might be going on is very believable — to the point where I've thought of it almost every day since finishing the book. He has expressed a point of view that would explain experiences that I have daily.

As you know, the first category in the Doescher Advisors Executive Health Check-up is "Spiritual Health." With that in mind, *The Final Quest* is something you may want to at least consider reading and reflecting upon. What if what Joyner reports is true? How might it affect you?

Tribute to Jae Doescher

May 26, 2014 // Tom Doescher //

On February 16, 2014, my 29-year-old daughter died, and, in this blog, I hope to pay tribute to her. I wasn't sure exactly how I was going to provide business advice to you and, at the same time, honor Jae, but then it dawned on me.

Just like you, there were things in Jae's life that she knew were out of her control. Despite those limitations, she managed to rise above her circumstances, and, through her loving care, she positively impacted hundreds of children and parents all over the world. My wife and I continue to receive notes from so many people, telling us how much Jae meant to their families. One mother made the comment that her teenage children don't know life without Jae. A sobbing young man told us he didn't know Jae, but he had come to the funeral representing his deceased father, who had worked with Jae in the church nursery and always spoke fondly of her.

In many ways, Jae was like you (a business owner or an executive running a business). Owning and/or running a business is a lot more difficult than most people think. If you own a business, your family's wealth is at risk every day. Many of you operate in a world filled with giants, where your customers are large multinationals who often treat you unfairly and/or continually ask for price concessions. Your suppliers, too, are giants, and they dictate pricing. It seems like the federal, state, and local governments continuously pass laws or regulations that increase your costs.

To stay in business, you — like our daughter — need to rise above your circumstances. For Jae, the experience of caring for hundreds of children over the years was worth it — and your perseverance in your endeavors is worth it, too. Think about it this way: How many families does your company support? You provide great training and opportunities for advancement. Your team members are mostly good citizens in their communities who pay local, state, and federal taxes. Many of them serve on their local PTA or volunteer their time on their church's boards and committees.

Yes, like Jae, you make a huge impact on this world. And, like Jae, you may never get any special recognition for the efforts you put forth. But what you do is important, so keep it up. I'm cheering for you.

Doescher Advisors Celebrates 5-Year Anniversary

December 12, 2016 // Tom Doescher //

It's hard to believe Doescher Advisors is celebrating our five-year anniversary.

Pinch us! We are so blessed.

As I've told many of you, we're living the dream. If you're a client, former client, someone who has referred a client, or someone who has helped us, we sincerely thank you for the trust you have placed in us. We are humbled, and it has been a privilege to serve you.

Here are a few factoids from our first five years:

1. We have served 40 executives from 25 companies. Currently, we meet monthly with 15 executives.
2. Both of us have joined business networking groups, which have been very beneficial.
3. We have posted 160 blogs and 24 Food for Thought (FFT) articles, which are now read by more than 200 subscribers.
4. We have connected with more than 700 business executives through LinkedIn.
5. We have administered dozens of LFYS assessments.
6. We have read more than 75 business books, from which key takeaways have been summarized in my blog posts or FFT articles. My readers have told me this is a nice service that saves them time.

As you know, our passion is for helping businesses increase profits *and* jobs. To that end:

1. At no charge, we've helped more than 90 people with job interviews (including interview prep); business referrals; career counseling — some early in their careers, and others who have felt like they needed to make a mid-course correction; and gratis meetings to provide

second opinions on important business decisions and strategies; and we've conducted meetings with executives who just needed someone who understands to listen to them.

2. We introduced 10 people to companies that became their future employer.
3. We placed three interns, two of whom were offered and accepted full-time positions.

A special thank-you to Ken Kunkel, Dan Doescher, Jennifer Ballarin, Ellen Krugel, Demoree Elbing, and Anne Daugherty, whose assistance and support have been invaluable.

We are so appreciative of you and, in the years ahead, we pledge to strive to continue earning your trust so that we can serve you and those you refer to us.

Merry Christmas, Tom and Barbara

Advisor or Coach? What is Doescher Advisors?
July 19, 2016

The following is a summary of my "Advisor or Coach?" blog series. Hopefully, it answers the question: What is Doescher Advisors?

Scene 1: My wife, Barbara, and I are often asked if we're "coaches." For some reason, it was bothering me to be called a coach, and I wasn't sure why. Many of you know my original career goal was to be a high school football coach, but my failure to make the Western Michigan University football team changed that plan. So, while it would be natural for me to consider myself a coach, something was troubling me about that label. Then I realized that we're actually "partners/peers" with our clients, not coaches.

Scene 2: Barbara and I recently rented the movie *The Intern*, starring Robert De Niro as Ben Whittaker, a 70-year-old intern, and Anne Hathaway as Jules Ostin, CEO and founder of a ragingly successful e-commerce startup. One of Jules' executives suggested piloting a "senior intern" program (i.e., hiring  seasoned executives to work alongside the 20s-30s workforce). Jules reluctantly takes Ben on as her intern.

I'm not a film critic, but I found it to be a wonderful story.
For a week or so, my thoughts kept going back to the movie. I couldn't get it out of my mind. Finally, I had an epiphany. Ben was me. I was Ben.

(No, I'm not saying I am Robert De Niro, although he did look great. I'm saying his character, Ben, is what Doescher Advisors strives to achieve.)Before I lose you, hang in there. First of all, Ben behaved as an advisor, not a coach. To me, a coach calls the plays and is generally in a superior position to the players. That definitely is not what Doescher Advisors is!

213

Hopefully, I won't ruin the movie for you, but the following are takeaways from the film that correlate with what we aspire to bring to our clients as we serve them:

1. Jules was thriving without Ben. She didn't need him.
   Our clients are talented, successful executives who are leading great companies, and they will be successful with or without us.

2. Ben was comfortable in his own skin. He wore a business suit and tie every day and carried a classic briefcase. He didn't try to be a 20-year-old but acted his own age.
   We recognize our "seasoned" state, and don't try to pretend we're younger than we are, although we do use Apple products.

3. Ben was willing to learn. He observed and asked a lot of questions of many different team members.
   We are committed to being lifelong learners. And we learn a lot from our clients.

4. Ben earned the respect of team members by the way he behaved. He tried to help and give to everyone and did not hog the limelight. *We look for unique ways to add to our clients' businesses. And we are not looking to take credit for suggestions that work out.*

5. Ben wasn't a "know-it-all," although in this startup environment he could have acted that way.
   We don't understand our clients' businesses like they do. We look for gaps where we can add a new idea or two.

6. Ben wanted the best for Jules, based on her definition of best.
   Our advice is based on our clients' business and personal goals, not ours.

7. Ben was willing to take calculated risks, like hacking into Jules' mother's computer (this was a great and hilarious scene).
   If we believe something is an opportunity for our clients' business, we'll bring it to them — even if it's an idea that's way out there and nontraditional (i.e., out of the box).

8. Early on, Ben was slow to offer advice and express his views/opinions. *We try to learn the client and their business first, before offering our thoughts. As I've been reflecting upon Ben's approach, I've realized that our clients will benefit if we're more like Ben.*

9. Ben was humble. Nothing was below him. He cleaned up a mess in the main office, and he helped deliver the interoffice mail.
   Our goal would be to follow Ben's example and do whatever needs to be done.

10. Ben wasn't judgmental of Jules or any of her team.
    After years in business, we recognize situations often look simpler to an outsider who's unaware of all the circumstances and compromises that led to a particular decision.

11. Ben was others oriented. He was there to help the team.
    At Doescher Advisors, our two primary metrics are:
    - As we're driving to our client appointments, we ask ourselves: "Are we really excited about meeting with this CEO/president/business owner today?"
    -Then, as we're leaving the appointment, we ask: "Did we offer them anything that will help them be a better business leader, or a better person in general?" If the answer to either question is "no," we'll resign from the job. We believe our clients deserve our best.

12. Ben was willing to take the initiative to figure out how he could help Jules and her team.
    In our standard business advisory agreement we state, "During initial meetings and ongoing, through active listening, Tom will quickly learn The Client's most important goals, both business and personal."

13. Ben gave credit to others on the team.
    Doescher Advisors' goal is to help our clients be successful, not to take credit for their success.

14. Ben was upbeat and positive.
    There is more than enough negativity in the business world. Our goal is to be a positive influence on our clients and others.

15. Ben encouraged Jules and her team.
    We believe one of the reasons clients retain our firm is our ability to encourage them. As the saying goes, "It's lonely at the top" — and we've discovered that our clients appreciate recognition from someone who really understands what they've achieved.

16. Ben was comfortable talking about anything (there are some

hilarious scenes where he gives advice to some young men on the team who have asked him about very personal matters). *Although we're not counselors, from time to time we find ourselves listening to issues related to children or elderly parents, or discussing practical exercise programs.*

17. Ben was good at providing clear, practical, and actionable feedback to Jules and her team.
We are committed to modeling well-timed, effective, and sometimes unpleasant, hard-to-hear feedback.

18. Ben had a great sense of humor, and could laugh at himself.
We, too, try to catch the humor in life and often find ourselves laughing with our clients. Sometimes that happens when we're telling a story about something, we did wrong.

19. Ben was a truth-teller.
We promise our clients that we'll speak the truth in love (which we interpret as carefully selected words at the right time).

20. Ben focused on the "whole" person. He recommended Tai Chi exercise and more sleep to Jules.

    In the Doescher Advisors Leaders Health Check-up, I cover the whole person — spiritual, mental, emotional, relational, physical and financial health.

21. Because of all of the above, Ben fit in really well and was well-liked and respected by the team.
Again, we strive to be like Ben.

In the closing scene of the movie, Jules says, "It's moments like these when you need someone." As I stated at the beginning of this blog series, our clients do not need us, but they do find us to be very helpful. I hope you have enjoyed hearing about Ben and the similarities between him and Doescher Advisors.

Looking for Career Advice, or Do You Regularly Give Career Advice?

September 9, 2019 // Tom Doescher //

 TOM DOESCHER //

If your answer is yes, I would highly recommend reading *Strategize to Win* by Carla A. Harris, vice chair of Morgan Stanley. I try to be careful not to suggest too many books, but Harris provides some common-sense (or not so common) tips regarding jobs — or, as I like to say, careers. She's a very good writer (or has a great ghost writer), which makes it a quick, easy read. You can tell she's a consultant because she also offers some great checklists at the end of each chapter and poses thoughtful rhetorical questions. Maybe the only caution would be that she's a Wall Street investment banker, so for some her advice may not be as helpful.

Here are my takeaways:

1. Sadly (to me), she suggests people entering the workforce today should plan six to eight five-year modules at different companies. As a guy who spent 40 years at the same awesome firm, that's hard to hear — but I understand.
2. I think that much of Harris's wisdom would be beneficial, even if you're in a great place and intend to stay.
3. In my experience, today's workplace reminds me of a fast-forwarded video. There never seems to be enough time. Customers are more demanding than ever, and technology has sped up the way we receive and share information, but humans are still humans. Harris is very clear that you need to take charge of your own career.
4. Harris is talking about the workforce (both leaders and associates), but I believe her advice applies to customer/client relationships, as well.
5. Sorry to bring up introverts again, but Harris's advice will encourage introverts to step out at times. Harris says she often hears people (probably introverts) erroneously say, "I don't need to go out of my way to build relationships; I'll let my work speak for itself." This observation applies to both your company and your customers/clients.
6. She also provides her spin on being a leader. According to Harris, a leader should have leverage, be efficient in communicating, be willing to act, be diverse, engage, and be responsible.

When I reflect on my daily conversations with owners and associates, I realize that Harris addresses so many of the common challenges faced today. If she lived closer, I would probably figure out a way to meet her and would use her as an advisor. She has obviously experienced many different "real life" business situations and has an ability to simplify a lot of facts into some practical, logical action steps.

Let me stick my neck out. If you engage in business (as an owner or associate), I would highly recommend reading this book.

The Happiness Equation
December 2, 2019 // Tom Doescher //

TOM DOESCHER //

Recently, I heard author Neil Pasricha speak. I enjoyed his comments and decided to read his book, *The Happiness Equation*. In the book, he sheds light on why so many people today are unhappy. Here are my takeaways, plus a few editorial comments:

1. The more physically active people are, the greater their general feelings of excitement and enthusiasm.
2. None of us can control our emotions (Editorial comment: As a very emotional person, I found this statement liberating); we can only control our reactions to our emotions.
3. In 1927, Paul Mazur of Lehman Brothers wrote the following in the *Harvard Business Review*: "We must shift America from a need to a desires culture." (Editorial comment: Wow, I would say Mazur got his wish!)
4. Men and women in Okinawa live an average of seven years longer than Americans and have the longest disability-free life expectancy on Earth. The word "retirement" literally does not exist in the Okinawan language. Instead, the Okinawan language has the word "ikigai" (pronounced like "icky guy"), which means, "The reason you wake up in the morning." (Editorial comment: It's their purpose, or their "why.")
5. Pasricha includes his (and also one of my) favorite quotes from Lewis Carroll's *Alice's Adventures in Wonderland*: "One day Alice came to a fork in the road and saw a Cheshire cat in a tree. 'Which road do I take?' she asked. 'Where do you want to go?' was his response. 'I don't know,' Alice answered. 'Then,' said the cat, 'it doesn't matter.' "

(Editorial comment: We use this quote when we're encouraging clients to establish a purpose, or a "why," for their life and/or business.)

6. In 1889, the Germans created the concept of retirement to free up jobs for young people by paying 65-year-olds to do nothing until they died (the average life span at the time was 67). In 1880, 78 percent of American men over age 65 were still working; in 2000, 16 percent of men over age 65 were still working.

7. When we're presented with too many decisions (choices), we either do nothing or do poorly. (Editorial comment: 30 years ago, I was a member of Michigan Future, a think tank, and was blessed to spend time with some really knowledgeable, futuristic business owners. Referring to the auto industry, they would say that we're moving from mass-production to mass-customization. In other words, the customer was going to be able to design their own vehicle to suit their personal preferences. Well, we still aren't there in the auto industry, but one of my biggest complaints today is that there are too many choices among relatively insignificant products. I think this creates a lot of wasted time. I'm sure I've just offended someone, but remember this book is about happiness.)

8. In 1955, the Parkinson's Law was defined as follows: "It is a common-place observation that work expands so as to fill the time available for its completion." (Editorial comment: Here's a practical application: Are all your major meetings routinely scheduled in one-hour blocks, or do you schedule 15- or 30-minute meetings? If you've accomplished the purpose of a meeting, do you adjourn the meeting early? Sadly, it wasn't until the end of my first career that I started the practice of scheduling shorter meetings, ending meetings early, and even canceling meetings when there weren't enough important agenda items. My partners were definitely happier!)

9. Multitasking is a flawed concept. (Editorial comment: Yes, you can work on two things at the same time, but you do a disservice to both. There have been numerous credible studies that have dispelled the myth of multitasking.)

I was quite surprised to discover what topics Pasricha selected to mention in a book about "happiness." And these aren't just his opinions, as he references many studies, researchers, and other authors' work to support his findings.

Pasricha's formula for happiness: **Want Nothing + Do Anything (for others) = Have Everything.**

I believe it's very similar to Adam Grant recommending that we be Givers vs. Takers.

A Life Without Anxiety

January 13, 2020 // Tom Doescher //

Living a life free of anxiety is the promise of Dr. Gregory Popcak, author of *Unworried.* According to Dr. Popcak, anxiety tends to be a fear response triggered by something that either happened a long time ago, has not yet happened, or may not actually be happening at all.

For instance, have you ever been afraid you said something embarrassing (or wish you hadn't said it) while out to dinner with your friends (or client/customer), so you kept replaying the scene in your head and experienced a low-grade sense of dread? Or, say you emailed or texted a friend (or client/customer) and didn't get a response — have you felt anxious that something must be wrong?

(Editor's note: I confess this is me. I'm a world-class worrier. Ask my partner.)

TOM DOESCHER //

Dr. Popcak begins by differentiating between fear and anxiety/worry. He would say fear is the natural, biological, and appropriate response to an imminent threat. When the fear systems in our brain work properly, they serve a protective function, warning us of danger and then easing off once the threat has passed. In contrast to fear, anxiety is when the brain's natural fear circuits get hijacked by something that isn't an immediate danger or could even be good for us. Think about your life — where you work, live, and play. Now think about your parents or grandparents. I bet your life is filled with way more activity and travel. You may live in an urban setting that's more stressful, or your kids have endless sports and other activities (I grew up surrounded by farms, where in the summer, the neighborhood kids met every day to play unsupervised baseball; I think you get the point). And you wonder why you're feeling stressed!

I won't attempt to summarize the book, but if anything, I've said resonates in your mind, I would highly recommend investing some time in *Unworried.* Like many authors of the books I've read in the past few years, Dr. Popcak describes the need to reprogram our brain, and he strongly believes we can. In explaining what to do, he uses the metaphor of creating surge-protection as well as a treatment called cognitive behavior therapy (CBT), and limiting or eliminating the use of medications. This book provides well-grounded hope for the worrier. As someone with anxiety, I plan to incorporate Dr. Popcak's advice into my life.

The Four Seasons of Adult Life

March 10, 2020 // Tom Doescher //

 TOM DOESCHER //

I recently heard a pastor/counselor speak about the Four Seasons of Adult Life. As I listened, I thought many of you might enjoy his perspectives.

Novice (17–28 Years)

Novice actually means new or beginner. You're transitioning from adolescence to adulthood. During this period, the rational portion of your brain is developing. You make a lot of choices (friends, higher education, vocation/job) that will impact the rest of your life.

Challenges:
1. Will I grow up? Will I put away my childish things and ways? Think of a childish habit you had. Do you still have it?
2. Who do you spend time with? It's said that you're the sum total of the five people with whom you spend the most time. Who is the best person in your life today? **Tip: Try to never be the smartest person in the room**. (*Editorial comment: Be a lifelong learner.*)
3. What is/will your life be about? What path will you take? Will you focus on something bigger than yourself?
4. What will your priorities be?

Common Pitfalls:
1. Going down the wrong path.
2. A tendency to be prideful.
3. A focus on "doing" versus "being."

Apprentice (29–39 Years)
This is (or should be) a transition stage.

Challenges:
1. Your priorities will be tested. (What are your tensions?) During this phase is when many people get married.
2. Face your family wounds. (Often, your issues from your family of origin will manifest themselves during this phase. Be ready and consider seeking professional help.)
3. Relational complexity increases (parents, spouse, children, co-workers, neighbors). You may experience relationship disappointments. Will you "lean in" or "run"?
4. There's frequently a tendency to compare yourself with others (job, bank account, home, vehicle, spouse, kids).

Journeyman (40–54 Years)
In this stage, life is accelerating and can be exhausting.

Challenges:
1. You begin the transition from young to old. Your energy level is decreasing, while at the same time your demands are increasing. You need to reposition yourself for maximum effectiveness.

   Tip: Consider a reverse bucket list. In other words, what should you eliminate from your life so you can focus on your highest priorities?

2. How will you respond? Will you become a "victim," or will you accept the responsibility to change? Is there an area of your life where you failed? What role did you play?
3. Will you become isolated or connected?

   (Editorial comments: 1) I refer to this as the "Perfect Storm" phase of life. We have high demands at work, at home, at church, in the community. You have to learn to say "no," or you'll become overwhelmed. 2) In my experience and observation, this stage goes into the 60s for many executives.)

Mentor (55+ Years)

During this phase, you'll cash in on your previous choices. You may retire from your longtime career/vocation. You could become an experienced, trusted advisor. (*Editorial comments: 1) As you know, I'm not a big fan of retirement. 2) While you're in an influential position, it's an ideal time to begin mentoring others. 3) I would also encourage mentoring until you can't.*)

Challenges:
1. Will you be a consumer or an investor? (*Editorial comment: Said another way, will you be a taker or a giver?*)
2. Will you pass on wisdom, skills, and your experience? (Mentor, or initiate/engage, ask questions versus lecture, be available and give of your time, tell stories, encourage others.)
3. When will you step aside? (*Editorial comment: When will you transition to your "Next Season"?*)

Concluding reflections: 1) What's the best thing in your life today? 2) What's your biggest challenge and how will you address it?

Thoughts For The Next Season – Last Life Marathon

The following are some thoughts and suggestions to consider in your next season. We welcome feedback and other suggestions. Our goal is to assist people maximize their gifts to help others.

Designing The Next Season Game Plan

1. It may seem obvious, but even if you're not a plan-ahead type of person, we would strongly urge you to spend some time thinking about your next season before you get there.
2. We would recommend reading the Phil Burgess book, Reboot! We have met Phil, who has some refreshing advice for those navigating through this next season.
3. Phil talks about the fact that retirement is a relatively new concept since the 50s. In the last chapter of his book, Thou Shall Prosper, Daniel Lapin states there is no Hebrew word for retirement and provides some interesting points of view.
4. Study other people to observe what they have done, but do not be overly influenced by them.
5. Read Chapter 6 of *The Noticer* by Andy Andrews, who reminds us of the impact of several "Next Season" people, like Colonel Sanders, Nelson Mandela and others.
6. Interview others who have gone ahead of you. Tom reconnected with his long-time mentor, Ken Kunkel, and his experiences and advice were invaluable.
7. Consider contributing your time and talent to a charitable and/or educational organization.
8. Know yourself. Get out your old personal assessment tools or take them again, and have a professional interpret them for you, through the lens of this new season.
9. Don't follow the herd. Design your next season based on who you are.
10. Determine about what you are passionate in.
11. If it is your passion, stay involved in business.
12. Stay involved in "your" business; just make sure you have a real, clear succession plan. We know an auto dealer, who has turned his dealership over to his son, and the dealer, who is good at and loves to buy used cars, now works in the used car department.
13. Evaluate your unique experiences and skills and figure out a way to share them with others.
14. Read books about subjects that have always interested you (i.e. Civil War).
15. Pursue hobbies you are passionate about.
16. Listen to oldies music and reminisce a little.
17. According to Al Doescher, "The Golden Years Ain't So Golden".
18. According to Betty Davis, "Growing old is not for sissies."

19. Another book with some interesting points of view is *Teach Us to Number Our Days* by David Roper. For years he was a contributing writer to Our Daily Bread and is a Christian author. That being said, his sage advice is spot on.

Our Non-Negotiables

1. Be focused on others. Seems as we age, we become more self-centered. Fight the urge and find healthy, fun ways to contribute to others.
2. Related to others, consider continuing to mentor/help/coach/stay in touch with, those who helped make you successful.
3. Think about how your life could be a positive influence on others during this next season.
4. If you're a Type A personality, avoid filling your schedule up and losing your well-earned flexibility.
5. As you plan your activities, think about whether you want to be around people your age or those who are younger. We have been deliberate about spending a meaningful amount of time with young people.

In The First Few Miles, Make Adjustments

1. Consider taking an extended sabbatical between seasons. You can use the time for further planning.
2. For many of us, our life's work became our identity (i.e. We will leave the merits of this to professional counselors to deal with). So, one point of view would be to create a new identity. At cocktail parties, one of the first 2 or 3 questions is, "What do you do?" In this next season, we need to be prepared to have an answer.
3. Maybe another way to express it would be a comment from a colleague of mine who said, "Once you say you are "retired", to many you now become irrelevant."
4. You may need to try a few different things to determine what works best for you. So, give yourself permission to experiment.
5. Realize that you probably have less energy now but may not know it. We love to tell the story of Frank Moran in his 70s racing through the Birmingham Athletic Club locker room to get ready to play squash. I was at my locker and exhausted after a long day at the office, debating whether or not to work out. I went over to say hello to Frank and asked him where he got all the energy. He looked me in the eye and said, "What makes you think I have a lot of energy?"
I will never forget that scene and actually have had the same feelings in recent years. So, a doable pace is important.
6. For many people, slowing down will be difficult and will be a necessary but painful adjustment.
7. People will be happy to fill up your schedule for you. Protect it!

8. Realize that people will say stupid things to you. Until you go through this transition, you don't really understand how you will feel.
9. You may want to meet with a counselor.
10. If you are normal, you will need to go through a grieving process unless you had a lousy career. The following is a helpful article on grieving: *Loss, Grief, and Manliness: What Every Man Should Know about Losing a Loved One* written by Brett & Kate McKay • August 4, 2009 Last updated: March 16, 2020

Pace Yourself and Finish Strong

1. Develop good eating and sleeping habits and have a regular fitness program.
2. If you have something you really would like to do or say, do it. Don't assume there will be another day.
3. Back to energy & health, if there is something you really want to do, don't wait. Go to Mongolia or Antarctica.
4. Make a list of friends with whom you want to stay in touch; and take the initiative to schedule breakfast, lunch or dinner. If they have less flexibility than you (due to work demands), make the time and place convenient for them (and be respectful of their time/schedule).
5. Get help managing/investing your money; and set your spending budget at manageable level for the long-term.
6. Evaluate the impact on your spouse.
7. Consider doing more activities with your spouse.
8. Consider relieving your spouse of certain chores.

Do You Know Your Calling?
June 22nd, 2020 // Tom Doescher //

TOM DOESCHER //

Many of you know that my most common response to the greeting "How are you doing?" is "Living the dream!" There are several reasons I feel that way, but one would be that I'm living out my "calling." Some people might think that's a religious term, but to me it's the best way to describe operating in the space you were designed for. Sadly, it has taken me decades to really understand this concept.

When I completed Marcus Buckingham's StandOut assessment, it labeled me as a "Performance Coach" and offered the following words to describe what that means:

"People who come to you for advice will not only get forthright, practical guidance, they will also get a system to track their progress. You love to keep score. And while this logical, disciplined approach creates security and certainty with others, you temper it with a heartfelt belief in them and what they can achieve. Your goal is to create self-reliance in others. You don't want them to have to keep coming to you. And then you stand proudly on the sidelines and watch them deliver."

If you're a regular reader, you know I prefer the word "advisor" over "coach." That being said, I'll accept being a "performance coach."

So, I guess my "what" or "why" is advising/coaching, and my "where" is business — and in recent years, I've realized how much I love this role. As a former athlete, I assume I enjoy the competitiveness of business and, as Buckingham would say, "I love to keep score."

Back to "Living the dream." Advising my clients isn't work; it's who I am. One of my favorite authors, Matthew Kelly, would say that when I'm advising, I'm the "best version of myself."

In addition to working with my clients, I mentor both a young man who lives at a children's home and a felon who's spent most of his life in prison. A few weeks ago, I was talking to a longtime friend who asked about the mentoring. During our conversation, he said, "Well, that makes total sense." To which I said, "What?" He replied, "You're coaching."

Now you know a little more about me — but how about you? Do you know your unique calling?

Discover what it is, engage, and join me in "Living the dream!"

Emotional Intelligence

July 13th, 2020 // Tom Doescher //

TOM DOESCHER //

As I advise clients with regard to their teams, we often end up talking about a particular team member's emotional intelligence (EI), or lack thereof. You've probably experienced someone who is referred to by their colleagues as a "Bull in a China Shop"; and that's who my clients frequently want to discuss. In looking through more than 200 blog posts, I discovered I've never written about EI. I still remember reading Daniel Goleman's groundbreaking book, *Emotional Intelligence*, in 1995. Although the term emotional intelligence was introduced in the 1960s, it really gained popularity with Goleman's book. My recollection is that it was truly a WOW idea, but Goleman didn't provide any practical tools for utilizing the concept. Since then, several consulting firms have created practical, easy-to-use tools that business owners without a psychology degree can implement in their companies.

The book/tool I use with my clients is *Emotional Intelligence 2.0*, written by Travis Bradberry and Jean Greaves. When you purchase the book, you receive one online assessment code. I suggest to my clients that they first take the assessment and then refer to the book, which is structured a lot like the owner's manual for your vehicle.

There are four skills that make up emotional intelligence: Self-Awareness, Self-Management, Social Awareness, and Relationship Management. The assessment report provides a numerical score from 1 to 100, with a subjective evaluation for each of the four skills and suggests what you should focus on.

Let's assume your area for development is Social Awareness. You go to the "owner's manual" (the book) and look up Social Awareness. It provides an executive summary of what that means, a list of strategies for improving your social awareness, and a brief write-up on each strategy. I'm currently working with a client who completed the assessment and shared the results with me. The assessment suggested development in one area, so we selected three strategies from the book and the client is now incorporating these suggestions into their daily life.

Let me give you an example from my own life. Over the years, I've received developmental feedback telling me that, at times, I can be very intense and direct with my communication style. If you're my partner, Barbara, or Uncle Dan, you just tell me to "lighten up," but others may be taken back or offended. So when I'm in a situation where my directness may manifest itself and I'm working with others who may not know me well, I try to be aware, attempt to tone down my natural tendency, and watch people's reactions — and sometimes I need to apologize or explain my intensity. This strategy seems to be working.

If you've never taken an EI assessment, I would strongly recommend that you do.
Then, if you have a team member who could use some help, it's very powerful to share your assessment with them first, and then ask them to complete an assessment and share it with you.

Forgiveness
July 27th, 2020 // Tom Doescher //

TOM DOESCHER //

I'm stepping way out of my area of expertise, but one of the more common issues I observe is lack of forgiveness. I've found a really simple, practical summary of forgiveness and how to deal with it from a Mayo Clinic article entitled "Forgiveness: Letting go of grudges and bitterness."
The following are excerpts from the article, without any editorial comments:

Who hasn't been hurt by the actions or words of another? Perhaps a parent constantly criticized you growing up, a colleague sabotaged a project, or your partner had an affair.

These wounds can leave you with lasting feelings of anger and bitterness — even vengeance.

But if you don't practice forgiveness, you might be the one who pays most dearly. By embracing forgiveness, you can also embrace peace, hope, gratitude and joy. Consider how forgiveness can lead you down the path of physical, emotional and spiritual well-being.

What are the benefits of forgiving someone?

Letting go of grudges and bitterness can make way for improved health and peace of mind. Forgiveness can lead to:

229

- *Healthier relationships*
- *Improved mental health*
- *Less anxiety, stress and hostility*
- *Lower blood pressure*
- *Fewer symptoms of depression*
- *A stronger immune system*
- *Improved heart health*
- *Improved self-esteem*

Why is it so easy to hold a grudge?

Being hurt by someone, particularly someone you love and trust, can cause anger, sadness and confusion. If you dwell on hurtful events or situations, grudges filled with resentment, vengeance and hostility can take root. If you allow negative feelings to crowd out positive feelings, you might find yourself swallowed up by your own bitterness or sense of injustice.

What are the effects of holding a grudge?

If you're unforgiving, you might:

- *Bring anger and bitterness into every relationship and new experience*
- *Become so wrapped up in the wrong that you can't enjoy the present*
- *Become depressed or anxious*
- *Feel that your life lacks meaning or purpose, or that you're at odds with your spiritual beliefs*
- *Lose valuable and enriching connectedness with others*

How do I reach a state of forgiveness?

Forgiveness is a commitment to a personalized process of change. To move from suffering to forgiveness, you might:

- *Recognize the value of forgiveness and how it can improve your life*
- *Identify what needs healing and who needs to be forgiven and for what*
- *Consider joining a support group or seeing a counselor*
- *Acknowledge your emotions about the harm done to you and how they affect your behavior, and work to release them*
- *Choose to forgive the person who's offended you*

- *Move away from your role as victim and release the control and power the offending person and situation have had in your life*

Does forgiveness guarantee reconciliation?

If the hurtful event involved someone whose relationship you otherwise value, forgiveness can lead to reconciliation. This isn't always the case, however.

Reconciliation might be impossible if the offender has died or is unwilling to communicate with you. In other cases, reconciliation might not be appropriate. Still, forgiveness is possible — even if reconciliation isn't.

What if the person I'm forgiving doesn't change?

Getting another person to change his or her actions, behavior or words isn't the point of forgiveness. Think of forgiveness more about how it can change your life — by bringing you peace, happiness, and emotional and spiritual healing. Forgiveness can take away the power the other person continues to wield in your life.

What if I'm the one who needs forgiveness?

The first step is to honestly assess and acknowledge the wrongs you've done and how they have affected others. Avoid judging yourself too harshly.

If you're truly sorry for something you've said or done, consider admitting it to those you've harmed. Speak of your sincere sorrow or regret and ask for forgiveness — without making excuses.

Remember, however, you can't force someone to forgive you. Others need to move to forgiveness in their own time. Whatever happens, commit to treating others with compassion, empathy and respect.

Another Re-Recruiting Story and Much More

TOM DOESCHER //

Recently, a client was telling me a story about one of his staff members who left his company. He said, "Yea, now I have a new client."

When this staff member, a recent college graduate, started with his company five years ago, his wardrobe was seriously lacking. (Editorial comment: At this point, I had no idea where this was going.) My client said the new staff member was very smart and hardworking, but his appearance detracted from his overall effectiveness.

So, one day, my client gave the staff member an envelope and said, "Why don't you take the afternoon off and go shopping." Inside the envelope was a list of suggested business clothes and enough cash to purchase them. Wow, what a great story! But that was only the beginning.

Over 20 years ago, my client's mentor gave him an envelope with a business apparel shopping list and the necessary cash. My client went on to say he still has lunch with his now retired mentor. He said that action had such a positive impact on him that he has paid it forward with a number of junior associates over his career.

The story gets even better. He said, "Yea, I now have five clients who were former colleagues, whom I helped with their wardrobe."

Wow, what a great story about mentoring, re-recruiting and new business development all in one.

The Infinite Game

TOM DOESCHER //

Private equity groups/firms (PEGs) have provided an outstanding exit option for owners of privately owned businesses who wish to sell their company. Based on what I have experienced and learned from others, for the right situation, PEGs are willing to pay the founder/owners a very fair price, and often allow the owner to continue with minority ownership to participate in a second sale. The PEG owners are smart, experienced, connected and often bring resources, financial and otherwise, to the company. They provide a financially disciplined approach with annual budgets/plans and regular monitoring of the actual results.

So, all good stuff. For some reason, I have had a reservation about PEG ownership and Simon Sinek in his latest book about Infinite Companies helped me understand my concern. Most of his comments/observations/examples would be related to publicly owned companies, but I believe his theories would apply to some PEGs.

In a nutshell, his definition of an Infinite Company is one that bases its decisions on the long-term versus a Finite Company that is short-term focused. He shares stories about how both Infinite and Finite Companies behave.

If you are a founder, with what Sinek would call a "Just Cause", and desire to leave a legacy, I would highly recommend reading *The Infinite Game*.

If your company has gone public or sold to a PEG and you are no longer comfortable with it, I would highly recommend you read his book.

Originals-How Non-Conformists Move The World

 **TOM DOESCHER //**

Recently read Adam Grant's latest book. It helped me piece together situations in which I have been involved my entire business life. As many of you know, I like to start new businesses & initiatives. Grant's book helped me understand the many challenges I have faced over the years. More recently, based on my life choices, I have claimed the song by Micah Tyler, Different, because at times, that is how I feel. Again, Grant helped me better understand why I have chosen this path.

He concludes the book with these Actions for Impact:

1. **Questions the default**. Instead of taking the status quo for granted, ask why it exists in the first place.
2. **Triple the number of ideas you generate.**
3. **Immerse yourself in a new domain**. Originality increases when you broaden your frame of reference (e.g. spending time in a foreign country with locals.)

4. **Procrastinate strategically**. (Editorial comment: Grant suggests there are times when procrastination (or waiting) is the right approach.
5. **Seek more feedback from peers**.
6. **Balance your risk portfolio**. (Editorial comment: Hedge your bet.)
7. **Highlight the reasons not to support your idea**. (Editorial comment: This is counter intuitive but a great idea, due to confirmation bias.)
8. **Make your ideas more familiar**. Repeat yourself. It makes people more comfortable with an unconventional idea.
9. **Speak to a different audience**. Instead of seeking out friendly people who share your values, try approaching disagreeable people who share your methods.
10. **Be a tempered radical**. If your idea is extreme, couch it in a more conventional goal.
11. **Motivate yourself differently when you're committed vs. uncertain**. When you're determined to act, focus on the progress left to go – you'll be energized to close the gap.
12. **Don't try to calm down**.
13. **Focus on the victim, not the perpetrator**. In the face of injustice, thinking about the perpetrator fuels anger and aggression.
14. **Realize you're not alone**.
15. **Remember that if you don't take initiative, the status quo will persist.**

Conclusions:

If you are an innovator, I would highly recommend you read *Originals – How Non-Conformists Move the World*. It will be encouraging and help you understand why change is so hard. You will also get some great ideas to be more successful; and you will realize you are not crazy.

If you are a business owner, who wants your team to be more creative, it will provide you with potential obstacles that may inadvertently discourage people from suggesting or making change. You cannot have it both ways.

New Ideas for Your Elevator Speech

 ## TOM DOESCHER //

Somehow, I missed another great author, Donald Miller, who many of you probably already know. He has lead a pretty diverse life, that includes a movie based on his book, *Blue Like Jazz*. In his book, *Building A Story Brand*, he does a wonderful job of helping organizations script there elevator speech. I have experienced and agree with most of his advice.

In his StoryBrand Framework, he recommends seven categories:

1. **A Character**: The customer is the hero, not the brand.
2. **Has a Problem**: Companies tend to sell solutions to external problems, but customers buy solutions to internal problems.
3. **And Meets a Guide**: Customers aren't looking for another hero; they're looking for a Guide.
4. **Who Gives Them a Plan**: Customers trust a Guide who has a plan.
5. **And Calls Them to Action**: Customers do not take action unless they are challenged to take action.
6. **That Helps Them Avoid Failure**: Every human being is trying to avoid a tragic ending.
7. **And Ends in Success**: Never assume people understand how your brand can change their lives. Tell them.

Miller summarizes the above with three questions:

1. Identify your customers problem.
2. Explain your plan to help them.
3. Describe a successful (happy) ending to their story.

As you know from Adam Grant's book, *Originals – How Non-Conformists Move the World,* sometimes we need to take risks, so here I go. The following is the Doescher Advisors StoryBrand Elevator Speech:

"Over decades we meet business owners who are lonely. They lack an experienced, objective, confidential partner. Doescher Advisors fills that void through active listening and practical advice, like a member of the owner's executive team. The result: Our clients sleep better. Try us out for a month with no further commitment."

For those of you, who have read StoryBrand, please let me know what you think of my new elevator speech.

It's Easy When Things Are Going Well

 **TOM DOESCHER //**

Over the years, I have learned that it is easy to talk about and live out your values during the good times.

The real acid test comes during recessions & crisis.

Back in the early 80s, I was a young partner at Plante Moran. The firm had an opportunity and made a very unique confidential investment. In the partner meeting to vote on the investment, it was stated that 10% of the profits would be shared with the staff. Well, it turned out to be a fantastic investment that matured and paid out in 1983, which was a deep recession year that significantly impacted the partners' earnings. So, I was very curious, if the plan to share with the staff members would be honored. Keep in mind that the staff had no idea about this confidential windfall. Well, to my delight, we (since I was a partner) did share our good fortune with the entire Plante Moran team. I was re-recruited to the Firm. Our walk matched our talk.

So why am I telling you this decades old story? The Covid Pandemic has challenged businesses, who have had to make some really tough decisions. Barbara & I are very proud to be associated with our clients, whose actions matched words on the plaques on the company walls. We cannot share all the heartwarming stories but will highlight a few.

- A professional service firm whose competitors almost immediately laid off employees and reduced salaries. Although, it was gut wrenching, the CEO concluded to not make any reductions. Recently, I asked, "Now that we are past the worst of it, how do you feel about your decision?" To which he responded, "It was the right thing to do!"
- Another client, whose manufacturing plant could have remained open due to some "essential service" customers, closed his facility. The CEO was very concerned about his workers contracting the virus. That was not good enough. He also continued to pay all salary & hourly workers during the Stay-at-Home Executive orders. Really!

- Finally, an essential service client, decided to provide their $12-13 per hour workers with a $1,000 bonus. It gets better. The CEO and two other top executives personally handed the bonus checks to their 500 hourly employees working all over Michigan and thanked them for their service to the company, especially during these difficult times.

Every company I have ever known says they really value their employees. These three owners proved it, just like Plante Moran did back in 1983.

So, my question for you would be, "Can you substantiate with real evidence that your employees are important to you?"

If you have any cool stories that occurred during the pandemic, I would love to hear about them.

Sales Management 11.0

August 10th, 2020 // Tom Doescher

TOM DOESCHER //

If you're looking for practical, actionable ideas to help your sales team land new clients/customers, I would highly recommend *Sales Management Simplified* by Mike Weinberg. On a scale of 1 to 10, this book is an 11. To be clear, this is about "new" clients/customers, not cross-serving existing relationships. I found Weinberg's stories to be very relevant, and he describes situations I frequently observe with my clients. He divides his book into two sections: Part One – Blunt Truth from the Front Lines, and Part Two – Practical Help and a Simple Framework to Get Exceptional Results. In this post, I'll present Part One. The blog could be used as a checklist for you or your sales manager.

Part One – Blunt Truth

1. Today, sales managers are often distracted by trying to appease their overly involved private equity group (PEG) owners.

2. (Editorial comment: The CEOs and sales managers of my PEG-owned clients spend endless hours estimating and re-estimating the projected annual EBITDA.)

3. Playing CRM "desk jockey" doesn't equate to sales leadership. (Editorial comment: I had a CEO client whose parent company required my client to have the general ledger agree/match the *salesforce.com* records. I'm not kidding!)

4. Top sales producers tend to exhibit a characteristic Weinberg would describe as being selfishly productive. (Editorial comment: This is a tricky one, but the point is the best "hunters" know how to spend their time.)

5. The player-coach sales manager role can create mistrust and bad feelings. If a small company can't afford a full-time sales manager, Weinberg recommends that the owner, president, or another key senior executive serve as a part-time sales manager.

6. If there's anything guaranteed to deflate the heart of a salesperson, it's when the sales manager steals the glory and limelight. Often, the sales manager's competitive nature and strong desire to solve all problems gets in the way of doing their primary job: leading the sales team.

7. Hunting for new business involves risk, conflict, and rejection. Think carefully before putting account managers, sales support, or sales engineers in new business development sales roles. (Editorial comment: Based on my observations of hundreds of companies, most sales professionals are *not* hunters, but many of them are in hunter roles.)

8. The leader who is constantly preaching about holding people accountable for results and doesn't follow through does more damage than if he hadn't said anything in the first place. Sales. Is. About. Results. Period. Salespeople aren't paid to do work, or to be busy. Their job is to drive revenue — specifically, new revenue.

9. Weinberg would argue strenuously that keeping your lowest sales producers around *does* cost you, even if you're not shelling out commission dollars.

10. In his work providing new business development advice to companies, Weinberg observes many counterproductive sales compensation plans. He would also say there's nowhere near enough difference between what the very top and the very bottom performers earn.

11. Weinberg says other team members tend to be more jealous or unappreciative of those in sales than in other roles. (Editorial comment: I've observed where hunters are expected to complete too much paperwork. Often, they don't have the time or the aptitude, which creates tension with the operations, service, and accounting departments.)

12. Sales managers are working less in the field and not developing their team. The best mentoring happens out in the field, where they join their salesperson on trips to see the prospective client/customer. They

can coach and prepare them before the sales call and, following the meeting, they can discuss what went well and where they could improve. (Editorial comment: I can still remember sitting in my mentor, Ken Kunkel's, car before and after sales calls. He would always ask me what I thought. Then he would ask me if I noticed the prospect's reactions to certain comments. He would explain why he went in a particular direction after the client had provided some facts.)

13. Poor salespeople talk too much and listen way too little. Discover the customer's real issues before making a presentation — always. Poor salespeople give off the vibe that they're there to "pitch at" the prospect.

I'll end Part One there. On pages 100-101, Weinberg summarizes 21 common causes for sales teams' underperformance. Hopefully, I hit a hot button or two. In the next post, I'll summarize Part Two, which offers some practical advice for the issues identified above.

Sales Management 11.0, part 2
August 24th, 2020 // Tom Doescher

TOM DOESCHER //

This blog is a follow-up to my last post, which highlighted the common issues Mike Weinberg, author of *Sales Management Simplified*, experiences when he works with his clients.

Part Two – Practical Help and a Simple Framework to Get Exceptional Results

1. The 4 Rs of sales talent management: Put the Right People in the Right Roles, Retain Top Producers, Remediate or Replace Underperformers, and Recruit.
2. If I confidentially polled your salespeople, would the majority say the leadership of your company is "for" the salespeople or against them?
3. According to Weinberg, sales managers "invest" (waste) most of their time: They're slaves to emails, they have a ridiculous number of meetings, they get caught up playing assistant general manager, they focus too much on administrative items and unnecessary reports, and they don't protect their calendars.

4. Sales managers' top three activities should be: 1) Conducting monthly one-on-one meetings with individual salespeople, 2) Leading sales team meetings, and 3) Working alongside (observing, coaching, helping) salespeople when they're with customers and prospects.

5. During monthly 20-minute one-on-one meetings: 1) Compare actual sales results with goals, 2) Quickly review the salesperson's pipeline of potential deals and sales opportunities, 3) Review sales activity going forward, especially in situations where the salesperson fails the first two tests.

6. Two great sales activity questions to ask: 1) Can you name the new opportunities that are in your pipeline that weren't here last month? 2) Can you name the existing opportunities that you moved forward in the sales process since last month?

7. Sales team meeting agenda potential items: 1) Give brief personal updates, 2) Review sales results and highlight outstanding performance, 3) Share stories, 4) Conduct product training, 5) Share best practices, 6) Brainstorm deal strategies, 7) Have an executive or other department guest presentation, 8) Conduct a book or blog review, 9) Work on sales skill coaching/training, 10) Give business plan presentations, 11) Have a brief, controlled bitch session, 12) Share some non-sales-related inspiration, and 13) Talk about takeaways.

8. Riding along with your salespeople provides an opportunity to observe them in action.

9. Working in the field presents a priceless opportunity to coach a salesperson before and after sales calls.

10. Windshield time and mealtime provide a rare opportunity to learn more about your salespeople; this will make you a more effective sales manager.

11. Getting out of the office provides you with a firsthand look at what's taking place in the market.

12. Fieldwork helps you develop important relationships with key customers.

13. When with your salesperson, be present with your salesperson.

14. Don't do your salesperson's job.

15. Free up your excellent sales hunters so they can maximize their time hunting.

16. Most sales managers wait too long to address underperformers.

Hopefully, you've identified a tip or two that you can incorporate into your business. My suggestion would be to get a copy of *Sales Management Simplified* and use it like an owner's manual. Pull it out when you have a specific issue with your sales team and take advantage of Weinberg's wisdom on the subject. He obviously has seen it all.

The Churchill Wart Factor

TOM DOESCHER //

Obviously, I knew who Winston Churchill was, but until I read *Churchill Walking With Destiny* by Andrew Roberts, I was ignorant of his life story. That being said, if I were asked to name the ten most impactful people of the 20th Century, he would probably have made my list.

Well, assuming Roberts is an objective historian, in excruciating detail he chronicles Churchill's political life from one failure to another. The phrase "foot in mouth" disease or "bull in a china shop" would be appropriate. I was shocked to say the least. In the last chapter of the book, Roberts attempts to summarize Churchill's many failures and his few, but significant successes. Roberts would say that early on, Churchill was the only major Western leader who was on to Hitler and Stalin. His taking a strong position and sounding the alarm may have saved Western Civilization.

So, you are wondering, why did I entitle this post, "The Churchill Wart Factor". Well, in my humble opinion, we all have our "warts". That doesn't mean, we won't save the world someday. One of my many bad habits is judging others, often without all the facts. Studying Churchill has helped me see that it is often easier to see the "warts" and miss the brilliance. So, I thank Roberts for opening my eyes, not only to Churchill, but to the rest of humanity.

Winner of the 1978 Re-Recruiting World Cup

TOM DOESCHER //

When I say, "I am a lucky guy", I mean it. Recently I was reminded of a 4-decade old experience. I was a relatively new Plante Moran staff member when Barbara & I decided to sell our condo and begin our lake adventures. We had never sold a home before, so I went to my supervisor/mentor, Ken Kunkel, to seek his counsel.

For example, how do you get the timing of the sale to match the purchase of the new home. Anyway, as always, he had a lot of good, solid, practical advice plus he helped me to relax. Although I am a calculated risk taker, this was my first home swap out.

We met several times. After each session, I would have some homework assignments. As an aside, Ken knew quite a bit about the City of Novi, where our condo was located, and the local officials, since it was his client. Near the end of one of our meetings, to my shock, Ken said, "I may be interested in buying your condo for my daughter." Really?

So, now I am thinking, how is this going to work – selling to your supervisor. Ken suggested I get a couple of independent real estate appraisals and then we could discuss pricing. As you can imagine, I went from relaxed to nervous again. In addition to the appraisals, I did some of my own investigating, since we had a lot of friends living in Novi condos at the time.

In typical Tom Doescher fashion, I was very well prepared. You would have thought I was selling a Manhattan high rise. Well, the day came for our "pricing" discussion. I shared all my findings with him, and he studied the materials carefully. He took the highest appraisal, added several thousand dollars to the total, and said, "You & Barbara have made many nice improvements and are leaving several built-ins behind, so how does $X thousand sound?" He was definitely offering us a premium, plus now I did not have to worry about having my condo mortgage as a contingency on our new home offer since he was offering a cash deal immediately.

Not sure who was more surprised, me or Barbara. It was like we won the lottery.

I had been Re-Recruited, and this was only "one" of the many reasons the "Lucky Guy" stayed with the firm.

Made in the USA
Monee, IL
19 November 2020